Praise for the Barbarians:

"If you dislike a genuine love s[tory with]
cutting edges, don't read this b[ook.]"

— Gopal Baratham, *Singapore writer*

"In 1955 he was sent to Saigon to cover the war. The computer had not yet replaced the typewriter, nor had the Internet arrived to revolutionise the speed of human communication. But the hour of the Bloodworths' meeting was star-crossed. ... He was a true-blue 'red devil' with an Anglo-Saxon upbringing, she a 24-carat Chinese-Chinese with definite Confucian leanings. Then, as now, they would readily concede theirs was a genuine mismatch of cultures. ... I have known Ping and Dennis for almost 40 years. This has not stopped me from being amazed by their account of their life together. They have not ceased to mine each other's culture, customs and habits, and to flower in their relationship. Their differences have been rich fodder for both personal and professional growth these past four decades. ... Their frank, witty and often provocative reflections make for a hilarious good read."

— Wee Kim Wee, *President of Singapore, 1985-93*

"Not a clash of cultures but a sensitive and endearing account of a union of hearts and minds."

— Michael Leifer, *Professor of International Relations, London School of Economics*

"Leo Tolstoy wrote that happy families are all alike; but then Tolstoy never knew the Bloodworths. This couple — a proud Chinese girl married to a Western news correspondent and writer of bestsellers — found happiness in their own very special way.

Now they have written this highly controversial account of their more than 40 years together — a record of prejudice, insights, understandings, frustration, guerrilla warfare and growing affection — and have never stopped discovering new aspects of each other's world. Other people's happiness can be highly irritating but this book is the exception. It shows what can happen when East and West really do meet."

— Anthony J. Lawrence, *broadcaster and author, former Far East correspondent of the BBC*

"Dennis Bloodworth is the foreign correspondent's correspondent. He gave unparalleled coverage of Asia in the fifties and sixties. He was one of the first reporters allowed into Mao's China from which Liang Ching Ping had fled. They met in Hong Kong and proved that East can meet West and live with love, despite the differences. This fascinating intertwined biography is more than a romantic tale, it provides keen insight into the cauldron from which the modern Asia was formed. Part love story, part cultural guide, part history, it is wholly absorbing."

— Ray Heath, *South China Morning Post*

"The twain met. The sparks flew. The result 44 years later is a marvellous and instructive memoir."

— Nigel Holloway, *Forbes Magazine*

"This is a shrewd, funny and very honest description of a mixed marriage. Although the authors insist that their experience is unique to them, their growing understanding and acceptance of each other's cultures during a 42-year marriage provides a valuable lesson to anyone mired in incomprehension of another nation and its ways. But this is not just a personal history. As respected sinologists, Dennis and Judy Bloodworth have the historical knowledge to put their own experience into a much wider context. This is not just a good read, but a valuable handbook of the potential pitfalls and rewards of trying to understand someone else's viewpoint and culture!"

— Elizabeth Wright, *Head of Region, Asia and the Pacific, BBC World Service*

"Four eyes are better than two for observing, especially when one pair belongs to a British journalist and the other to a Chinese whose mother called her 'Tomboy of the Pearl River'. Their marriage in 1957 became a yin-yang partnership for writing about Asia. This book is a distillation of that journey and their life together. They take turns to write on these pages. Needless to say, each perceives things differently. The result is a marvellous melange, full of insight, humour, philosophy and sparks — a meeting of East and West.

— Michael Richardson, *Asia Editor, International Herald Tribune*

Two voices, two cultures, love story. What happens w a proud Chinese woman meet Western foreign correspon dent...

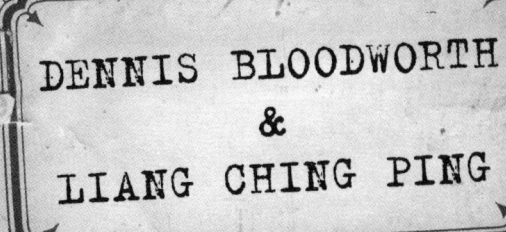

DENNIS BLOODWORTH
&
LIANG CHING PING

I Married a Barbarian

Marshall Cavendish Editions

© 2000 Dennis Bloodworth & Liang Ching Ping

Cover art by Opal Works Co. Limited

This edition published 2010 by
Marshall Cavendish Editions
An imprint of Marshall Cavendish International
1 New Industrial Road, Singapore 536196

All rights reserved

No part of this publication may be reproduced, stored in a retrieval system or transmitted, in any form or by any means, electronic, mechanical, photocopying, recording or otherwise, without the prior permission of the copyright owner. Request for permission should be addressed to the Publisher, Marshall Cavendish International (Asia) Private Limited, 1 New Industrial Road, Singapore 536196. Tel: (65) 6213 9300, Fax: (65) 6285 4871. E-mail: genref@sg.marshallcavendish.com. Website: www.marshallcavendish.com/genref

The publisher makes no representation or warranties with respect to the contents of this book, and specifically disclaims any implied warranties or merchantability or fitness for any particular purpose, and shall in no events be liable for any loss of profit or any other commercial damage, including but not limited to special, incidental, consequential, or other damages.

Other Marshall Cavendish Offices:
Marshall Cavendish International. PO Box 65829 London EC1P 1NY, UK • Marshall Cavendish Corporation. 99 White Plains Road, Tarrytown NY 10591-9001, USA • Marshall Cavendish International (Thailand) Co Ltd. 253 Asoke, 12th Flr, Sukhumvit 21 Road, Klongtoey Nua, Wattana, Bangkok 10110, Thailand • Marshall Cavendish (Malaysia) Sdn Bhd, Times Subang, Lot 46, Subang Hi-Tech Industrial Park, Batu Tiga, 40000 Shah Alam, Selangor Darul Ehsan, Malaysia.

Marshall Cavendish is a trademark of Times Publishing Limited

National Library Board, Singapore Cataloguing-in-Publication Data
Bloodworth, Dennis.
  I married a barbarian / Dennis Bloodworth and Liang Ching Ping. – Singapore :
  Marshall Cavendish Editions, 2010.
  p. cm.
  ISBN-13 : 978-981-4302-86-9

  1. Bloodworth, Dennis. 2. Bloodworth, Ching Ping. 3. Spouses. 4. Interracial marriage. I. Bloodworth, Ching Ping. II. Title.
DS610.72
920.7 – dc22   OCN657936682

Printed by KWF Printing Pte Ltd

For Each Other

Note

WRITING this book presented an obvious language problem, for Ping's English is picturesque rather than precise, and could be defined as a lively British vocabulary struggling in the inexorable grip of Chinese grammar — *Pinglish*, perhaps. While I wrote in English, therefore, she wrote in Chinese and produced her own translation (with the close collaboration of a massive dictionary), which I then edited to clarify the meaning where necessary without, I hope, eliminating the flavour of her egregious style. My part of the book is printed in roman, hers in italics.

I have used the past tense, in the main, since although much that we say of each other still applies today, our story does cover a period of more than 40 years. For the romanisation of Chinese names I have adopted the modern *pinyin* spelling, with some exceptions where the old Wade-Giles rendering may be more familiar to the reader ('Tao' and 'Taoism'), or *pinyin* would look anachronistic ('The Viceroy of Canton', not of Guangzhou). Sun Yat-sen University, as it is more commonly called, is referred to here as Zhong Shan University to distinguish it from the Sun Yat-sen University the Russians had opened in Moscow.

Preface

AT FIRST glance we might seem to have no excuse whatever for inflicting our story on the long-suffering public. True, I am British and my wife Chinese, but that does not necessarily signify. We live in Singapore, where all Chinese are now educated in English and raised like kids in Europe and America on the Muppets and Microsoft, McDonald's and — occasionally — Macbeth. In this westernised Asian society the record of a mixed marriage between a couple officially registered as Dennis and Judy Bloodworth would appear to have nothing of interest to say about the international clash of cultures so dear to the hearts of doomwatchers.

But while I am a straightforward open-plan Englishman with an honest-to-God no-nonsense Anglo-Saxon name that hides nothing (unless you count a full-blooded Hungarian mother), that 'Judy' is misleading, not to say downright deceitful. For unlike all the other Chinese Judys in Singapore, where it is common to take a Christian name even if you are not a Christian, Judy is not Judy but Zhu-di. This means, rather ominously, 'Tomboy of the Pearl River', and was originally a nickname given to her by her mother after an exceptionally disgraceful episode in which at the age of five she showed a precocious sense of poetic justice.

My brother was a big strong boy, but afraid of girl. There was a girl in the neighbourhood always asked him for lot of butterflies, and when one day he refused, treated him very badly. So I netted a spider with long feet fully covered black hair, put it carefully into a box, tied it up, and gave it to the girl. She was gladly accepted the gift, but when the box was opened, extremely frightened, crying loudly and ran back to her house, the spider climbing on her clothes followed. Afterwards she fell ill. Mother knew about that and looking very angry she caught me and beated my bottom madly. In same time she scolded me in a hard voice: 'How could you do such wicked thing? You are evil. You are worse than any tomboy. From now on your name is Zhu-di.' My bottom felt burning hot, very painful, but my brother bought me a little white mouse on a moving wheel, very funny ...

Her real personal name is Ching Ping, and this is shorthand for an esoteric classical tag from the ancient *Book of Poetry* which — even more ominously — translates as 'Apprehensive Ice'. (Nowadays that would be spelled 'Jing Bing', but we are sticking to 'Ping', for that is what I called her in *The Chinese Looking Glass*, a book I wrote thirty years ago with which this account will now and again cross references.)

So what's in a name? The whole point is that Ping is no domesticated English-educated Singaporean, but very much an alien 'Chinese Chinese' from China, which is why I do most of the talking in this book. She was born in Beijing and brought up in a proud, strictly Confucian family who were horrified at the very idea of her wedding a pink and white 'red-haired barbarian' and promptly ostracised her for five years. On my side my mother was furious, and even a favourite aunt wrote to me saying simply '*Don't*, Dennis, don't do it!' So we can in fact claim that ours is a genuine mismatch of cultures.

In principle that still does not mean we have something to offer in a wider context, that we can pretend our union is a microcosm of a macrocosm, that it mirrors the confrontation of East and

West in a domestic setting, the predicted 'war of civilisations' in a teacup. For one thing, there is only one of Ping and one of me. We are not the moulds from which our entire peoples were cast. On the face of it, we can only speak for ourselves.

And yet ... Stereotype is a much maligned word. But if someone talks of a 'typical' Frenchman or German or American we recognise at once the image he has in mind. Yes, each person is unique, but you don't have to dig far beneath their individual idiosyncrasies to find that people of the same tribe or nation do have certain fundamental characteristics in common, derived from a shared history and heritage. 'Even dragons have nine kinds, but all dragons,' as Ping says in her corner-cutting English. Despite the diversity of his origins, there is even such a thing as an American, the distinctive outline of whose profile is etched by ingrained convictions and concepts, stubborn prejudices and misconceptions. Men from all backgrounds in the most multiracial mix in the world will rally to defend the Stars and Stripes, western democracy and the US Constitution, the First (and the Fifth) Amendment, the Pursuit of Happiness, the World Series and Apple Pie à la Mode. And whether they like it or not, the female of the species from Bryn Mawr to Brooklyn, from Katherine Hepburn to Fran ('The Nanny') Drescher, are daughters of the same revolution.

Similarly I, like all my countrymen, was conditioned by a fermented witches' brew of Judaeo-Christian, Greek and Roman ingredients, while Ping, like all hers, was the product of a very different but equally ancient Confucian, Taoist and Buddhist tradition that lies beneath the thin crust of modern Communist China. In consequence the basic grammar not only of our languages, but of our psychologies was different. And when your knee jerks are not the same, you cannot walk in step. We inevitably started out together with minds poles apart, like the protagonists in all East-West encounters.

Including Washington and Beijing. Happily, that did not stop President Clinton from saying he would seek an 'engagement' with China before his meeting with President Jiang Zemin in October 1997. But — engagement? By that time we had already been married for 40 years. So it could be that although our object in this book is to entertain rather than to enlighten, we do have something to say that might, here and there, contribute to better mutual understanding, if only at ground level. After all, *Chinese Looking Glass* was one of four books that President Nixon was recommended to read before his historic visit to Beijing in 1972 to re-establish relations with China in the first place. And it doesn't seem to have done any harm. That is, assuming he actually read it.

Dennis Bloodworth & Liang Ching Ping

1

IT WAS a sheer fluke. I was walking down the middle of rue Catinat in Saigon, empty even of mad dogs in the midday sun of the Indochinese siesta hour, when I was hailed from the terrace of the Hotel Continental Palace by Benny Chau. Damn. I really did not want to stop. I had just acquired the most precious gift a foreign correspondent could sell his soul for, a visa for Chairman Mao's China. It was July 1955. No Americans had got there before me, and only a handful of British journalists. It was so rare a privilege that one of them had written a book about China after being allowed in for only six days. And I was to have six weeks, all to myself. I was leaving for Hong Kong at three the following morning by Pan-Am, and I had a thousand things to do. I smiled, waved a hand vaguely, and kept going.

But this equivocal gesture got me nowhere. 'Come and have a drink,' Benny called, 'I want you to meet a friend.' A friend. What sort of a friend and how much I would owe him I was only to learn with the passage of years. For a second I hesitated, not knowing my whole life depended on my next move. Then I shrugged mentally and crossed over to them. I did not know it, but that was one of those moments in life when fate makes nonsense of all our plans for the way ahead by suddenly turning a sharp corner without signalling.

I shook hands with them both, sank into a chair, and ordered a '33' beer. Benny's companion was a fair-haired, pink-faced Californian with a lazy air but still blue eyes, a little older than my thirty-six. To cut things short, I said I was off to Hong Kong the following morning and could only stay a minute. Oh, said Rupert Bond, where would I be putting up? He was going there too and we might meet up for a drink sometime, as a matter of fact there was to be a dinner for a secretary at the US Consulate there three days later, he would get me invited, and he would ask Laura, the Chinese painter he was eventually to marry, to bring someone to make up a foursome, OK? Good. So that was fixed.

By then I was on the ropes and could only murmur a weak yes. The lazy air and laid-back West Coast drawl had been deceptive. We duly met for a drink two evenings later in Kowloon, and almost the last thing I recollect of my old life was the beer puddle on the wet bar. The barman's name was Chee, I remember, and he wiped it with a bandaged hand, as if wiping out my past. He had cut his finger on a small electric fan. I can still see the fan. Then they walked in, Laura and this anonymous friend of a friend of a friend whose name I learnt was Ping.

I am over six feet tall and at five-foot four she seemed, as the cliché runs, small but perfectly formed. She was nothing like the monstrous regiment of pretty, round-faced, pert-nosed Cantonese girls in Hong Kong who are often so difficult to tell apart. She had an oval face and a long, straight nose and phoenix eyes like polished damsons, a high forehead and brushed-back hair. But I did not take in any of this in detail at the time. All I saw was that she was not pretty at all. No, she was just — I am forced to use that sinfully overworked word — beautiful. And with her low voice and the slow dance of her movements, soothing as a sigh of relief. I silently blessed Rupert Bond.

When I looked in his eyes just first time, I suddenly knew how much I owe Laura. I was always so fond of her, so kind and good-natured, and she and Rupert wonderful couple often asked me join them for dinner. Laura was a painter, like to paint carp, because Chinese believe fish lucky. But this time she had used magic brush to put a rainbow in my life.

The dinner was for John Holdridge, who seventeen years later would become Henry Kissinger's China expert and accompany President Nixon on his historic visit to Beijing. With ourselves as two extra guests, we were twelve at the table, and I was not seated next to her. Whenever I stole a glance at her she seemed withdrawn and preoccupied and spoke little. But afterwards the four of us went on to some sort of nightclub, where we found ourselves sitting at a table at the back together, and Ping and I began to talk our way fast out of the growing tension between us. When the lamentable floor show came on I gave her my hand so that she could stand on her chair and see better. It was at that moment that someone up there snapped his fingers. She did not let go. Nor did I.

I suddenly bewitched. Of course he is charming, amusing, pleasant manner, interesting companion, godknowwhat; also Chinese believe his long 'mu'-shaped face with wide 'jia' forehead, big flat ears, pair blue eyes under thick bushy eyebrows, firm round chin, long gap between lips and nose, all put together means confident, resourceful, artistic, sensitive, compassionate, kind, lucky, long life, healthy stomach. But not just like that, the way. We were both so surprised and so happy, it was like miracle. Although this our first meeting we did not feel like strangers, and especially his few Chinese words made our conversation gay and lively. Then his face also immediately familiar like old friend, made me think someone I had seen — Gary Cooper, Burt Lancaster, Rex Harrison —?

Rex ...? 'For Christ's sake, Ping, you simply cannot say flattering things like that about me. People will hate my guts before we get to Chapter Two.'

'But that is the way I saw you.'

'Yes, but only because love is blind.'

'Of course. So is Justice. Why you complain?'

For nine days and nights he transformed Hong Kong for me. When I think it back I remember wandering on The Peak above the harbour overlooking the city, here and there dazzling lights, the whole island like mountain of lanterns floating in a dark sea like a dream. Also sampling Western cocktails in bar — 'Grasshopper', colour in green, 'Bloody Mary' in red, 'Persian Cats' in golden orange, and 'Pinkie Lady' like milk and ice cream. I tasted them all and seemed like walking into the floating air. And especially one evening the crowded typhoon shelter at Causeway Bay. We hired a sampan and were rowed out to sea, the light of so many boats reflected in the water like golden snakes moving on the ripple. People in other sampans were playing mahjong, or drinking wildly, while one boat with Chinese music circulated among us, and floating kitchens with peddlers crying out what food and drinks they sell. Then D and I reclined on the big cushions at the back of the cabin which like a soft cradle in this simple world of the past all through the whole noisy night.

And I remember when the time we went to crowded ballroom trailing tantalising Paris perfume under changing lights with lively music and dancers shaking and twisting and turning. I clung to Dennis, and he asked if I am happy. I said I felt I could fly. So fly now, he cried, and suddenly held me up high, floating in the air, flying gently to the clouds, heaven and earth spinning round and round.

But when I asked her the one thing I had to know before I left for China, a single tear rolled down her cheek. Marry her? What was I talking about? What did I mean? Was this a British joke? I said I was serious. But was I? It was our last day. The dream was dissolving. After all, let's face it, what did we really have in common? I was English, she was Chinese. We came from frighteningly different backgrounds. I mean, take me:

It was remarkable that I had survived even my first five years to savour this encounter. My earliest memory is of living by the River Thames near the Hurst Park racecourse, where at the age of four I contrived to escape from my mother and dodge into a neighbouring field to tease the only other occupant, a pawing, ill-tempered sixteen-hand stallion put out to grass. I was rescued by my frantic parents, and thus lived to sneak into their bathroom a few weeks later, climb on a stool, and imitate my father shaving in the mirror of the washbasin. It appears that I did this as realistically as I could, using his cutthroat razor, and on finding my face covered with blood, tried to repair the damage by rubbing in handfuls of my mother's Pond's Vanishing Cream. It was she who discovered me a little later, looking like a slightly apologetic strawberry sundae. A few hours afterwards, as if to wash the last of it off, I managed to fall into the river. But this caused less comment as I did it frequently, my record being three times in one day.

The next hazard I recollect was my early sex education. My father was an engineer who liked his Scotch too well, and by the time I was five we had been reduced to living in one room over a milk shop in Soho, the sort where they scooped it out of pails for customers who brought their own jugs. The milkman had two daughters, Lily and Joyce, aged six and four, and on one memorable day they lured me into their claustrophobic lavatory and proceeded without further preamble to pull down my shorts. I was terrified, despite the usual qualified promise: 'If you show us yours, we'll show you ours, but you're not allowed to touch.' Touch? I couldn't believe what I saw. The girls also taught me my first four-letter words — 'only they're secrets and you must never

ever say them in front of grownups.' I dutifully hugged them to myself for years.

Secrets? But I was already leading a double life even at that tender age. In the morning I was taken by hand across Regent Street to the Burlington College for Young Ladies (I think it was called) in Mayfair, where — I suppose for a token payment as my mother was an old girl — I was taught to speak impeccable King's English and to comport myself like Little Lord Fauntleroy. The afternoons, however, were free, and once back at home and up to the ears with twelve times twelve, I would wolf my lunch and rush out into Carnaby Street to join the less washed kids of Soho, roaring around in soapbox cars, yelling derisively at strangers in raucous cockney ('Giddy, giddy gout, yer shirt's 'angin' aht!'). My world split down the middle by Regent Street, I spoke two languages but belonged nowhere.

My mother divorced my father when I was seven (I was told he had died, but kids know better), and went to work in a pleating shop, where she scraped together enough money to send me to a small prep school at Birchington-on-Sea in Kent. From there I won a scholarship to Sevenoaks, and in all spent ten years of my life as a boarder. At Birchington I remained in school even during the holidays, as my single working parent had no time for me. But then I acquired a stepfather who had the virtue of being a teetotaller. The only trouble was, he liked girls instead. His success in business was also uneven, and I would come home at the end of one term at Sevenoaks to find us living it up in a smart apartment on Park Lane with Lord Beaverbrook in the flat below, and at the end of the next back in Soho in two small rooms above a Chinese restaurant. It was a little like my former Mayfair-Soho shuttle, only more leisurely.

When I was just short of seventeen, my stepfather's affairs went down for the third time, my mother divorced him in his turn, and we were penniless again. I left school and went out to work, first analysing pig food in a London laboratory, then as the sidekick of a small-time press photographer (I lit his magnesium flash when he did posed portraits), then as a cub reporter writing three-line obituaries, and finally as the editor of a somewhat obscure newsletter that nobody much wanted although it was free.

World War II broke out when I was twenty, and I spent the next seven years in the army — tramping through North Africa, Sicily, Italy, Hungary under the Russians. In 1946 I married a Hungarian in Budapest and was promptly demobbed for fraternising with the enemy. Back in London a grateful government nevertheless gave me a sports jacket, a pair of flannel trousers, a raincoat, a piece of paper which authorised me to collect a gratuity of 30 pounds from the War Office in 1976, and then let me loose on civilian life. For want of a job in journalism, I became the office manager and salesman of a tin-roofed sheet metal fabrication plant in Peckham employing 35 workers, which predictably collapsed under me in 1949. By then I was down to the same salary I had earned when war had broken out ten years before — four pounds ten shillings a week, or just over sixteen US dollars.

Broke again, I managed to get an introduction to David Astor, the editor of the London *Observer*, who read a test piece I wrote for him, shook his head sadly and said that unfortunately he could not possibly offer me a job. My heart sank like a pebble.

Unless, of course, I was prepared to go to Paris ...

I worked for the *Observer* for five and a half years in Paris. But my wife, who was very trendy, duly found herself a boyfriend there, and when he went into shock after a particularly disagreeable experience, left me to comfort him like the soft-hearted girl she was. (An acquaintance in the apartment above his had leaned over the old-fashioned lift gate to see why the car did not come up when he rang, whereupon it came down from above and chopped his head off.)

As his flat was just down the street I decided to put more space between us, and asked the *Observer* for a transfer. David Astor sent me to Saigon for four months to cover the end of the Indochina War, and then, in the spring of 1955, suggested out of the blue that while I was in the Far East I might as well apply for a visa for China. Why not? No harm in asking, was there? No, as it turned out.

About three months later I received a cable saying the visa was granted, but it would be valid only if I crossed the frontier into China at Shenzhen on 16 July, so on the seventh I flew to Hong Kong to report to the China Travel Service, then the one narrow door into the vast People's Republic. Luckily it was a fine summer's day, for the landing at Kai Tak airport could be dicey, partly because of the sharp, scarred hills that flanked it, the most prominent being the Lion's Head. But what was to prove far luckier for me was that at the foot of the lion was an obscure shantytown of muddy lanes and illegal wooden houses knocked up around a Taoist temple, where fortune-tellers read the future of anxious suppliants from slips of yellow paper.

They needed hope, for they were in limbo. Huangdaxian had no electricity and there was no proper postal service, for the houses did not officially exist and had no numbers — all the mail went to the local medicine shop, to be collected from there. A no-man's-land shunned by the colonial police and written off by the Hong Kong government, it was then a nest of triad gangsters and a ghetto of impoverished refugees who had fled Mao's paradise with what they could carry. And among these — did I but know it as I headed for my comfortable hotel — was a certain Miss Liang Ching Ping, who was living hand-to-mouth trying to raise three small boys by any means that would give her a handhold on life, from selling pigeons to working illegally for a miserable pittance as an unregistered schoolteacher. But it had not always been so.

2

I HAVE to confess that I never lived in one room over a shop with my father and mother in China, but my fall into poverty even steeper. I was born into influential Confucian family of wealthy landowners, our ancestral home in South Guangdong province a walled maze of courtyards and moongates and pavilions where four generations of the Liang family with their wives, concubines and children, a hierarchy some 500 souls in all (I was 'Seventeenth Son's Eighth Daughter'), were waited on hand and foot every step of the day by almost so many servants. At the entrance were great double doors, and inside, the Ancestral Hall with incense-bearing altar and ranks of red and gold tablets commemorating distinguished dead of the family.

The living also distinguished in their own way. My father, Liang Shu-hsiung alias Liang Hsin-ch'ang, was three years in gaol in Hanoi after he been arrested in the French concession of Guangzhouwan in South China for planning an abortive uprising against ruling Qing Dynasty. He had already rallied six counties to the cause of Dr Sun Yat-sen, leader of the revolution to unite China under a president, and when Sun became Generalissimo of the 'National Military Government' in Canton in 1917, my father was his confidential secretary.

One year later Sun was ousted by unscrupulous rivals and left Canton. But my father stayed. He had taken Imperial examinations to become a mandarin but also studied Chinese herbal cures under famous master. Now he quickly made contact with other comrades, hid them in his surgery, and then with my mother help got them away to safety. After that he continued work for Sim's republican movement, going on long journeys around the country, openly practising medicine but secretly rallying support.

He was capable, honest, upright. He had felt those running the national affairs under Qing Dynasty had been corrupt and incompetent, so the country subjected to foreign aggression, and now Qing was gone Chinese divided between rapacious warlords.

He threw himself into the torrent of revolution until his firm spirit followed him buried into the grave.

My mother, his second wife, was daughter of poor peasants in North China, even never studies in school but she was generous, heroic, brave, her body large and strong, full of spirit, lots energy. She had taken the risk to save my father when pursued by officers of the Qing Dynasty. It was then both realised they had a common goal in life, and although my mother 20 years younger did not stop them to join to be revolutionary partners for rest of their life.

After Sun Yat-sen established himself once more as head of government in Guangdong in 1921, my father held posts as prefect of several prefectures in succession, put down gangsters and local tyrants, gave free medical treatment to the poor, helped the needy, and popularised elementary education. Finally his health broke down from overwork and he died in office age only fifty-three. His last words were that his sons must remain devoted to the country, while daughters should study medicine or education to bring benefit to society, and the older should protect the younger, guiding them to carry out his wish.

Two of my brothers rose to become Nationalist Kuomintang (KMT) generals in the army of Chiang Kai-shek, after trained at the Whampoa Military Academy in Canton. Han Ming was a *corps (later army) commander, distinguished himself in the battle for Changsha in 1941. Under his command the main Chinese force tenaciously defended this key city against three frontal attacks of Japanese and wiped out their effective strength — the only success China could call as 'brilliant victory' in the war. Hua Sheng, my honorary second brother (actually a distant cousin, but the son of a member of the Liang clan who was a blood brother of my father) — eventually became Vice-Commander of Manchuria and Governor of Jilin Province; and another brother Han Yao, fiscal chief of Guangdong Province.*

I was born in Beijing, but went to high school in Canton, and then to Zhong Shan University, which was forced to evacuate to Yunnan province by the advance of the Japanese and their wanton and indiscriminate bombing of coastal cities. The war lasted eight years, during which I saw my brothers only on and off, as in a broken-down movie. But because I was the youngest, everyone took pity on me, I was the 'pet piglet' and spoiled rotten, as D would say. I could ask for anything I liked except a teddy bear — my superstitious mother said I would grow to look like one.

But my brothers, who were very close to me, also told me what I should do all the time. 'You are growing up. Do not forget father's upright spirit of Liang family. You must not be affected by vanity and seek pleasure, you should study hard and temper yourself through manual labour, then do your bit for society,' said Han Ming. He seemed to have a lump in his throat.

Hua Sheng, too, was a stern teacher. For example one year in Manchuria he took us on a trip in heavy snow falling without stopping, the wind seemed coming from far places with damp chill which got through my bones. We rode in jeeps, and I wore a long pair of leather boots and gloves and a hat that kept the ears warm and had a cover over nose and mouth up to the eyes, but even so a thin layer of ice formed over my eyelash, the whole body so clumsy like a robot.

Then he decided to visit the Cave of the Virgin Mary at the foot of the mountains. The Cave was long and narrow cavern with figure at the end; surrounded by thin mist, grey fog outside and closed off from rest of the world, it was peculiarly calm, quiet and lonely, a fairy place with unimaginable power. In freezing cold, Hua Sheng said, 'If live among green hill and clear water too long, ambition will die out; I ask you come here not only to build up good physique but also strengthen your will power.'

He then began to run in the snowfield that stretch to the horizon, the snow falling softly, steadily, fortunately strong wind blowing the way exactly I wanted to go. At last he stopped and looking at gloomy sky, said, 'I chased the communists so many years but they will come back. When I first came here I called together 3,000 teachers for training, revised the course of study, reprint the new textbooks, give free to all schools. Because the only way to save China from communism is through the people's political consciousness. That is the mission of education and you should achieve that goal.' Lying in bed exhausted that night, I examined my conscience in the stillness. How was I to do it?

We had followed my father's wishes; one sister became doctor and I studied education and did teachers' training course before going to Zhong Shan University. Stealthily this led to me feeling warmer towards communists although my family prominent in Nationalist Kuomintang. Why this happen? That time the university engaged few dramatists to give lessons, and they explained theatre was effective place to arouse the masses' thinking, the plays always analysed human nature evil, hypocrite, cheating, greedy, shameless and all social crime, so dramatic movement could reform society and solve all sorts problems of actual life. I very fond of literature and art and my mind full of emotion to save the nation from extinction. I threw myself into the dramatic movement, performing and producing many plays.

Now Dean of College of Literature, Hong Shan, a famous

authority on drama, was a powerful giant, quick-tempered, very strict with progressive views. The left-wing students obviously worship him and studied hard and didn't care a comfortable life. I was curious about their politics, having learned to admire them. But as communism continue to expand very fast, many famous orthodox scholars attacked Hong, and in the end he left the university. When I said goodbye to him I felt overpowering stinging melancholy, because in this tune of war against foreign enemy our country should not be divided as a possession belong to this or that party or clique. I seemed to hear the howling of dragon and tiger.

But when I explain my sadness to Han Ming, I found myself divided from my Kuomintang brother. I said trouble was that in China prosperous people wallowed in luxury, there was collusion between business organisations and officials, corruption and degeneration everywhere, while the people became destitute and homeless, hungry and cold. So idealistic youth thinking was naturally radical, and want very much to go in for thorough reform. Therefore hard not to turn to Marxism-Leninism. I just want get all disgusted feeling off my chest.

'Now we are facing to a matter of life and death,' he answered, 'but your youth do not understand Marxism-Leninism and continually criticise the Kuomintang government, never think about society must base on stable situation. No! They have completely no concern the country ruin or not.' His face was sullen and there was a frown between his brows. Silent and upset, after a short moment he continued, 'You should know communism is incompatible with Chinese traditional benevolent government idea. Marx suggested all credit should go to workers, but Sun Yat-sen wanted ownership by all five classes of the people.

'We want revolution for all Chinese, not just domination of proletariat. Yet your young people still shout blindly to worship communists. Your questioning attitude is a shock to me. I begin to

understand the reason of the failure of the KMT, it is the ideological confusion in the youth mind.' Suddenly he held my hand very tight, made me feel really painful. At all time I saw shadow of my father at Han Ming's back and after this talk felt bitterly lost, the suffering of self-contradiction between revolutionary KMT and communism deeply in my mind, as in mind of most youth in the late forties.

My confusion continued. My youngest brother Han Chao (Number Seven), a naval officer, was specially close to me. When he married in Qujiang, I took the train and went to the wedding. The wedding feast full of noise and excitement but the feet soundless on the luxurious carpets, the wives wearing pretty cheongsams or fashionable long dress, people very elegant and poised with fine manners. Han Chao's bride, Kwai San, was one of my dearest friends. We all loved her, and this was my mother's happiest day in a hard life — until one notable literary drunkard, who had been swallowing champagne, talked wildly, 'The daughters-in-law of the Liang family are exceedingly beautiful which shows they are an example of a powerful petit-bourgeois family,' he cried.

This discordant note, struck at such a moment, left my mind a blank, disillusioned as I tried to think, not knowing which way to go in our divided country. I yearned for a direction, the right middle path, an ideal career that I could not find. Everything was a big muddle that time, including my love troubles (mostly I asked for it). Somebody said 'you have just entered into a dark room attempting to catch a black cat that is not there'.

After a deeper self-examination, I determined to plant my feet on solid ground. I began to study vehemently and wrote solemn articles on ideological problems and educational policy for a monthly magazine published in Luochang, which was under my brother Han Yao. I became happy with the idea of taking up writing as a profession. That was a way to do good, influence affairs. One day I talked to him frankly about what I felt.

At the end of the war in 1945 and after I graduated Han Yao arranged for me to take a job as educational inspector and also in charge of the public library in Qujiang, as a step to guide me into politics. He said, 'In Qujiang all high schools are controlled by the provincial government. The main task of your job will be mass education in the countryside. You should campaign to eliminate illiteracy, teach people understanding their own rights and duty, bring in the democratic work-style. As to the library work, there are plenty banned books worth to studying, a rare chance to engage in advanced studies.'

I had a queer feeling in my heart. It seemed full of joy, anxious and expectant. The library stood on the bank of a river with a garden round it with a small thatched cottage for me. Most banned books were kept in a separate room behind a locked door, and when I opened it a strange, musty smell came from the old volumes. Set along the shelves in serried rows, there were books everywhere about Marx, Marxism-Leninism, and the writings of Engels and Stalin. After cleaning, the room became an ideal study. I worked in the countryside most of the time, but I spent much time in the library.

I especially spurred myself to study Marxism-Leninism diligently, reading a great deal of forbidden books, and the more I read the more I hated 'class struggle', the communist morality and their outlook on life. I wanted overthrow their cold-blooded theory and the Marx way of mechanical thinking, the idea to destroy all classes but the proletariat, building one's ideology on bloodshed. And then once in power the proletariat not masters, but just tools for the Party, the new society to be governed by a group of super-communists, a supreme new class. What a horrible theory obviously!

When I read enough this deceitful empty talk I just locked up the study and went to the countryside to draw a deep breath of freedom. Here everything quite different. At first there was only one primary school in the vicinity and the education level of the teachers quite poor, and I had to guide them. The office in this village looked after all surrounding villages, and the big central hall open to all of them for people flocking together in their leisure time, but few people had ever used it.

First I suggested using the hall as a branch library, and prepared to supply suitable books and magazines to attract the better-educated, and the hall also became a meeting place to discuss about urgent matters to improve living conditions that should be done at once — for example, to repair the broken main road to the villages, extend electric current supply. I would then speak to the prefect personally about these questions. It made all villagers gradually realise the spirit of democracy worked.

My tall young bespectacled assistant, whose plump wife called him 'Four-Eyes Kid', was help me enthusiastically. I encouraged him tour the villages tell tales of classical Chinese literature and its heroes and lessons to be learned, and because he was very skilful the crowds getting bigger and bigger. There were many other activities. I chose some clever teacher from the primary school to start an adult evening literacy class, the heads of villages began teaching people to play Chinese chess, we instructed the young kung-fu enthusiasts, and also got them to practise lion-dancing at night, and whenever festive occasion we arranged get-together for all in front of the main temple. It was an exhilarating scene. I was happy. I had found my vocation and my work to benefit society.

And then it all collapsed, my dream of Utopia dashed. Defeated by the communists, the main forces of the KMT retreated to Taiwan. My mother went to Hong Kong. My two sisters stayed in China but because belonging to landlord families were persecuted and reduced to miserable condition. The husband of the elder was publicly tried and killed, and both were soon driven to suicide. Under land reform all the property we owned in the country was swept away, nothing left any more. I followed my mother to Hong Kong. My life was full of utter helplessness and contradiction, the future grim. But my mother said, 'poverty is not guilt, so not a thing to be afraid of.' And I clung to that.

3

THE LIANGS were an eccentric and impulsive lot, as I was to learn. In 1962 they finally forgave Ping for marrying me (my family had got around to forgiving me for marrying Ping only in 1960), and we visited the family in Taipei. My first memory of the sixty-year-old Han Ming, the hero of Changsha, is of his demonstrating a tennis smash for me at the dinner table with a full box of chocolates, which spewed out in all directions over the food, a stroke that would have baffled even a Sampras. Thirty years later and by then 91, his brother Hua Sheng visited us in Singapore and left us exhausted within 48 hours (among other things by blithely trying to jump a monsoon drain). But we had got off lightly, for he next flew to Manila where his daughter lived, and was so smitten with the cockfighting there that he bought fifty prime birds on the spot, which he then left with her with orders to look after them for him before swanning off to America.

Ping's sister, the doctor, had stayed in China in order to serve the new regime after her marriage broke up, but because her position was inevitably delicate given her Kuomintang background, her mother had brought her three small children out of China to Hong Kong, from where she could be in touch with her daughter across the border.

A strong, resourceful woman, 'big as a mountain', she had

rented a piece of land from a Buddhist nunnery on the outskirts of Huangdaxian because it was cheap and she had little money. On this plot — with the help of friends — she built a little cement-floored box of plastered concrete, its four rooms separated only by thin beaverboard partitions, its kitchen, shower and toilet in a courtyard outside, the whole surrounded by a low wall. To make ends meet, she and a friend bred pigeons for sale to a group of restaurants financed by an acquaintance from the good old days in China. When Seventeenth Son's Eighth Daughter, born with a jade spoon in her mouth, arrived in Kowloon in 1949, it was like the end of the known world.

I came to Hong Kong full of memories of good times, so proud in spite all my doubts, because in China I can do anything I want. But now the life and loves of the past seemed flowers in the mirror, the moon in the water, firecrackers in the sky, as the river had gone and never return. Old family friend warned me I could not even get job as teacher because my Zhong Shan University degree not recognised in Hong Kong, so hardly can work. So I helped my mother with the pigeons. I also wrote articles and poems for local Chinese newspapers in little wooden hut in my mother's courtyard, but only paid just few dollars, cannot earn living that way. My big shot friends could not help me. So many in same situation. Hong Kong completely twisted all our lives. I carried my $200 Italian handbag from China in Hong Kong but now only three four local dollars inside.

When I did not cry as a baby, my mother thought I would bring the revolution good fortune and my father called me 'a little piece of hard bone', strong in character. So I had great ideas about future of China. But those great ideas had proved entirely a dream. And now I woke up. My mother's humble pigeons kept us. Her daughter even so educated cannot help. I had lost myself. I was nothing.

I was deeply frustrated and dissatisfied with myself, so threw myself into full-time work in a subsidised school as a 'black market' *supply teacher. At the same time, three nights a week, I crossed the harbour to Hong Kong Island after school closed at 5:30 to give private tuition to a rich family's children. The pay very poor, so before I went on the boat I ate my dinner (meat bun $1.20, soft drink 80 cents) in a public toilet near the ferry terminal to avoid doing so in front of other passengers. Then four hours later cross the ferry back to Kowloon and make long way home late at night. I saved as much money as I could for my mother and talked to her cheerfully, and for two years it was hard but not unhappy life. When I enjoyed the peaceful evening with mother and the children, actually did not felt miss anything.*

But it was not to last. In 1952 her mother sent Ping's sister across the border a message asking her to join them in Hong Kong. When there was no reply, she decided at their insistence to join the rest of her family, including her seven other grandchildren, in Taiwan. But there was a good reason for the failure of Ping's sister to reply. Almost inevitably, the communists had got around to denouncing her publicly as a 'capitalist and counter-revolutionary.' Hounded, insulted, singled out and humiliated at public 'struggle and criticism' sessions, she had finally jumped off a roof to end it all. Her much-loved sister dead, her mother gone, left alone in Hong Kong to feed and clothe and raise her three orphans, Ping was in despair.

It was a thunderbolt from the blue and my deep feeling of grief almost suffocated me. In front of me seemed only world filled with death and darkness. But I had to earn living to keep the kids, no time for sorrow. They were now the meaning of my life. Apart from help my mother's partner with pigeons, teach at school, give tuition at night, and still writing articles, I began to do weekend voluntary service for Catholic Church. My sister had been converted Catholic, and Peter, a Catholic school principal who was a cousin of my best friend, had suggested it. It could lead to a way to educate the boys for little money, he said.

The Catholic organisation sent a little van took me to different hospitals. I visited many poor patients, most illiterate, and wrote letters for them to their husbands working in New Territories. I deeply sympathise their loneliness, but most spoke peasant dialects I cannot understand, and often cannot express their love. So I cheated, and in my own style wrote very warm loving letters for them. They very happy. So the nuns gave me a lot of powder milk, vitamin pills, and all kinds of meat cans for the boys.

Peter was then able to arrange for them to become boarders in the convent school of the Salesian Brothers in nearby Macau. He did all the necessary paperwork, but she naturally wanted to see the convent for herself. The night ferry was not cheap, but the uncle of a friend who had been a senior official in China in his day was now the ship's cook, and arranged for them to pay their passage as extra weekend crew, serving drinks and washing dishes.

We wore blue jeans, rubber shoes, and joined the ferry on Saturday as waiters, and on Monday returned to Hong Kong with two nights' salary; also the cook gathered the bone part of chicken, duck and meat left over in kitchen, put all in box, and gave us to take home for delicious banquet. He also comforted us. In old days, he said, if gentleman even turned up sleeves to work, everyone say he is a ruffian. Now all must work. No way out. 'You both actually look very nice in jeans, why you worry? Come again soon.' But although his friendship very touching, I felt as an olive inside my mouth, very bitter.

However, the Instituto Salesiano in Macau proved to be everything that had been promised, and would give the boys full board and an education for next to nothing. The Church had removed a major worry and, deprived of her ambition to work for China like her father, Ping considered being converted and becoming a nun. In that way she could still serve the Chinese poor — at least in Hong Kong — and in return she could hope to find security and peace of mind. But there was a slight snag. 'I was still doubtful, because where is God?' Could one be a nun without believing in him? After wrestling with her Confucian conscience, she decided she could. Her argument was simple. While she did not believe in a Catholic God, she did not disbelieve in one either, did she? So that meant she was free to do as she wished, didn't it? But before she could apply this very Chinese logic to life, I turned up.

I always felt there were two kinds of western people on earth, one who turned a blind eye to eastern civilisation, the other eagerly facing to it. And here was Dennis, international correspondent ardently attracted to Chinese culture. Perhaps he would be a voice like spring thunder to wake up the West to China, and I could help him. He told me even when he was only 18 he bought a book to study Chinese characters, and went to see ancient Chinese costume play in London and said I look like leading lady.

Love is certainly blind — she was an English actress called Thea Holm. But it was true that I had become fascinated with things Chinese in a typically superficial fashion at a tender age after seeing an exhibition of paintings (and a remarkably pretty Chinese girl) at a London gallery, and an open-air performance of *Lady Precious Stream* in Regent's Park in which Thea Holm had played the lead. And, yes, I had even bought an elementary Chinese grammar at Foyle's, the second-hand bookshop in London, as it was going for only sixpence. I learned nothing from it, but I had shown willing, and I still had it to prove it. So in the end I won. For the Fishers of Men, Ping was to prove the one that got away.

We were both adrift. Ping had three boys on her hands and 'no way to go'. My divorce had come through the month before we met, and all I had was a dead past at the other end of the world and a hotel room in Saigon. When we clasped hands in the half-dark of that nightclub, we did not know who was rescuing whom, or which of us would love the other more for it. We still don't.

But by the end of the first nine days, we knew what was going to happen. That was why Ping bought the shoes.

When Dennis left Hong Kong for China and I said goodbye at the railway station, my mind was completely empty. I wandered aimlessly down Nathan Road, wondering how I could do something for him to express my full heart. Then, suddenly I saw it.

Of course! I walked into a shoe shop and bought myself a pair of western-style shoes with heels nearly three inches high. I had never worn such things before, but as Plato said, love is a serious mental disorder.

When you wore these shoes, it was said, they straightened the back and forced you to move 'with a graceful demeanour conforming to the standard of the top rank and fashion'. For me, walking in them was extremely difficult and uncomfortable, even on flat ground must be careful not to slip and fall. I felt the whole shape of movement rather comical and unnatural, like Chinese women with bound feet. But now I was willing to suffer, even feeling as if in shackles. Why ask for this trouble? The point was I would be only eight inches shorter than D now. Undoubtedly it is love.

Letters from D were the springhead of my life, with their ideas bounding from word to word and sentence to sentence. I had had my dream of escape, and now my escape was not a dream but right before my eyes, taking me away from unbearable narrow life-circle of Hong Kong to Singapore, which Dennis was to make his base.

When the time I climbed Lion Mountain to be among the flowers, the dewdrops at sunrise, the world bright and fresh at dawn, and expected ecstatic happiness, I also felt the hunger in my soul could be satisfied. For now I could write for China. D and I would have a dedicated task, working together and writing with our deep love to help East and West understand each other's culture, absorbing each other's essence and passing on the experience to all mankind in the world.

For the next 25 years Ping would be my right hand, guiding me through the fiendish intricacies of Chinese politics as I tried inadequately to pass on my growing bewilderment to the readers of the *Observer*; she would be at my side when I wrote three books trying to explain China and the East to the West; and she would co-author two more with me with the same object in view. By 1972 Nixon had been urged by his advisers to read my first book, *The Chinese Looking Glass*, before setting out for Beijing, and 17 years later an official of the British High Commission in Singapore would phone up to say the Queen proposed to make me an Officer of the Order of the British Empire. Had I any objection? An OBE? I asked him what it was for. 'They haven't told us exactly,' he replied, 'but it's something to do with serving British cultural interests in Asia and helping to create a better understanding between East and West.'

In October 1989 the Queen visited Singapore in the Royal Yacht, and after an evening reception on board for the President and government ministers and other appropriate guests, we were asked to stay behind when they all left. It was after eleven when we were summoned to the privacy of the Queen's day cabin, where she pinned the gong on me. There was no one else present. (The equerry was just outside the open door.) It was, so to speak, just Elizabeth and Philip and Dennis and Ping — for, exceptionally, Ping (up to her ears in cheongsam) had been allowed to be present. They did not know, of course, how much that exception was deserved, how much I owed this moment to her.

But that was many years ahead. Once in China and unaware that I had had a formidable rival in the Catholic Church, I was beginning to allow myself the luxury of a few treacherous doubts about mixed marriage. This was 1955. Was it really such a good idea, given the prejudice we might face? Might it not be a recipe for misery? Three weeks after I proposed to Ping I found myself dining with a crusty Old China Hand in Shanghai who had spent all his happy working life just down the road from the public garden whose entrance was quite erroneously said to have borne the infamous notice 'No dogs or Chinese allowed'. Here was a devil's advocate *par excellence*, and I decided a trifle ignobly to put the matter to the test to reassure myself. I was thinking of marrying a Chinese girl; with his long experience of the Far East, what did he feel about the idea, I asked him, taking a quick swig of his Hennessy. But I was fortifying myself against an avalanche of protest that did not come. 'My dear chap,' he said warmly in the accents of London Clubland, 'I do congratulate you. You could not possibly do better.' And, you know, the old boy was to be proved absolutely right.

So there was to be at least one thing we would have in common. At precisely 2:00 PM on 12 March 1957 at the Supreme Court Registry Office in Singapore we both married barbarians.

4

SINGAPORE. The setting was ominous. 'What kind people I marrying?' Ping asked herself a little belatedly when Nalini Schooling took her to Changi Gaol on her first Saturday, carrying a fierce homemade curry and a carton of cigarettes for her brother Devan Nair. (It seemed that while the prison diet had improved since the days of the Japanese Occupation, it still left much to be desired.) Ping had arrived in Singapore by sea in December 1956, having left the boys in their Macau convent for the time being. The problem of where to put Ping herself in order to observe the hypocrisies had been solved for me when Tony and Nalini Schooling, a left-wing English intellectual and his Indian wife whom I still knew only slightly, offered to take her in until we married.

Everything was new and strange to her in their old, sparsely furnished bungalow in Chancery Lane, of course, but it quickly became stranger. For even when she was alone in the house she was constantly running into miscellaneous young men in flip-flop thumb-sandals, shorts and flapping shirts, who wandered in and out as if she were not there, treating the place as their own, raiding the fridge for beer and snacks, lolling in the rattan chairs while endlessly talking anti-colonial sedition, and then disappearing again without a word to her, sometimes casually making off with

Tony's car or scooter, depending on which he had left behind when going to work at Radio Malaya.

But it was all perfectly explicable. The young men — 'light brown, dark brown, godknowwhat,' she could not yet distinguish between the Malays, Indians and Eurasians of multiracial Singapore — were the lucky ones who had been left at liberty when at the end of October Devan and other fellow conspirators in the Factory and Shop Workers' Union had been picked up and thrown into the political wing of Changi prison romantically known as 'Moon Crescent'.

The headquarters of the 'Factory and Shop' was the nerve centre of a subversive left-wing organisation whose hard core of pro-communist leaders were dedicated to the overthrow of the British colonial government of the island, if necessary by violence. From their barely furnished offices in the equally incongruously named Middle Road they mobilised and manipulated a mass movement of tens of thousands of workers and students, and their flair for getting troublemakers on to the streets had led to several years of disruptive strikes and disorders and some bloodshed. It was proudly claimed at that time that the riot squad of the Singapore colonial police was the most experienced in the world, and even the fatuous hippy farewell of the period — 'see you later, alligator'; 'in a while, crocodile' — had been parodied to suit the local mood — 'see you later, agitator'; 'when it's quieter, rioter'.

At the end of October I had moved from Saigon to Singapore ahead of schedule to cover the latest explosion of anti-colonial mayhem for the *Observer*. But when I asked around for Devan Nair, whose name a colleague had given me as a good left-wing source, it was to find that he had been locked up the day before I arrived. As an Indian, Devan was essentially a dedicated tool of the movement, useful because he could widen its mass action by attracting other Indians. But its red-hot core was, like Ping, 'Chinese Chinese'.

Colonial Singapore was run exclusively on the English language, and its administration had from the outset established English-language schools whose products could enter the civil service or become lawyers, doctors or teachers, and generally make themselves useful to their British masters. Immigrants from China who wanted their children to have a traditional Chinese education had to fend for themselves. Their clan societies and the philanthropic millionaires among them had therefore opened their own schools and brought in teachers from the mainland. But since their graduates could not speak English, they were marginalised, excluded from careers in government and the professions, many of them forced to take ill-paid jobs in factories or on the buses.

The illegal Communist Party constantly worked on the discontent and bitter sense of humiliation of these 'Chinese Chinese' underdogs to serve its own revolutionary ends, and when the government took the first timid step towards ending the discrimination against them by bringing the Chinese schools more into line with the English-language system, its popular front demagogues promptly denounced this as a dastardly plot of the unspeakable British to 'destroy the Chinese language, education and culture'. That above all was well-calculated to bring Chinese of all persuasions springing to their feet — students, workers, and the tycoons with the money to finance mischief — for it was a threat that flicked all of them on the raw.

And Ping? I still knew too little about her and discovered too late that she was not only a political animal, but a highly emotional one with whom, as she told me, the excited atmosphere of student revolt in Singapore at once struck a sympathetic chord. For it had not been so long since as an irrepressible firebrand at Zhong Shan University, she herself — faithful to her father's memory — had agitated against the corruption and nepotism of the Chiang Kai-shek government, a hot-headed idealist whose words and acts had more than once knitted the brows of her betters and mentors. I now had to remind myself that she, too, was a Chinese Chinese, which in the context of Singapore meant that she was one of them, while I was one of us: we had been born into opposite, hostile camps and could prove victims of the surrounding smog of mistrust and hatred. Ping was anti-communist, but if she believed the British were 'destroying Chinese culture' it was an obscenity that could have her, too, springing to her feet.

The trouble was that there was no way of shielding her from all the strident left-wing propaganda, especially as I had put her into the Schooling household where 'everybody filled with strongly intellectual revolutionary ideas — the anti-colonial struggle like in a volcano.' She seemed to be getting disconcertingly close to the Schoolings, moreover, notably to Nalini, who was proud that her brother Devan had been thrown into prison by the colonial power and prophesied great things for him (gaol was a good recommendation, and he did in fact become President of the Republic later). I began to fear their political influence over her, fond though I was of them, for if her patriotic passions were roused against the British as they had been roused against the shortcomings of the KMT in China, it could even threaten our marriage. ...

At first I was comfortable living in the Chancery Lane house; Nalini was a very pleasant young woman with easy manners, and welcomed me in a most warm and friendly fashion. They are treat me well, the atmosphere was lively, and of course when I heard about the strength of the Chinese school movement to safeguard Chinese education and culture, naturally I was very excited and in favour it. For Chinese civilisation inherited from 5,000 years past must be defended, and Chinese education and culture cannot neglect. My skin, my blood, my mind all demand I shoulder the responsibility for it, no matter which country I lived. In front of foreigners, once mention about this problem in Singapore I always felt uneasy and fidgety.

But anti-colonialism is another matter completely, and I want nothing to do with it. And especially I learned all stories of British destroying Chinese culture were rubbish, just propaganda trick of Chinese pro-communists fooling the people to start anti-colonial violence, I began to feel most uncomfortable and worry very much. Not about me, of course. I was anti-communist and not anti-colonial — I thought myself very lucky come to Singapore. So I just listened all the talk, say nothing. But I began to worry about D.

Of course for his newspaper he must know about left-wing politics, but he seemed getting very close to Tony, and I wonder how much political influence Tony being such anti-colonial Englishman was having on him. I came to Singapore with my heart and soul wanting to set up ideal home here. Now I feared if D drawn into left-wing struggle manipulated by communists, peace and happiness of our marriage only could be temporary, because we just like a blind person on a blind horse rushing headlong to unpredictable future. ...

This ludicrous comedy of errors, which had each of us fearing the other might be lured away, seduced and ruined by the scheming Maoists (which neither of the Schoolings were), was a sharp lesson in mutual ignorance. But seen in perspective it was just one more hazard to overcome. The myth of the 'destruction of Chinese culture' was quickly exploded once we got around to confiding our secret fears to each other, but myths had been leading to misunderstanding and mistrust between East and West for millennia.

According to the Ancient Greeks, the distant and uncharted Orient was largely inhabited by one-eyed monsters; and beyond them — if you were foolish enough to proceed further east — by griffins who guarded a land of gold; and then beyond them. ... Ignorance is a hardy weed, and 2,500 years after Herodotus a

Grand Secretary was to tell the Chinese Emperor confidently that the best way to deal with the marauding British was to cut off all exports of rhubarb to them, whereupon they would quickly die of constipation.

Both sides have been fed horror stories about each other — all the more horrible because they had simply been rehashed from the vulnerable truth. 'The Heathen Chinee' with his inscrutable face and inch-long fingernails drowned unwanted baby girls, didn't he? Of course. But then, inconceivable as it might sound, white Christian nuns ate them. And that was not all. The more devout among the red-haired barbarians went even further. They not only drank the blood of their god, but consumed small biscuits made out of him every Sunday. Unbelievable.

The Chinese have always taken a condescending view of 'foreign devils' from the West, for even when they displayed superior virtues, they were not Chinese, and were to be regarded much as Christian missionaries might look kindly on a well-mannered cannibal who didn't pick his teeth. When in the nineteenth century Lord William Napier of Merchiston was sent to China to parley with the Viceroy of Canton, that gentleman noted, 'The said barbarian is of reasonable intelligence. ... If he applies himself with perseverance, he may yet distinguish right from wrong.'

Morals? The confrontation was intensified. It was the perfumed decadence of the East that had corrupted the austere Roman Republic of upright senators and chaste matrons, wasn't it? It had turned a sober homespun democracy into the plaything of lecherous and sybaritic emperors surrounded by wantons in transparent silk and capable of any unbridled excess. No wonder, when in China itself 10 out of 25 Han Dynasty emperors had been queer. And the Chinese were polygamists. Every home was a private bordello of multiple wives and concubines and bondmaids who, I was assured by my elders and betters at school, were equipped, you know, down *there*, with horizontal not vertical smiles (though how that would work always puzzled me). There was no depravity of which they were not capable. Why, they would even shut the head of a live duck in the top drawer of a chest and then. ... No, I mean, really, old man ...

The Chinese naturally took a different view. Han Dynasty emperors queer? And what of Socrates, Plato and company? In China love was well-organised and straightforward. Parents arranged a marriage between a suitable bride and groom through a go-between. There was no nonsense about couples choosing each other. A husband might then acquire concubines in the traditional manner (often after consultation with his wife), and when feeling like a change of air frequent the approved pleasure houses or boats of 'flower girls' properly trained to entertain him with song, repartee and other arts. All was open and aboveboard. Everyone knew where they stood. Or slept.

But although three of Ping's brothers were wedded to brides chosen by their mother, all were soon divorced, and all then chose wives of their own. Han Ming fell in love with a winsome student who gave him a bouquet at a welcoming ceremony for his troops in Guizhou; Han Yao only had to cast an eve on the fetching daughter of his host at a dinner; and when Fifth Brother Han Qiang was appointed prefect of Wuchuan he promptly married one of its eighteen famous beauties. And all the marriages survived.

However, when Ping and I tied the knot after knowing each other for more than 18 months, we were looked at askance. In the monogamous West, the Chinese insisted, all was anarchy. It was customary for men and girls to marry on impulse for ephemeral love, and quickly live to regret it. With only one woman in the house, a man naturally had to find himself an illicit mistress or two whom he would then have to frequent clandestinely, or even more furtively pay unlicensed females of dubious repute for their favours if he wanted peace and quiet in the home.

Instead of the order and system of a Chinese household of perhaps a dozen or so women, all was haphazard, hole-and-corner, complicated by primitive and hypocritical taboos which nevertheless did not stop people from indiscriminately hopping in and out of each other's beds on the quiet. It was a culture of unconfined promiscuity and vulgarity in which, it should be added, pornographic paintings of grossly overweight women in the nude were universally treasured in national museums as incomparable works of art. No wonder the Chinese communists attributed all 'unhealthy tendencies' to the white man.

Nor was that all. By the very nature of things, what is covert and forbidden becomes an obsession. In time the West had developed a mania for sex in all its manifestations, so that press and television were flooded with shots of selected bimbos flaunting their boobs and bums (as they so crudely called them) in provocative poses, of naked passion in grunting action, obscene innuendo and hitherto unspeakable four-letter words. Instead of the mystery and the magic under dim lights, the whole business of joy was exposed to glaring publicity at every turn as if the world spun on it, and the result was not only squalor but surfeit and ultimately boredom. What should have been a delight had become one big yawn.

The East had corrupted the West? It was the West that had corrupted the East with its loose morals. When I explained what the 'missionary position' was to Ping and why it was so called by the innocent natives of Polynesia, she commented without surprise 'of course they taught the people that as well as God'. However, my first 24 hours in Saigon did not impress me with oriental virtue. Seated on the terrace where I was one day to meet Rupert Bond, I was at once assailed by small children carrying trays of rings. That might happen anywhere, but these rings were not for the finger. They were coils edged with a halo of hairy spikes, which when fitted over the male organ were guaranteed to raise to almost unbearable heights the pleasure of one's inamorata of the moment — possibly the child who sold it. As an Australian colleague remarked later not without pride and a hint of white supremacy the kids would be out on the streets and accosting one at seven in the morning; there was no time of day when the inexhaustible Caucasian could not be tempted, it was assumed. Saigon also boasted what must have been the biggest whorehouse in the world — the Bullring — offering a wide choice of several hundred amenable girls from all over Asia. But what impressed me most was the first vivid account I heard of The Game.

It was essentially a form of Chinese roulette, and these were the rules: A party of men would sit at a round table in a Chinese restaurant in the suburb of Cholon and order, say, an eight-course dinner. They would then unzip their trousers and carefully extract their masculine members, while engaging in animated conversation on some deceptively lofty topic. Next, a small boy or girl would be inserted beneath the overhanging tablecloth, and, after critically appraising the array of talent exposed, select one individual and proceed to give him a taste of fellatio. If the chosen recipient of this strictly *sub rosa* attention betrayed himself by voice or gesture during the performance and was correctly challenged, he would have to foot the bill for all. If he was not detected, the Game would move on. It was a neat way of avoiding the usual sordid argument about who was to pick up the tab, it seemed.

But this is anecdotal evidence, and there was a prudish side to the Chinese. Western writers unblushingly churned out hard porn for an expanding market, but the Chinese insisted that their smut was improving literature, designed to educate the unwary in the dangers of overindulgence in sex and thus meeting an essential social need. The author of the famous novel *Chin Ping Mei* was so intent on making absolutely clear to his readers the hazards involved (his hero died a total wreck below the belt) that when it was first translated into English it could be published only after long passages had been put into Latin. On the other hand *The Before Midnight Scholar*, another classic with the same high moral purpose, falls back on the more common convention of reverting to coy euphemisms — his hero's male organ is an 'ambassador' presenting his credentials at 'court'. Others speak of sex circumspectly as the 'game of clouds and rain' or 'fish and water'.

Ping herself could be straight-laced. On one occasion she simply stared open-mouthed at a private exhibition of nudes, and on another was reduced to helpless laughter, a sure sign of embarrassment among Chinese. I was early made aware that she could not bear to hear bad language, whereas I thought it had ceased to exist, having vanished into everyday speech. When the three boys first went to school in Singapore, they were jeered at unmercifully because when speaking Cantonese they did not use all the wrong — or was it the right? — words in what is a notably colourful dialect.

I had to remind myself that if lurid tales were told of the Chinese male, in old China the unmarried female was sternly protected and knew life only from peeking shyly from behind a painted screen or the corner of a fan. When we stood side by side in the Supreme Court building in Singapore and made our vows on that fateful day, I suddenly forgot Hong Kong and had a vision of Ping as the traditional Chinese bride her grandmother must have been, a young girl with bound feet dressed like a doll in stiff brocade and crowned with an elaborate headdress, a fringe of beads veiling the painted mask of her face. She would be impassive but filled with foreboding as she sat alone and invisible in a curtained palanquin and was carried blind through the streets by four bearers towards a groom she might well have never seen.

As we signed our names and left, I saw Ping for a moment as this unblinking image from an alien culture, remote and untouchable, an enigma whose thoughts I could not know. What had I done? I remembered the Confucian tag from which she derived her very name — 'Be apprehensive, as if on the brink of a deep gulf, as if treading on thin ice'. Dressed in a long cheongsam of virginal white with a chaplet of jasmine in her hair, Apprehensive Ice looked back at me for a frozen moment through fathomless black eyes, expressionless as an idol. But once we were through the door the ice broke, and she gave me a sudden gleeful grin. 'So now we have the government paper,' she said, waving our marriage certificate, 'we can jump into bed any time, and nobody can say *one word*.'

5

THE STORY of the next 42 years is soon told. We held our wedding reception in the old Cockpit Hotel, a gracious colonial building before it was inevitably vandalised by the architects and replaced with a repulsive tower block. The reception was followed by a small dinner under the palms on the terrace for a few friends, mainly our four witnesses, Nalini and Tony Schooling and Rosemary and Russell Spurr, then Far East Correspondent of the *Daily Express*, who suggested this book and its title 30 years ago.

The next morning Ping and I drove to Mersing on the east coast of Malaya for our honeymoon. We hired a small boat and spent much of our time swimming with the gaudy fish in the crowded coral reefs and basking on the beaches of the nearby island of Babi Kecil when not otherwise engaged. But joy was not unconfined. On the first evening I was trapped in the Rest House where we were staying by the local British bore, who buttonholed me and would not let go despite all protestations. Desperately I told him I was on my honeymoon, but that was a gross error. '*Honeymoon?* Good show. We must have another drink on that. My shot. No, I insist. *Boy!* Did I ever tell you about. ...?' Yes, he already had — twice, but I was young and he was on the brink of senility. I could not in all conscience refuse to listen, so another interminable anecdote was repeated. And when I finally got away and joined Ping in our room, 1 found that 1 was so badly sunburned that the first words of love I uttered as we sank into bed were (so *she* says) 'For God's sake be careful! Don't touch me! Don't touch me!' For a day or two we could only make love in the sea. ('Like a volcano under water,' says Ping.)

I always had a deep feeling for the sea, and the honeymoon gave me an unforgettable recollection. Babi Kecil is a small island, and on a sunny day under the cloudless sky the sandy beach looked like a huge golden blanket, while the coconut and areca palms inverted in the water moved softly up and down as the sea surged, all a marvellous peacock blue. At that time this place was without human habitation, no sound of men or animals. Such a miracle! At last we had found the Garden of Eden where, according to the Bible, our remote ancestors Adam and Eve did not wear any clothes. So we followed the trend, took off everything, and went into the waves.

When people peel off their clothes they shed their false, obstinate, arrogant, conceited character and become just themselves, returning to their real origins. I felt so happy and part of nature. My love boundless as the sea and sky, I held my beloved partner closely, the rhythm of our breath in harmony, our hearts going pit-pat together full of thoughts of love, so in a twinkling I realised the meaning of the eternal, and the memory ever remained.

Perhaps as D already said, I am by nature bit prudish. I am entirely against stark naked exposing in front of other people, even John Lennon and his Japanese wife Yoko both naked on TV to protest against war and appeal for peace. That was not the right flavour to me. And famous case Christine Keeler swimming naked in pool in aristocratic house in England part of big scandal when Jack Profiuno, Secretary for Defence, lost his job. You must seek a private paradise completely your own for love. Only then can the desire be true and pure. I remember only vaguely the sound of the wind and waves on the return journey to Mersing, the rose-tinted clouds dancing across the evening sky. But the diamond stars whispered to me at night, and the rare treasures of my memory made me feel terrific, rich and satisfied.

Fortunately this idyll was ours before the arrival of the Schoolings, who drove up from Singapore for a few hours to see how we were getting on. But if it was friendly prurience that brought them, they were to pay for it. We bathed together, and Tony was at once bitten by a poisonous jellyfish in precisely the wrong place. How it got into his swimming trunks was a mystery, but it knew its business all right. We rushed him to hospital, pale with fears of future impotence. It was fortunate that art flourishes in adversity, for it was an episode otherwise calculated to shrink the most persevering of marital libidos. After all, it could easily have been me.

Tony recovered, but fate had not done with us. When a few days later we drove happily across the Malayan peninsula to Kuala Lumpur, having been warned that we must on no account stop on the road and risk being ambushed by communist guerrillas, the wind suddenly ripped the rotten canvas top off my old second-hand Hillman on a blind corner of the jungle, just leaving enough of it attached at the back for it to trail its full length on the ground behind us like the train of a wedding dress. It took long, long minutes to wrestle it free and abandon it before we could go on.

But we survived the honeymoon, if somewhat shaken, to settle down in a third-floor apartment overlooking a steaming, flat-roofed Singapore. (There were then, as I remember, only two buildings more than seven storeys high.) Ping taught Chinese literature and history to some 35 vociferously pro-communist senior girls in a Chinese high school almost opposite the home of the leader of the Opposition, a Mr Lee Kuan Yew. I was meanwhile promoted to be Chief Far East Correspondent of the *Observer*, and took on as my first part-time assistant an ebullient Eurasian named Gerald de Cruz who was between moral convictions at the time — born a Catholic, he had become a communist, but had later converted to Islam. (He got away with it, but then so — in a different way — had his successor, a thin, wiry Eddie de Souza. Eddie had dropped a hammer on the head of a Japanese officer while working on the River Kwai bridge and lived to tell the tale.)

For the next 25 years I was in and out of Singapore, covering the march of folly from Japan and South Korea in the east to Burma and Sumatra in the west, inevitably spending most of the time in Vietnam, Cambodia and Laos, but later concentrating on Mao's China. Ping sometimes came with me, especially when I was China watching in Hong Kong, and last accompanied me when I went to Saigon again at the end of the Vietcong Tet Offensive in 1968. But for the most part she stayed at home, for nine years earlier we had succeeded in adopting the three boys — by then fourteen, twelve and nine respectively — and bringing them to Singapore. This had been quite a feat, since iron bureaucratic logic ruled that they had to reside on the island for at least six months before we could become their parents, but could not be granted visas to enter it in the first place until we had done so.

I did not want separated from the boys too long. D already had plan to adopt them soon after we married, but I worried this charity as price of love not fair or healthy. Should I have right to ask him take on the heavy burden? Are you a fool, I asked him? Why you do this? You better should not.

My conscience trouble me, but then one day we went to Macau to spend a weekend with the boys. Everyone happy, but the biggest surprise D's behaviour before the boys quite something I never seen before. He had a facile fund of chitchat and himself became a merry creature and talked with a kind of eagerness, like a child bubbling over with zest of life, so the more he talked the more their little eyes shining. My heart swelled with joy, and words could hardly express my excitement. My doubts had gone, and after forty years the love between father and two surviving sons still perfect.

And meanwhile our happy marriage did make my family able to recognise Dennis as a trustworthy barbarian, especially because my mother deeply touched by his generous way to look after her grandchildren, and when we came to them in Taipei in 1962, everyone want to express their heartfelt feelings. More than that. I told her that D's mother is Hungarian, and gave her long explanation that when the Hsiung-nu, the Huns, moved west in fifth century because lacked grass and searching for pasture they vigorously attacked and occupied Hungarian plain, and ancestors of Hungarians in fact Hsiung-nu. This meant D had blood relationship with Chinese, because in Imperial times Chinese claimed Hsiung-nu one of five races of China, therefore Chinese flag had five colours.

My mother actually believed me. She looked fixedly at D's face, then beamed with pleasure and said, 'no wonder his hair not curly, his nose not like a hook, and without hairy body, and manner gentle and cultivated. Of course cannot be barbarian.' After that she gave a banquet for whole family, and when mentioned D always said he was 'my half-Chinese son-in-law.'

I was in. As the flat was too small for us all, we had rented a two-storey house outside the city limits at Bright Hill, and Ping resigned from her school to raise the boys and about 700 chickens. I said I was surprised that as an animal lover she could keep hens in batteries, but she retorted that it was a matter of priorities, as it had been when she bred pigeons for a living in Hong Kong. It was them or us.

As correspondent of the Observer *Dennis always running around those countries in Southeast Asia for news, and in Vietnam War go to dangerous gunfire places as newspaperman should do so. I say nothing, but I worry so much, my mind always perplexed and uneasy. He say keep chickens cruel but my idea in time to have 5,000 chickens, make enough money from eggs, he will not need to be a journalist and go away, but stay at home, write books. So keep chickens, keep husband.*

I remember once when D in Vietnam Creighton Burns, the correspondent of the Melbourne Age, *flew back from Saigon and came to see me, hand over to me a letter wrote by D, full of delightful thoughts and feeling, touched me very much indeed. But his mention about the fighting in Vietnam frightened me. 'Did you hear any guns?' I asked Creighton. 'Yes, but only when drinking in the bar on the top of our hotel, we heard shots and bombing in the far distance. We get used to it. Nobody really feel danger,' he said to reassure me. I knew better, but he was so kind and meant so well, I bursted into tears. 'No, I can't bear it! I hate war, I want Dennis back here with me', I said. Then I felt shamed. 'Do excuse me.' But it was truth. I felt so lost and lonely.*

She would not be happy until we bought our own home, so we took over the mortgage on a bungalow with more than an acre of terraced garden off Dunearn Road, only to discover too late that we were now inside city limits, and keeping chickens was illegal. After a sad farewell, Ping sold them and bought a gardenful of orchids with the money to cheer herself up. But despite her green fingers, they wilted. This proved a blessing in disguise, for she now set out to find another job, and was lucky enough to be taken on by Radio Television Singapore as a broadcaster and producer in Chinese (scriptwriting for peanuts had been another of her unprofitable activities in Hong Kong).

My dream suddenly fulfilled. I found myself not only fully distracted while Dennis away, but doing what I always want to do — write and work for society and country facing new era of independence. That was because in those days radio and television was government department under Ministry of Culture, and I was in Chinese-language section of the Central Production Unit specially created to guide the different races in Singapore to come together as nation, to reject communism, and to live in harmonious coexistence and united as one. My boss was P.S. Raman, brilliant middle-aged Indian educator, smoke heavily, with sharp mind and brooding eyes, a real thinker, full of ambitious plans for the future of Singapore.

'There is no doubt Chinese culture can help society be stable and conform to high standard of morality,' he told me, 'but to build up a multiracial nation, the traditional system of purely Chinese education of course not suitable. You must find a proper way to handle this situation, and dispel the prejudices in mind of Chinese by persuasion (especially because Mao Zedong now communist boss in Beijing). While Chinese important, they must also accept need for English as official language of Singapore because it is world language of science and also commerce and bridge between races here. Singapore only a man-made country, very fragile, different races as if in small boat sailing against wind and current; if not work together with one heart, boat will sink.'

There was only one other member of Chinese section. I took charge of a forty-five minute Chinese-language Forum once a week, which invited different noted public figures to join in the programme from time to time to make serious study of current problems so that the public could be moulded, and their opinion play a leading role. I also ran programme called 'In and around Singapore' explaining national economy and development like housing programme, and 'What Others Say', analysing world opinion especially in Southeast Asia about international situation.

That time most difficult for Lee Kuan Yew's government, struggling to found a slate. I covered separation of Singapore from Malaysia, Confrontation between Indonesia and Malaysia, and race riots between Chinese and Malays until after midnight, and followed footsteps of government to fight communism. I really believed there was a bright future for this newly independent multilingual country, which could promote understanding of East and West cultures. It seemed the revolutionary fervour of my father urged me to work hard. Meanwhile D sometimes invited to talk on TV about current situation in this region and he and P.S soon very close. I was completely happy.

But all good things come to an end; in 1966 Ping resigned on doctor's advice from her taxing job after undergoing a cancer hysterectomy and thereafter concentrated on the boys and their education.

The year before I had rather unfairly trapped David Astor into giving me a sabbatical to write *Chinese Looking Glass*. It was perhaps that experience, one calculated to lead to all sorts of stimulating fights between Ping and myself, that in 1998 eventually persuaded us it would be fun, even therapeutic, and now safe to write this book, all the skeletons in our respective cupboards having presumably crumbled to dust over the years. I had resigned from the *Observer* in 1981, and we were scraping along on the sale of my books and our savings. That was only possible because we had increased our reserves by selling the Dunearn Road house after 17 years for a useful sum, buying another in Windsor Park for much less, and selling that nine years later for another useful sum. We finally settled for a modest condominium townhouse with a little courtyard that cost only ten times what we had originally paid for Dunearn Road, which at current prices was a steal. For the moment, we were in the black, thanks to Ping's insistence on our buying a property back in 1961. God help us if we had relied on my earnings.

The boys meanwhile went to universities in England and took degrees, Bosco a Ph.D. All then worked in Europe for about ten years, but finally returned to Singapore to settle. They were hardly recognisable as brothers — Dominic, assertive and ambitious, an irrepressible trader whose dream was to make his million, retire and fish; Bosco, a stocky, gregarious beer-drinker, a rebel and a karate black belt with a dangerously quiet voice who was nevertheless to become a Principal Scientific Officer in the Singapore administration; John, tall, shy, modest, a meticulous accountant but laid back about absolutely everything else in life.

The three contrived to marry Chinese wives from three different countries speaking three different dialects — Dominic a Hokkien from Taiwan, Bosco a Chaozhou from Hongkong, John a Hakka from Singapore — and they in turn produced our three Chinese grandchildren. So what chance did I have, one against ten in a DIY Chinese Tower of Babel? Well, after 42 years Ping and I work today in almost identical studies, one above the other, amicably writing the same book separately yet together. How did we make it this far? That is the real story, and will take slightly longer to tell.

6

WHAT was the secret? Talking on the same wavelength? Certainly not in terms of linguistic fluency. Rather the reverse. I don't wish to imply that our first wondering exchanges were on a Me-Tarzan-You-Ping level, but she used to say that fortunately we spoke each other's language so badly that we could not quarrel. In Tokyo they distrust you if you speak Japanese too well, and I sympathise: as my division advanced through Italy during World War II, all the local characters who spoke fluent English and were eager to act as our interpreters turned out to be deported gangsters from Chicago bent on skinning us.

And of course speech is a trap, a medium for misunderstanding — as Shaw said, England and America are two countries divided by a common language. For one thing, definitions can be different. When Ping asked me to show her the poor in London, I shamefacedly took her to a squalid, rundown slum, only to be told, 'no, I mean *reary* poor.' These people were affluent compared with the wretched of China. They weren't even starving. And you said you would show me the beautiful scenery of England; where is it?' she asked, as we travelled down to Somerset by train. I pointed to the fields, the parkland, the gentle hills rolling by. She shook her head, dissatisfied. Scenery to her was a painting on a Chinese screen, improbable mountains wreathed in cloud surrounding unfathomable lakes smooth as glass.

Then if it was not language, was love the whole secret? Again, the very word is a pitfall. It depends what you mean. 'Apples, love?' a barrow boy once asked Ping in a London market in that affectionate way they have when grossly overcharging you. It was the summer of 1965 and we had been on a tour of Europe. 'I know apples,' said Ping, 'but what is love?' Good question. I tried to explain. Her reaction was censorious.

I hate these kind honeyed words in London market, sometimes this title they change to 'dear' or 'darling' or if customer young girl 'duckie', but no meaning. Not sincere. How can they be? Just sweet mouth talk, talk not from heart. Language too rich means words too cheap. Chinese say 'Much politeness must be false'. D complains we also say 'Much politeness offends no one.' But that is for foreigners, I told him: I talk to you as if you are another Chinese. Even we often just call each other 'Mouse', which is like code for everything — beloved, sweetest, affectionate, dearest, godknowwhat. No need to say. (As in man or mouse, for Christ's sake?) Of course. Means want live husband not dead hero — warm home, peace, love, especially now getting old. Chinese wife and husband don't ever call each other anything. No such thing. Just 'you'.

Love was too real for it to be devalued by trite clichés, but may often be expressed obliquely — when she dropped me off somewhere, Ping might say: 'go inside, or my car won't move.' It made my day. Better still: 'there is only one moment I forget you.'

Don't waste words on the Chinese. 'Fine words and an insinuating appearance are seldom associated with virtue,' remarks Confucius. They distrust language, for their own is often too scented with flowery euphemisms specifically designed to deceive everybody including themselves. The philosopher Han Feizi pointed out that the corrupt bureaucrat who gave his friends hand-outs from state funds was called 'benevolent', and only those who twisted the law to suit their family were 'men of loyal principle'.

That was more than two thousand years ago, but matters did not improve with age. In the early 20th century a warlord's take from drug traffic was a 'tax to discourage opium', but a 'laziness tax' was imposed on those who failed to grow it for him, while a 'goodwill tax' paid his penniless soldiers, its object being to dissuade them from creating ill will by robbing the peasantry he was thus robbing himself. The communists stopped all that nonsense, merely to replace it with their own prevarications — 'There is no crime in China', 'Ours is a happy life under the correct leadership of Chairman Mao', 'Joyous are the peasants working on the hydroelectric schemes', and most notably 'All our economic targets under the Five-Year Plan have been basically achieved' — 'basically' meaning they had not been achieved at all. Mao Zedong's disastrous economic experiment of 1958 was called 'The Great Leap Forward' even after some 16 million people (figures vary) had died of starvation or from floods or disease as a result of it. The masses were described as 'well-fed and supremely content', and it was all 'thanks-to-Chairman-Mao-and-the-Chinese-Communist-Party', according to sanctimonious cadres who would be flogging watered-down penicillin to sick old widows of the dead once the old man was gone.

So when in 1997 the United States and Japan strengthened their military links by signing a new 'security treaty', but issued a joint communiqué that 'stressed the continued interest of both countries in furthering cooperation with China', Colin Powell had cause to remark unhappily, 'I think the first reaction from China was a little bit sharp.' That figured, bearing in mind the recent massive display of American naval strength in the Taiwan Straits. The Chinese know how to translate words like 'security' and 'cooperation' in such circumstances. They greet political speeches with slow uniform clapping, which seems eminently suitable to me: it sounds so like barracking. They judge men and countries only by their actions. In consequence, they are a race of Eliza Doolittles when it comes to love: 'Don't talk of moon, don't talk of Fall, don't talk at all! *Show me!*'

In 1956 we were separated by a bloody riot in Hong Kong, and it was Ping who 'showed me' by dodging through the roadblocks and concertina wire and running the gauntlet of glass-strewn streets to find me. Within the traditional Chinese family, as I had to learn, no one says 'thank you' at every turn, because loyalty and gratitude are taken for granted and expressed in reciprocal acts, not verbal cop-outs. If one of his younger brothers began making grandiloquent promises, Dominic's sceptical response even as a boy was always limited to two words — '*do it*'. When I accused Ping of starting to say thank you for everything, she retorted, 'only because by now half-barbarian', and her invariable response to my 'good morning' is, even today, an absent-minded 'yes?'

It is small men have big mouths, talk too much all time, the more talk the less act. Cannot trust them. Like politicians. Good men who even die for country use only few words. My mother very quiet woman, when I say a lot, tell me I am vulgar. Most talk is nonsense. Someone make all sorts of promises, I say go to hell. Show me.

I did, and so did she. Action was the real language of married love — thoughtful gestures, giving way, understanding each other's wishes, a silent hug, the right gift (but a tortoiseshell backscratcher for my birthday?).

About any small detail in life such New Year, Valentine Day, of course my birthday, he never forget to surprise me by nice presents. I remember the first year after married I heard sound nearby Christmas tree, I looked around, there was rattan basket tied up with beautiful ribbon, when I undone it, suddenly a white kitten jumped to my feet, just like snowball rolling, and made more noise to bless good wishes. I had once complain have no cat, so just exactly my dream was coming true, better than pearls.

I am not underrating the importance of the spoken word, and we did in time progress to the point where we could quarrel quite effectively. But not disastrously because we never did acquire a talent for each other's native tongue. I staggered along in Mandarin like a drunk on cobblestones, the language made even more incomprehensible thanks to what the French would doubtless call the pernicious spread of English, and the tendency of Chinese to use it whenever they thought it would be helpful. (In Japan they practise it on you, which is even more baffling.)

After I had hugged a precious bottle of Scotch to myself during a three-day rail journey to Beijing from Hong Kong, I finally opened it in my hotel room and, after consulting my phrase book, confidently ordered *qi shui*, only to find when I had added it to three fingers of irreplaceable White Horse that it was not soda, but lemonade. 'Ah, yes,' a kind friend told me too late, as they always do, 'but you see in a hotel for foreigners the Chinese for soda is "so-da".' And that was back in 1955. Years later I asked for a glass of *pi jiu* in a crowded bar in Singapore, only to have the wretched waitress look at me dumbfounded; my face was saved when Dominic said, 'Dad, in a place like this the Chinese for beer is "beer".'

'The Mandarin for "guard house" is *men fang*, right?' I asked Ping just the other day.

'Of course, but you won't use it. No one will understand. In Singapore they say *jing wei shi!*

'*Jing wei shi*. Good.'

'Yes, but only for writing, really. They also won't understand if you say it.'

'So what do you say when you say it?'

'"Guard house", of course.'

Terminology can be another trap. When our younger daughter-in-law applied for a civil service post Ping told me on my arrival home one day, 'John says Ivy failed her medical test, because too *fat*.' Too *fat?* Ivy was beginning to show a little comfortable cushioning here and there, but no more. But in any case what was the government doing recruiting officers according to their *avoirdupois*. Why not according to the size of their feet? It was monstrous. I would write a stinking letter to the *Straits Times*, I would phone Rex Shelley on the Public Service Commission and tell him just what I thought of him (the Commission was not involved, but never mind), dammit, I would damn well... I was denied these pleasures, however, for John later confessed that he had not told his mother that the adverse report was about a blood test, not a physical examination, and he used the word 'fat' on the phone because he could not think of the Chinese for 'protein'. Ivy got the job, and I subsided.

Then I had always to adjust to Ping's idiosyncratic Pinglish. This was not just a question of pronunciation, of separating almonds from onions and polish from porridge and melons from marrow, or even untangling everyday expressions like 'that is I got'. In her mind everything was a sharp picture, perhaps transposed from Chinese characters. Abstract phrases, like soft words, were out. Hard metaphor came as naturally to her as bad grammar. She thought in graphics. When she had to have traction for a spinal problem they 'hung her every morning' she told shocked friends unacquainted with the joys of physiotherapy, and when she was tired she felt like 'bread soaked in tea'. Refugees had a 'here without a there.' Resignedly making welcome a tiresome guest was 'unrolling a red carpet for the dog', but there was no avoiding him, because he was always running around his friends 'like a revolving restaurant.'

There was no affectation. It was as natural to her as swearing is to a soldier. It was her world, a world that was a series of images seen through other eyes than mine in which caterpillars ate leaves 'but left the bones', the chattering classes were like 'bunch birds', and when she went out I had to 'keep my ear up for the postman.' Sometimes it was a little baffling, as when she said of the car, 'we can nearly seat three in front', or for a shopgirl when told 'I want something exactly different', or perhaps 'a dress without underneath' or 'paper soup' (soup in packets). She once complained of a market purchase, 'chicken so small, cook too much will become like bird', and of an unsatisfactory laundry 'why the people wash the shirt so dirty?' And what of the fabulous 'butterfly', that most oxymoronic of all oxen (or lepidoptera)? But then when I said of Watergate that the *Washington Post* coverage exposed President Nixon's villainy, it was her turn to be fazed. How could covering *expose*?

The pitfalls were endless, but Singapore was a good school for partners in a mixed marriage to learn to think twice before judging each other too quickly by their words — or deeds. Singaporeans do not speak Pinglish, but they do speak 'Singlish'. When Ping says 'Why you worry?' she means it. When a Singaporean says it in answer to a question it can mean 'mind your own business'. To the newcomer Singlish appears to be a terse, crude, insulting pidgin that is to English what a squeezebox is to a Steinway, or like playing Mozart on a mouth organ. It is incapable of the frilly refinements of the mother tongue. If you ask a shopkeeper in England to sell you a flashlight he might answer, 'I'm awfully sorry, sir, I can't help you just at the present, as we are waiting for further supplies.' But in Singapore his reply would be reduced to a wooden-faced 'cannot', and if you had the temerity to ask for something else, 'also cannot', or the more informative 'no stock' if you were lucky. If you ask for someone on the phone, the abrupt response from his secretary is invariably 'Where you from?' (You only exist as a cog in some commercial enterprise.)

But unlike the oh-yeah-great-cool-man gibberish of the Anglo-

Saxon who is rapidly losing the use of language altogether, Singlish is at the same time wonderfully expressive. Take the robust comment on your limited intelligence, 'Small job your head, lah!' Or the equivalent of 'Forgive my asking but do you usually walk into a room just like that without knocking?' — 'Not shy, ah?' Or the Singlish for 'I'm so sorry about your trouble with the police, but you did rather ask for it, didn't you?' — a sarcastic 'Die for you.' 'Now don't tell me you too disagree with me' becomes 'you also another one' (like Brutus).

When Singapore Chinese speak English and not Singlish it may still come out as a string of sharp monosyllables as toneless as the mechanical clack-clack of a pair of high heels late for work. Listening to the stiletto voices of many of the young women, female clones in smart black suits with identical masks of makeup and identical casques of sleek black hair, you might be tempted to think this a society of dishy automatons. And when they do give life to a sentence they may put the stress in all the wrong places, like a child reading aloud a text he does not understand, as in 'I left the sports *page* on the *armchair* in the sitting *room*,' so that you wonder if they know what they are talking about anyway. And then what do they talk about? Food, shopping, the price of everything ('how much you pay?'), the 'five Cs' that are the dream — modified only during the economic crisis of 1998 — of these seemingly two-dimensional creations of the Maker: cash, credit card, car, condominium, country club. ('Like children in a toyshop, Singaporeans are trying to hold as many goodies in their small hands as they can,' as someone put it in the *Straits Times*).

Do they sound cold and unfeeling? When asked in court why he had not apologised, a senior secondary school teacher who had scalded a colleague by upsetting a cup of hot coffee on her back replied coolly in 1998, 'I've not cultivated the reflex to say I'm sorry.' Note it is a mere mechanical 'reflex' anyway, and therefore devoid of feeling. Too bad. And what about their actions? Unfortunately these, too, may often seem to match their speech. Some appear to be both deaf and blind, for they will shout at each other even when walking only a foot apart, and meanwhile stride past your nose as if you were not there. Give up your seat to a golden oldie in a bus, and you may be rewarded with a suspicious glare as she pointedly brushes it clean with her hand before sitting down. Put out a gift box for a children's home, and it will be filled in no time with unwanted, dirty and broken toys, armless dolls, and board games with missing pieces that people have been just waiting to dump. Offer free school books to the poor, and the rich will rush up in their Mercedes and trample each other to grab first. Knock a dollar off the price of an entrance ticket to something, and a mile-long queue may be there by dawn. When a man is killed in a fall from a high-rise block, a bystander asks if the wristwatch on the still-warm body is a Rolex; and when a police car arrives at the scene of a drowning, another notes the registration number as a possible winner in the next social service lottery draw. At times, Singapore Chinese can seem as ill-bred as they are well-educated, or like peasants without an agriculture.

How wrong can one get? That is only the downside of the stereotype, if sometimes too close for comfort, and one must not go by appearances. Many Singaporeans speak better English than the English, and as for their being cold, more than half of all murders committed in 1996 were hot-blooded crimes of passion, which must prove something. Unfeeling? A Bangladeshi worker who illegally enters the country and is crippled after being mugged and left in a drain to die is inundated with gifts from Singaporeans who queue up to file shyly past his bedside with their offerings, including the whole day's earnings of a taxi-driver, a one-thousand dollar note from a young man in jogging shorts, a five-thousand-dollar cheque from a middle-aged woman with a card reading 'forgive us'

— $60,000 in a few days, most of it anonymous. The *Straits Times* carries a report of a poor Malaysian housewife suffering cruelly from elephantiasis and is at once flooded with telephone calls from Singaporeans wanting to help pay for her $50,000 operation. And both beneficiaries are foreigners.

So is Princess Di, but when she is killed in a car crash in Paris a thousand Singaporeans queue up for hours under a scorching sun at the British High Commission to sign the book of condolence and offer flowers. This was the country in which the British suffered their most humiliating defeat in World War Two and abandoned the local population to the purely imaginary mercies of the Japanese. Yet never in more than 40 years has any Singaporean made the slightest derogatory remark about it to me.

Of course there are the good and the greedy everywhere. But there is more to it than that. This is a society with an idiom of its own. The man who pushes past you rudely as if you do not exist will stop and oblige with a smile if you ask him the way; the driver of the BMW behind you who blares at you insistently for holding him up may pull over and change your wheel for you when you explain you have both a bad flat and a bad back. I am brushed aside by an uncaring crowd of shoppers in a supermarket, but when I fall two men — a Chinese and an Indian — at once rush up to haul me to my feet and wind a handkerchief around my bleeding elbow. The same Singaporean can appear thoughtless, selfish and uncouth, and yet warm, friendly and helpful almost simultaneously in the eyes of an uncomprehending foreigner.

I edge my way past a woman blocking a narrow path with a bicycle, and she moves aside slowly without an apology. But when I thank her in tones of heavy irony, she gives me a gracious 'you're welcome', as if she had gladly done me a favour. And the point is she means it. I stand patiently at the desk of a salesman who ignores me while he writes in an account book, finally glances up at me expressionlessly, and goes on writing. He then stops for a moment to take my money without a word, tosses it into a till, and bends again to his ledger. Affronted, I decide to make myself a nuisance and ask him if he can direct me to a nearby Italian restaurant I've heard of, just to see what he will do. He gets up, takes me by the arm, tells me the food is excellent and I should not miss the spaghetti à la carbonara, and walks me to the door to show me the way. I am left scratching my head.

It is too easy to be misled by one's own conventions. I think the penny dropped at last when I stopped my car near the entrance of a driveway to a block of flats and a Chinese woman barked peremptorily from 20 yards away, 'I don't think you should park there!' Walking up to her, I asked her just who she thought she was, yelling at me like that, whereupon a husband appeared from nowhere and demanded in an injured tone, 'Why are you so rude to my wife, when she speaks to you so politely?'

Politely? He actually thought she was being polite? And then I saw it. Of course he did — by his lights. A well-disposed Singaporean is uncompromisingly direct, as he would be to an old acquaintance. By the same token, Singlish is not rude; it is just that its pithiness makes it seem so. When Ping cannot find briefs to fit her, the sylphlike saleswoman says, 'This kind made for pretty, slim girl. You too fat. Get much fatter, any size cannot wear, lah.' Ping (at 110 lbs) merely laughs — 'she means friendly'. It is the right response. Blunt speech can be a compliment, a gesture of intimacy, even a form of straight-faced kidding. The girl feels she can be frank with you as if you were her sister.

The possibilities of mixing signals are endless, and the whole comedy of errors was epitomised for me by an encounter with an open pick-up full of workers in the back which cut in on me sharply before a traffic light one day. I shouted angrily and raised two up-yours fingers, whereupon the workers broke out in broad smiles and gave me the V-sign in return. It was a vivid lesson in instant incomprehension.

It was Ping who pointed out the obvious. If I was offended by the way the Chinese went on, it was my own ignorance that was at fault. *Tout cornprendre c'est tout pardonner.* To understand all is to forgive all. And to know the Chinese one must not only study their customs, but get down to the roots from which they have sprung. Why did they simply ignore strangers until there was some reason for recognising their existence? Because it was second nature; their whole society was a series of concentric circles founded on an age-old tradition that put loyalty to the family and clan first; friends, fellow villagers, even people of the same province second; outsiders nowhere. Ignoring you was dictated by custom, helping you by the heart. Why were they so materialistic and grasping, so devoted to the stressful chase for the five Cs, so anxious to grab something for nothing? Their forebears had suffered centuries of dire poverty, sometimes semi-starvation, and this had made them *pa shu* — 'fearful of losing'. Why did their English sometimes sound so soullessly singsong? It was not for lack of feeling, but stemmed from the fact that their own South Chinese dialects were essentially a series of sharp-edged monosyllables. Moreover, each monosyllable had its own tone, which left the sentence as a whole without any. The lesson for me was that only after I had explored the whys and wherefores of the Chinese would Ping and I be able to live in harmony, for we started with so little in common.

People more important to understand than words. Otherwise in real life how can our love last? First, must accept gap between cultures, realise other side ideas not too bad, so appreciate each other but agree to be different. Then can sail safely through conflicting waters of two civilisations. You ask me teach you Mandarin. What is the use, when you know nothing about 5,000 years tradition behind the Chinese character? What good is Chinese man speaking perfect English with Oxford accent who never read one word English history, never heard Robin Hood, William Conqueror, Magna Carta, Waterloo, godknowwhat? No, first you learn China, then you learn Chinese.

So I read it all in translation — Chinese history, philosophy, literature, science — and was quickly hooked. It means that my Mandarin is still 'no better than she should be', as they used to say of fallen women, but we now share an understanding of each other that requires no words, for 'those that know do not speak', as the Taoists say. It crosses without effort the linguistic faultline in our marriage that could otherwise start a domestic earthquake. Talk of Taoist fables or the Taiping Rebellion, *The Taming of the Shrew* or the Tower of London and we will greet the allusion with a nod and not a blank stare. Ping often takes a shortcut to English literature by reading simplified versions of well-known novels, but when she reads the original version she now shows an uncanny appreciation of style — 'good writing like crisp apples'. (Gobbledegook is 'bloody nuisance words'. How right. But language never grows old gracefully.) On my side I learned that while her writing might sometimes seem unblushingly lyrical to me, it would be accepted as a matter of course by educated Chinese, for whom the line between prose and poetry can be tissue-thin.

When I asked her what she was reading in bed and she replied 'just some rubbish', turning the cover of the book to reveal that it was *Pride and Prejudice*, I did not bristle. I knew that this was not a criticism of Jane Austen, but a definition of the genre — in China even the most renowned fiction was traditionally regarded as disreputable, and the mandarins who wrote it were usually careful to remain anonymous. But one had to know that.

We had our weak spots, we soon discovered, mine too numerous to catalogue. On her side it emerged that Ping had no bump of locality and her knowledge of western geography remained obstinately vague, despite her reading. England was always 'London', and Scotland was 'England', and she foxed me by assuring me that 'America' began with a 'U' until it dawned on me that, in fact, much of it did. She further mystified me when she phoned from Florida once to say she was going to fly to Panama for the weekend. *Panama?* For fun? She had confused it with the Bahamas. I consoled myself with the memory of the British prime minister who said, when shown a map of China, 'So Canton is down *there*. I always thought it was up there,' pointing towards the Manchurian border.

When she toured the US without me, I was worried stiff as to how she would get around the map, and visualised her swallowed up forever by some nightmarish ogre of an airport like O'Hare while trying to change planes. She disliked travelling anyway, wanted to stay at home forever with her garden and her dog and her piano and her tennis and me, though not necessarily in that order, I hope. Going down the road to the supermarket was a chore. How would she fare transiting Chicago? I should have known. She followed her own golden rule, which should be the golden rule of nations — be modest, never upstage.

When get lost I just behave I am stupid old Chinese woman know nothing, then the people very kind and help me. If you are too proud and clever, and try to do everything and find your way everywhere by yourself, you get lost. Then if you complain direction signs all wrong, say airport's fault you don't know where you are, they send you to Hell instead of New York.

No comment. (This was in the early nineties.) But the system worked. When I saw her off to Toronto from Heathrow in 1998 she was afraid of being late for her plane and hurried through the ticket barrier 25 minutes before the passengers for her flight were called. 'She'll have a long walk to Gate 20 by herself and there'll be no one at the other end,' the checker said gloomily, shaking his head. Helpless on the outside, I had a vision of a forlorn Ping alone and lost forever in the entrails of Terminal Four, and spent a panicky 45 minutes making a nuisance of myself before I could find out whether she had actually found and boarded the plane.

'Why you worry?' she asked me on the phone from Toronto the next day, mildly surprised. 'I just tell one British Airways girl I don't understand how to find the way, she introduce me to second pilot, he carry my bag to that kind motor trolley, and we rode together to the plane. Very comfortable. Then he very kind put me on board before all the other people.' Just so.

My ludicrous fears about Ping's ability to look after herself derived from the idea that when she was alone in the West she was a bewildered Chinese lost in a strange, sometimes incomprehensible environment. In fact she was not bewildered, but very Chinese, and attracted precisely and above all by the strangeness. We still had, of course, much to learn about each other's countries and cultures, but meanwhile our immediate problem when we settled down together in our three-roomed Singapore flat in March 1957 was to handle the everyday differences that grew from those roots — in our eating habits, manners, customs, tastes in colour schemes, furniture, ornaments, starting with the set of prints of bird paintings mounted on cork we had been given as a wedding present.

'I think look very nice in two rows on wall above bookcase.'
'But Ping, you can't, they're *table mats*.'
'So?'

7

'SO?'

The place mats very beautiful, total six pieces, and all birds different, their colour gorgeous and the movement absolutely splendid. So why not hang on wall? You say cannot because place mats should belong on dining table. Well, plates should belong on dining table too but I see allowed to hang on wall also sometimes. So why not place mats? English customs very odd, wasn't it? I mean how to explain ...?

Was this to be the first challenge? I was a prey to uneasy thoughts. What had happened to my vision of the submissive and trembling young bride being carried through the streets in a closed palanquin to her new lord? The answer was simple. Like most visions it was an optical illusion. The more man was the master in China, the greater the ingenuity woman showed in paying him only lip service while undermining his mastery. Within the wider Confucian realm, the Japanese wife might bow low and kneel humbly to serve her husband, but she took away his entire pay packet every month as soon as he got it and gave him only pocket money. While the wife of a Vietnamese stood humbly behind us to serve us both lunch in Saigon without sitting down herself, her husband glumly described her as the real 'minister of the interior' in their home; he was not even allowed into the kitchen from which it came. (Nor was I into mine.) A thousand years ago the women of Hunan conspired to get one up on their menfolk by inventing a secret script in order to exclude them from their private exchanges. Two thousand years before that only women had surnames in China. And since then the expression 'dragon lady' has not been coined for nothing.

The trembling girl in the palanquin? Behind the bridegroom she would now face for the first time a far more daunting figure — the matriarch of his family, the ultimate object of veneration described in the classic Chinese novel, *The Dream of the Red Chamber*. And in time the submissive bride would become the implacable matriarch in her turn. (Time *healed* all, did they say? At least in the good old days a young Chinese wife could be divorced just for talking too much. Not any more.) I remembered with distaste the Chinese joke about a club of ten henpecked husbands caught by their wives practising group therapy in a 'teahouse'. Nine bolted, but one was cheered by the bystanders for having the cool cheek to stay behind in his chair to face his spouse — until it turned out that he had died of a heart attack.

I glanced at the scroll I had hung over the bookcase where Ping wanted the table mats, a large portrait I had bought dirt cheap in Beijing of a magnificently clad old dame with a face of iron seated magisterially on what looked like a throne. Surely Ping must appreciate this epitome of a Chinese matriarch? The table mats would be kept in their place. 'Yes, must take that down, of course,' she said, her eyes following mine. 'That is why need table mats that wall.'

'Take it down? But it's beautiful. You Chinese venerate your ancestors, and they told me in the shop this was an ancestor picture they were getting rid of for someone because the communists disapproved of them.'

Ping turned a widening eye on me. 'Of course ancestor picture.

But not my ancestor.' I hadn't thought of that. And there was more to come.

Dennis say wrong put table mats on wall. But then how much more wrong hang this painting? This scroll is painting of someone else dead ancestor of high position and wealth and must be treated with solemn and respect. They are called 'happy god' and must be painted dressed in ceremonial robes as if to have an audience with the emperor. At ordinary time all such painting would be kept rolled up in big wooden boxes, only at Chinese New Year brought out and hung on wall of imposing shrine where all ancestral tablets also arranged, men on the left, women on the right. In front of shrine a long table full of flowers and fruits and other offerings, and candles and joss sticks burning. Then the whole family one by one come forward to kowtow, because they are not just paintings and tablets but the spirits of the ancestors. Dennis just think some sort of eastern traditional art, but they are like ashes of dead persons. How then can hang all year round on wall in strange house?

I blinked. Ping had gone; the alien girl in the palanquin was back. In my ignorance I had committed an even worse sacrilege than hanging table mats on the wall, it seemed. But we ended, appropriately, love-all — no ancestors, no place mats. In theory, furnishing the flat could have provided the first battlefield between East and West, but it seemed that that did not have to be. The Chinese have suffered terrible hardships during their unforgiving past, but when one considers their furniture, one begins to wonder if people get the history they deserve, for it suggests a strong streak of masochism and a devotion to excruciating discomfort. I was ready to make a last-ditch stand for bum-friendly barbarian armchairs as against the pitiless stools and carved wooden seats that the Chinese seemed to have specifically invented for getting rid of unwanted guests. And I was not going to celebrate holy wedlock on a gilded platform of hard planks with a porcelain pillow under my head guaranteed to give me a crick in the neck. But there was no contest, and each gave way to the other room by room, our two designs for living meeting in a bed with an unyielding inch-think kapok mattress on Ping's side and the latest twangling box-spring Slumberland Special on mine.

I frowned out of the dining room the resident enamel washbasin that unaesthetic but practical Singaporeans were wont to install. Ping frowned off the wall an otherwise banal painting of flowers which I had hung for the elegant string of Chinese characters — presumably lyric verse — scribbled down one side of it. 'Oh, picture not too bad but writing rubbish,' she said. (Chinese characters can always catch out the unwary. The Royal Navy once put a recruiting ad in the *Observer* weekend magazine showing a particularly jolly jack tar on the loose in exotic Hong Kong. Unfortunately for the Admiralty, the graceful ideograms above the establishment behind him read 'pawnshop'.)

But Ping approved of much that I had picked up here and there simply because I thought it looked nice. I was enjoying beginner's luck, it seemed. A set of six colour prints turned out to be rather fine book illustrations for *The Dream of the Red Chamber* (including one depicting the young hero lying in bed apparently having the dream); a rather ordinary gold-painted carving, she explained happily, depicted a famous incident in which Confucius was asked by a small boy why the sun was big yet cool at dawn, yet small but hot at midday. (The venerable Sage was baffled.) And it seemed that the meaningless lacquer work on a painted wooden sofa I had found in a Singapore junk shop in fact illustrated a classic tale about filial piety, in which a middle-aged man rolls on the floor like a two-year-old to persuade his aged parents they are younger than they feared.

True, I had mistakenly hung a plaque of the Chinese character for 'Fortune' the right way up at New Year; it should have been upside down so that the luck would go into the floor, not out through the roof. But then when we received the gift of a giant Dutch biscuit in the shape of a garland, Ping — having already seen wreaths pinned to people's front doors at Christmas — hung it up on ours, ignoring my protests, and when it finally began to breed life, sprayed it with insecticide and rendered it quite inedible anyway. You win some, you lose some.

D gave me a big flower vase and incense burner in pure green, made by China in Qing Dynasty, besides one Tang horse mixed with three different colours. During he worked in Beijing, he also came home with few beautiful figures, excavated copies of Qin Dynasty soldiers and palace musicians all made by pottery. But most exciting was picture by...

It was a long scroll depicting a delicious Tang Dynasty maiden they had shown me in an art gallery in Beijing after I had told them in Mandarin with many gestures (thank Heaven for body language) that I didn't want landscapes, but paintings of people.

She examined it critically. 'How much you pay?'

'About $30.'

'Thirty dollars?'

'Well, I liked it, and it was the right size for the wall, and I was told the communists were making curio shops sell everything off very cheap,' I answered apologetically, 'and it didn't seem very much at the time.'

Ping turned opaque eyes on me and shook her head. 'Worth fifteen, maybe twenty —'

'Well, even so —'

'Fifteen, maybe twenty thousand American.' She pointed to the characters in the right-hand bottom corner. 'It's by Chang Daqian, most famous Chinese painter today.' She was over the hill, ignoring the fact that I hadn't the faintest idea what I was doing when I bought it.

Perfectly wonderful. But the real reason made me happy was that things he buy mean Chinese art and culture slowly but deep-going influence on D's mind.

When Ping wrote that later, I looked around suspiciously. There had been some give and take. The green-and-white awning I had had fixed over the veranda had been condemned as 'like ice cream cart', but the fitted wall mirrors in the bathroom had passed muster: 'without them feel lonely, with them like going to party'. The bum-friendly armchairs had been duly sanctioned and were in place, and two identical mattresses now levelled out the bed, both five inches thick but stuffed solid and laid over planks, an acceptable compromise.

But apart from a few sticks of strictly utilitarian furniture, I was surrounded by Chinese tables, Chinese chests and Chinese cupboards, Chinese carpets, Chinese paintings and Chinese calligraphy, Chinese vases, bowls, figurines, pottery and crockery, and even two red-and-gold pieces of carved wood which Ping explained were our 'carpenter's grandmother's front legs', for which she had paid him five dollars — they had come from the foot of the lady's marriage bed. About the only western thing in sight was a clock I objected to but Ping treasured. I said it should be relegated to her study; she wanted it in the sitting room. We settled the problem in our usual spirit of compromise — so of course it hangs in the sitting room. And then I realised what had happened.

The Chinese empire was essentially a cultural concept. The most suitable emblem for it would be a pair of chopsticks, not a flag. 'Chinese expansionism', as a military proposition, is a grossly overrated bogey, as the wiser men in the West are aware. It was less the tradition of the Chinese to conquer the neighbours with arms than it was to soak them up by converting them to their own Confucian civilisation, if occasionally with the prod of a pike. Conversely, when rude barbarians invaded China, as they did with monotonous regularity, they were not flung out again by force, but simply absorbed, swallowed up by the omnivorous Chinese way of life so that they often became more Chinese than the Chinese themselves. And now it seemed that after the hapless Tatars, Kitans, Kins, Mongols and Manchus, it had become my turn. But I was not totally absorbed.

Chinese are used to treat Sunday like happy new year, always polish shoes put on best dress and go out to enjoy ourself together with family and friends. But for some English Sunday could be most dull day in the whole week. Depends. D liked to put on comfortable disgraceful old dress, even not shaved, stay at home to read, or mess with car, won't see friends. Very peculiar. So because I must be with him of course I don't go for picnic or anything but also mess with car, work in garden and give dogs a good wash. So after such weekend car run much smoothly, the garden more beautiful, the dogs shining, so I suppose make some sense. But funny, and hard to get used, and when D not in Singapore I dress up and rush out on Sunday to be with friends in lots amusing places, talk and laugh in Cantonese or Mandarin and don't worry about difficult questions in English like whether dinner means lunch or supper which still don't exactly understand.

There were limits to the extent to which I could be beguiled, and music, I feared, might be another language that divided us. For Ping was a devotee of Peking Opera, which to me sounded (when I first heard it) like a caterwaul of concupiscent tabbies screeching on a hot tin roof while someone below tried to scare them off by banging a kitchenful of saucepans together. On her side Ping felt much the same about mindless pop as she did about modern western art in the shape of a cow sawn in half to make a statement in a prominent London museum, and her reaction to duodecatonic Schoenberg was 'You mean that is music?' But if the carpenter's grandmother's front legs symbolised the conquest of the East, our secondhand upright symbolised the counterattack of the West, since we had not bought it for myself, but for Ping.

Ping's love affair with Chopin et al. has lasted a lifetime. With nearly a quarter of a century to go, she swore in 1957 that she would subdue the piano by the time she was fifty, and now in her seventies still fights a stubborn rearguard action against it. She had meanwhile bought tapes of all the etudes and nocturnes, and was delighted when our two Alsatians showed a predilection for singing counterpoint whenever she played them (while having a definite thing against Delius) — 'so musical, the dogs'.

As soon as the sound of music came from the house to the garden, instantly the two dogs rushed on to the terrace started to sing in unison, Morgan howling in sonorous voice to follow the melody entirely, then Seagoon joining in barking or yelping to show the lively rhythm, with D conducting their performance making the evening with guests most enjoyable. One lady asked me how to teach the dogs to sing. I told her frankly I did nothing, and gentleman explained to us 'don't forget they are German, of course have a gift for music'. He was also German, of course.

Ping will sit through any programme of the Singapore Symphony Orchestra provided it includes a piano solo or concerto. She is not averse to Beethoven's Sixth, either. But much orchestral music is 'just noise'. Noise? I was almost surprised she knew the word. I discovered at battle school in Scotland during World War II that when we practised blowing up railway lines (be sure to stagger the charges so that you twist the rail) I would lose my hearing. 'Ears wax up,' said the A4O. 'When you're 50 you may be a bit deaf.' I was 24, and shrugged. Fifty? I ask you. But he was right. The unfair thing is that as the hearing deteriorates with age, one becomes even more sensitive to certain sounds. I can be driven berserk by screaming toddlers and bawling teenagers, as Ping has sorrowfully indicated, and when our soi-disant Shetland collie-cross barks I yell at him like the drill sergeant I once was, so that he now goes by the sobriquet of 'Shutup Charlie'. (Charlie is the vociferous successor of our four Alsatians).

But Ping does not hear Charlie or me. She is immune to noise, for psychological deafness is the defence the Chinese have developed against their own bedlam. She might well remark with wonder that, be it ever so humble, an Englishman's home is his castle, where he can bolt the door and relax in peace and quiet in front of the TV. For I am sure the Chinese idea of home was never a castle. When it was not an entire walled village teeming with the progeny of some patriarch with a dozen or two wives and concubines, it could still be a cramped warren bursting with the uproar created by three or more generations of one family living under one roof, each member shouting louder than the last in order to be heard (and to prove he or she was right) above a general hullabaloo of shrieking, stomping toddlers, gossiping and bickering adults and the querulous calls of the old.

Today the Singapore Chinese household may amount to no more than a married couple, the odd grandma, two children and a maid, but the inherited razor-sharp voices prove that Darwin was right. As for their being disturbed by the noise of others, when a woman was murdered in a Singapore flat in 1997 it was three or four days before the body was discovered; the radio had been blaring nonstop day and night since the killing, but the neighbours had ignored it. They had not been alerted by their ears, but their noses.

If it is quiet outside, the Chinese will quickly remedy that lamentable state of affairs by finding something to celebrate with deafening explosions of long strings of firecrackers to frighten off devils, or a lion or dragon dance accompanied by the banging of drums and gongs and the clashing of cymbals. Firecrackers are outlawed in Singapore, so instead there may be a *wayang*, a Chaozhou or Hokkien street opera, the excruciating din thoughtfully amplified so that it may be enjoyed by thousands of people for miles around, even when there is no audience actually watching the stage because the singers are playing only to the gods.

Otherwise the excuse for the din may be a wedding, a feast day, a shop opening, a welcome for a distinguished visitor, or even a funeral, the all-night wake accompanied by shrill chatter and the hard rattle of mahjong tiles.

Oversensitive to this infernal racket on all sides, I began to fear I had married into the wrong continent, and drew no comfort from the airy theorising of academics who explained that Chinese have a different perception of sound, and regard it as a means 'expressing personal affection'. I can think of a dozen better ways. However, life changed for me when I acquired a pair of industrial earmuffs — the sort worn by pneumatic drill operators — which proved miraculously effective. 'But you don't wear them,' objected Ping. 'I don't have to,' I replied. 'Now that I have them and can put them on any time I'm disturbed, I don't hear a thing.' I had found my own psychological defence against the bedlam.

In any case the pandemonium was no longer so one-sided, for we now had ear-bashing karaoke in the pubs, the hot blast of electronic sound in the deafening discos, and hysterical rock concerts like the West. In 1991 the controversial satirist Bo Yang could still admonish his fellow countrymen for what he described as a 'noisiness' damaging to the nerves and offensive to Europeans. But in the modern world where the pollution is universal, the difference is not one of decibels any more, but style.

That has always been true of the 'sloppiness and filthiness' of which Bo Yang so woundingly accuses the Chinese in the same paragraph. When it comes to cleanliness, however, the customs of East and West may be said to dovetail rather than compete, because they are diametrically opposed. In English eyes, the closer you are to a Chinese, the more hygienic he appears; the further away, the more insanitary. In Chinese eyes exactly the reverse is true of the English.

Of personal cleanliness, the Chinese note with disgust that given half a chance the English will soak in their own dirty water in a bath instead of taking showers, and then use the same water to clean it. In some shameful cases, difficult though it may be to believe, they bathe and change their linen and their towels only once or twice a week. So of course they smell. When asked what I smelled like, Ping sniffed and replied 'Banner'. She was referring to our first Alsatian, Banner de Grandeur. I could only draw comfort from this by reminding myself of his long aristocratic pedigree, as against my own humble background.

The Chinese, on the other hand, are justly famed for their laundering, and our washing machine and tumble-dryer seem to be pounding away 24 hours a day for only two people and a maid. After the morning shower, Ping ruthlessly flings all the washable clothes and other linen she can find into a basket for immediate immersion, drying and ironing, and despite my feeble protests the items may well include perfectly clean towels that have not in fact been used overnight. Her dearest wish has always been to have one of those gleaming space-age American bathrooms that justify the existence of God's Own Country in her sight (among other considerations). But I had been brought up strictly, and we had no quarrel about personal hygiene except over whether the lid of the loo should be left up or down. The Chinese like it up, 'to air it', as Ping says. The English keep it down precisely to avoid doing so. But where there are two wills, there's a way. We compromised by having separate bathrooms.

At the next stage — the home — some of the more obsessed English wives can be inordinately houseproud, washing their floors every day, meticulously dusting and polishing their furniture, silver and brass, and hoovering everything that can be hoovered. They will sweep all dirt into a pan, throw all their rubbish into a bin, and hang out their washing only on prescribed days, 'and their sailors scrub the decks of their ships every morning', a well-travelled Chinese friend told a disbelieving Ping.

According my close friend Piroska Rajaratnam, the Hungarian wife of Singapore's famous foreign minister known as the 'Lovable Owl', told me when I first married, English women manage the household very well and good stamina too. Most have no maids and so have to tidy up the rooms themselves, make the bed, clear up everywhere — kitchen, bathroom, toilet — mop the floor, occasionally wash clothes, clean carpets, go to shopping. Not like Chinese middle class wives in Singapore who always with maid, and if no maid often still not work herself, just leave the messy situation there, then dress beautifully and go out for fun. Are there different philosophy of life between East and West, Piroska ask? Not all Chinese like that, I said.

But I did admire the English housewives for running house in perfect discipline way according Piroska. Among seven days in a week, each day what to do, what to eat, all worked out according to plan. For example Monday washed and ironed clothes, Friday ate fish, Saturday went out to shopping for food and household necessities for whole week. On Sundays some couple may go out together to relax and enjoy themselves like Chinese if husband not lazy, but on public holidays, if wives still doing housework, even not allowed husbands stay at home, probably sent to park to read newspapers for hours to avoid getting in the way. On other days if husband come home from office early without calling, wife be angry and blamed him she had not been trusted.

Housewives kept the habit of living according to formula as far as possible. This suited English husband's mind, because they firmly believe in behaviour with rules and regulation. 'You are very lucky marry Englishman,' Piroska told me, 'because the style English housewives control their husbands so successfully has been known in all the world.' Even Chinese say only low-grade husband beat the wife, gentleman always obey her. But according our tradition bossy wife not well-mannered, and I did have an old-fashioned mind. So in our family D was definitely 'Boss', as our Filipino maid called him. In this respect for sake of harmony I am not English housewife.

Or Piroska's idea of one, Heaven be thanked. But Ping is not to be outdone in the observance of their household rituals, and in addition has a mania for putting whatever is loose and therefore untidy into plastic boxes and bags that are neatly stacked up in larger plastic boxes and confided to fridges and cupboards or inaccessible shelves to be forgotten in due course. But while many Chinese are houseproud, too, the more civic-minded among the English would take things a stage further — at least until recently. For most would behave as if the streets and parks were extensions of their homes, refraining from dropping odds and ends — even bus tickets — on the ground, religiously throwing them into the bins provided, or stuffing them into their pockets or handbags to dispose of later.

Ping, too, will pick up any litter on the paths outside our townhouse, and takes pages of newspapers and a plastic bag with her when walking Shutup Charlie in the park in order to recover his daily output. But that is where, as an individual, she parts company with the Chinese stereotype, for while they may be particular about their persons (until recently they would complete their toilet with the assiduous plying of earpicks, tonguescrapers and backscratchers) and sometimes their homes, the Chinese are in general not to be trusted beyond their front — and especially their back — doors, for alfresco anarchy comes to them naturally.

In Ping it takes a mild form. She will look with disapproval at the regimented daffodils and tulips in a London park in Spring, for they are too orderly for her fastidious taste. She likes a garden to be 'woolly', a tangle of sealing wax and yellow palms and bottlebrush trees, straggling alamanda and hibiscus, bougainvillea, firecracker, catswhisker and mickey mouse. True, there may be stacks of pots and buckets here and there, but when I protest that they spoil the effect of all the designer chaos she replies serenely, 'I see the flowers; I don't see the pots.'

Fair enough, but while a modicum of chaos may be in the natural order of things, there is a time and place for it, like everything else. In respecting this principle Ping is atypical, and a better example of the Chinese stereotype could be said to be our first amah Ah Yee. Faced with the problem of disposing of the cartons and crates and miscellaneous rubbish that had collected in our flat when I first moved into it, her solution was simply to dump them somewhere else. Immaculate in black trousers and starched white tunic herself, she therefore carried them all down to the manicured lawn below our apartment block, poured half a can of kerosene over them, and applied a match. The fact that after the leaping flames subsided and the suffocating black smoke had finally cleared, the bonfire had left an unsightly mound of cinders and ash on a large patch of burned grass and bare earth was of no moment. *Her* floor upstairs was once again spotless.

Visitors to Singapore comment on how green and clean it is, but this is thanks to a government that employs a horde of workers, mostly Indian, to go around picking up behind its citizens. It also maintains discipline by imposing heavy fines on litterbugs, sometimes sending them back to the scene of the crime to clear up the mess — my assistant Eddie was once fined ten dollars just for dropping a cigarette butt into a monsoon drain. Even then one gets the impression at weekends that the streets are innocent of refuse simply because it has all been dumped in the parks and on the beaches, where the muckspreaders are more difficult to detect. You always know where Singaporeans have passed that way by the trail of discarded soft drink cartons and cans and bottles, polystyrene food boxes, plastic bags, discarded newspapers, and — in more secluded corners — used condoms and soiled kleenex.

If their marble-floored flats appear as pristine as new pins it is precisely because they have piled their broken tricycles and old television sets and bottomless rattan chairs and split cushions and the rest of their unwanted junk on the public landing outside their back doors for someone else to move. Obsessed with cleanliness, they will hang their daily washing over their balconies, sheets and towels sometimes flopping down to obscure their neighbour's balcony below 'like tongues of thirsty dogs', as Ping says. They may also leave trash bags filled with the gruesome remains of their meals and other kitchen waste beside the communal rubbish chute on their landing to feed the cockroaches, because sending them down it would involve their touching the dirty handles of the chute with their hands. Where public toilets are involved, it is obvious that for too many of them house-training not only begins but ends at home, and many will smoke and spit wherever they can get away with it no matter what the neighbours feel. There is a Chinese saying that you 'sweep the snow from your own door but not the frost from your neighbour's roof'. Confucian chauvinists boast that while the West considers only the rights of the individual, their superior society has always put the community first. Like history, this is just so much bunk.

But it must be added that the Chinese have less incentive to be civic-minded, simply because most are seemingly impervious to the unpleasant in their surroundings. They have a knack of using their senses selectively, and just as they may hear only what they want to hear, they will often see only what they want to see, and smell what they want to smell. The lotus grows out of the mud, so admire the lotus and ignore the mud — 'I see the flowers, not the pots.' It follows that Chinese 'food courts' can be as filthy as their customers are clean; it is the cuisine that counts. 'I don't care,' as one Singapore woman said, when questioned by a reporter on her reactions to squalid kitchens, sluttish waitresses, crabshells on the floor, and similar nationwide phenomena, 'I can sit beside a rubbish bin and still enjoy my food.' And, who knows, perhaps she has the right perspective. When in 1998 the government graded hawker stalls according to their hygiene, most customers said they would ignore a bad rating if the chicken rice was good.

But Ping does not go that far. 'It makes my skin nervous,' she once said, scratching her chopstick arm as we ate fish porridge in one of these hawker centres. So we agreed about the environment for eating. But what of the food itself? What was it to be? Seated opposite each other in our new flat we faced a crucial decision — West or East? T-bone steak or Cantonese fried rice? The choice could make or break our marriage. Fortunately the solution was obvious.

8

CHOPSTICKS? Or what one Chinese had caustically called the 'kitchen implements' favoured by the gourmets of the West? At first the matter was settled by Ah Yee, who told Ping scornfully when asked to serve us boiled rice that foreign devils did not eat rice, they only ate blood-soaked steak or roast chicken with roast potatoes and frozen peas followed by raspberry jelly. She could have been Mrs Danvers in Daphne du Maurier's *Rebecca*, and for three days that is what she gave us, night after night. But the girl who presented hairy spiders to her enemies at the tender age of five was no cringing Mrs Max de Winter. Once Ping had got her second wind, she decided that any Chinese who tried to stop another Chinese from eating boiled rice must be insane, and promptly sacked Ah Yee, who indeed ended up in a famous mental home.

What now? I had eaten my first Chinese lunch in the old Shanghai Restaurant in Soho in 1937 and not looked back. I loved Sichuan chilli prawns and sour hot soup with steamed buns, Peking duck, vinegar and ginger pigs' trotters, eight-week-old hundred-year-old eggs, and all that went with them. But there was always the hidden agenda, about which one had only heard tales of horror and imagination: the fresh monkey brains and unborn mice, the steamed fish with the head kept alive in ice, its mouth keeping time with those of the diners as they tucked into the body, the gall bladder of the king cobra (current price around $1,000), the drunken prawns leaping despairingly in flaming rice wine, the stewed dogs, and the contempt poured on the softhearted fellow who gave up eating them — 'What for? Even if you stop biting them, they will not stop biting you.'

A dog-eater once explained me if you don't like eat dog, can pretend the eating dog is some other kind animal — remember ancient Chinese philosopher said, 'white horse is not a horse'? — then cannot be hurt. Because this dog is one special breed, not the same as usual dogs — it is Chinese purebred, colour black, short hair, with pink nose. It must be young (but if eat cat just the other way round, should pick out a rather old one).

They say wherever there is water there are Chinese, and where there are Chinese there are Chinese restaurants, and so permeate every corner of the world. And Chinese will eat whatever animal on land or sea, their tricks to cook it unimaginable. But foreigners who even sneer at French eating frogs and snails, which most commonplace, are often scared and hardly recognise miracle of Chinese cooking by consummate skill. If show any favouritism for Chinese food it is only fried rice, chop suey, sweet-sour pork, dim sum and Peking duck. They do not appreciate there are many more delicious food. D refuse to eat stewed sea slug although full of vitamins, and for long time never touch my favourite dishes — fish head, chicken feet and spiced pig's ear. How strange. Why the people like that? In nineteenth century even Emperor Qianlong of Qing Dynasty came south from faraway Beijing six times to make inspection tour and eat such local delicacies as hairy crab in Shanghai, salt duck in Nanjing, and smoked fish in Suzhou.

And then of course there is snake banquet with succession of exciting dishes. Once chill in air, people scramble for it in South China. Ideal place to go is Wuyi mountain in Fujian Province surrounded by undulating hills where all kinds snake come and go unpredictably, so that to catch snake is lifelong career of local people. Up there in surrounding mountains plenty of snake restaurants with cage in front with many snakes in it, such as iron snake, water snake, rape flower and silver cup snake, hundred steps snake and cobra. Snake banquet begins with soup, then fried snake with vinegar and sugar, baked snake with ginger and spring onion, the skin of snake used as cold dish, fresh, crisp, smooth and palatable. While the banquet served, they also cut the snake's gall bladder and let the bile drop in liquor, immediately to drink as changes to gorgeous colour, jade green with bright crystal, full of fragrance and taste. But foreigners never eat this. Pity.

Not surprisingly, Ping confronted with admirable fortitude traveller's tales from the West of raw oysters swallowed whole, screaming lobsters plunged into scalding water, putrid grouse and snipe's dirt, raw beef beaten into submission, and haggis, sheep's offal boiled in the animal's stomach (alive?).

But fortunately none of the exotica of the two hemispheres had much to do with home cooking, and we settled down comfortably to a mixture of eastern and western. Sometimes it would be straightforward English or Chinese — roast lamb and cranberry jelly one day garoupa steamed in a sauce of black beans, chilli, ginger and garlic the next — sometimes dishes on common ground like pasta and paella and pork ribs; or our own hybrids like Chinese Hungarian paprika chicken (add chilli to make the paprika hotter), or disastrous mixtures that had to be offered to the dog, usually without success. But I never got around to eating fish porridge with garlic for breakfast, and Ping never took much of a shine to 'chicken food' (Kellogg's or other) — 'It tastes like newspaper.' It was all part of the deal.

That was only the beginning, however. The days of globalisation when the do-it-yourself stuffing and scoffing of deleterious fast food by the T-shirted young everywhere would unite the world were not yet upon us, and East and West were still divided by their different concepts of polite eating. I had remarked with some displeasure that even when they had been to university abroad, Chinese had questionable table manners once faced with western cutlery, and was at pains to make sure that Ping committed no social solecisms, like chewing at a whole chicken leg from the end of a fork. On my side it was different, of course. I was skilled in the use of chopsticks, and had no fear of committing solecisms at a dinner given by Chinese, for after all they had no etiquette worth mentioning, had they? Basically all they did was compete in picking titbits from a common dish with chopsticks that had already been in their mouths, put their rice bowls to their lips and noisily scoop in the food or, in some cases, eat with their fingers. It was a free-for-all, and I resigned myself to making free of it and mucking in with the rest. That is, until one evening shortly after we were married when Ping laid a placatory hand on my arm as we dressed for an upmarket Chinese dinner party and said, 'Please don't angry, but I think it better tonight you eat with fork and spoon, okay? I feel more comfortable.'

Fork and spoon? Like a *tourist?* But before I could find my voice, she sat me down and explained.

Of course naturally there were just few small things. He put his chopsticks right inside his mouth when he took food from them, which most vulgar. I point out he must take food only with his teeth without chopsticks touching his lips, which correct behaviour because that way everyone can eat from same dish and still not unhealthy. In fact in my mother's house we even use two pairs chopsticks — white and red — red for taking food from dish to put on plate, then white for putting in mouth.

Also wrong to leave his small bowl of rice on the table when he is eating from it; he must try to learn to hold it up close to his lips, and if large bowl, do not use chopsticks at all, only use spoon. A Chinese restaurant owner told me once, 'Foreigners skilfully operate chopsticks, but cannot hold the rice bowl near the mouth because the nose too big. It seems their mouth therefore never collaborate with the bowl.' D's nose not too big, but he tried to use the chopsticks to carry rice to mouth from bowl on table with ridiculous gentleness not surprising hardly got anything to eat.

D also pick up button mushrooms or quail eggs with fingers because slippery and clumsy with chopsticks. But cannot. Chinese custom only can use fingers for picking up food with shells or bones, like prawns and spare ribs. I also point out must not try to take fishbones from mouth with chopsticks, and spitting out bones also absolutely not allowed. Chinese people cover mouth with left hand and take them out quietly with right hand's fingers. And another thing ...

'All right, but then why do you Chinese chop up chickens and ducks so that one's mouth gets full of bone splinters, instead of disjointing them in a civilised manner as we do?' I unwisely counterattacked. Ping looked at me in astonishment. 'To let out the goodness of the marrow when you cook them, of course,' she answered. 'Your people sometimes no sense at all, even do not know how to treat food with respect.' 'But we do have respect for table manners,' I hit back, striving to get even, 'so when you use a knife and fork in future, kindly don't behave as if you were playing the piano. You should keep your arms close to the body, not stick your elbows out on either side.'

English people so funny, behave at dinner as if table manners more important than what they eat, seems. But even when use knife and fork in western style D picks up breadcrumbs from table with wet finger like a ant, and eats sardines without first take out all the dirty things inside, even bones. I cannot bear to watch. Yet setting of table must be perfect, so he also gives me lectures. When first married important shopping for me was kitchen utensils, but for D all kinds glass and cups in different shapes for drinking. 'Use bigger or smaller glass depend what kind of drink,' he told me. 'If need to add on ice or pour in water, soda or tonic then you just use big glass. If only drink something like sherry or port, of course use small glass can do. Remember whisky on rocks must be bigger glass, let the ice clash the glass giving some clear and melodious sound. If the person drink brandy, the shape like bowl, by that will smell it better sending wafts of delicate fragrance. For wine use glasses with stem, higher stem for white wine because temperature should be kept cold, so hand holding glass must not warm it. Have to learn these things, he said sternly.

We ended up pointing at each other and shouting in chorus, 'You are a barbarian!' But as if Ping's painful strictures were not enough, a new offensive opened after Piroska gave her lessons in western etiquette and I lost my advantage on that sector of the battlefield. If I tried in my amateurish way to help her lay the table, it was 'don't you know you should place the knives facing inwards, the one used first on the outside? And the dessert spoon goes here, not there.' Or it might be 'you should not pick grapes off the bunch with your fingers; we should use a small little elegant pair of silver scissors to cut them' (which of course we did not have).

This was too much. 'I'll have you know my mother was very strict with me about table manners when I was a boy,' I protested, and told her what it had been like — the admonitions, the nagging, the discipline. Ping was unimpressed. 'When I was child,' she retorted disdainfully, 'my nanny made me eat all my meals in front of a *mirror.*'

Piroska taught me many common courtesy of English daily life, as how to lay the dinner table correctly and how to serve tea. English very much care for tea; even workers have tea break at 11 AM and 4 PM, and afternoon tea at home always very elaborate, with thin sandwiches and cookies or pastry seemed like another meal. But

Chinese enjoyment of tea completely different. They drink tea from morning to evening, did not fix any definite time and never add milk or sugar, but kept the tea in pure taste, and very particular about quality of water — the best from mountain spring — and control of duration and degree of heating. Drinking tea calmly in a teahouse in the mountains guides the person's mind to the nature and he holds aloof from the world. But Piroska's influence over me very strong because of her successful mixed marriage with Raja, who came from, wealthy Indian family, so we religiously drink tea at four o'clock.

Piroska usually serious and wag the finger at me when make a mistake, but Raja amusing with innocent smile and perfect manner. Both very fond of animals and their garden full of blooming orchids the work of careful loving hands. Their house tidy and clean, tranquil and furnished in very good taste, the walls lined with books like a library. Piroska collected beautiful things, so that her dinner table gloriously dazzling with luxurious air of cut glass, crystal and silver which she cleaned herself with great pleasure. Even I prefer simple things, such as in our home, I cannot stop to admire.

I thought I had a chance to get my own back in the war of manners when we invited a few people for dinner shortly afterwards, and our Chinese guests had the impudence to take over the house unasked, the women crowding into the kitchen, meddling with the cooking, bringing out snacks and ordering me to eat them, the men rearranging the terrace furniture to their own liking, pouring themselves hefty drinks from the bar, and talking their heads off in Cantonese without a glance for me. Left sulking in a corner, I finally sprang to indignant life when one of these fellows clapped his hands from the top of the terrace steps and shouted in English, 'Dinner on the table, everyone. Come and get it.'

'*If* you don't mind, Chang,' I said loudly and pompously, rising to my full height, '*If* you don't mind, I happen to be your host, so be so kind as to allow me to announce dinner in my own house.' Dead silence, and I realised that somehow I had dropped an appalling clanger. The party continued on a hushed note. 'It was my fault,' Chang, a bosom friend of Han Chao, said to Ping. 'No,' she answered, 'you just forgot he is a barbarian.' 'Of course they behave like their own home,' she said to me sadly afterwards. 'Means they are our friends. Why you so rude treat them like stranger?' I had violated that old Chinese social custom of taking things for granted within your own circle and never standing on ceremony, just as you did not say 'thank you' all the time within the family.

Raymond Chang sent us a pair of pottery elephants in glorious blue. But he never came again. D didn't realise we were brought up in a custom not to put being courteous above our true feelings of closeness. D paid attention to manners and was fixed on the rules of politeness too much and could not release his true sentiment from ethical restrictions. Therefore he did not know how to relax and feel so easy and happy like me. Same in working hours, never chat with friends on telephone or write letters, cannot bear interruption. Work is work. I understood him perfectly, and sincerely wished the others would too.

When in Singapore Han Chao, who had commanded a destroyer in the Chinese navy but left it to become captain of a super tanker in order to make ends meet (having produced six daughters while trying for a son), would arrive unannounced at dinner time with a five-course supper in polystyrene boxes and three or four complete strangers — fellow captains or his own officers. He would then sweep aside what Ping and the cook had prepared and substitute his own takeaway dishes, filling the kitchen with his huge frame and bawling voice. Or I would come back from an interview to find him stretched out stark naked but for a pair of briefs on my study floor to cool off in the airconditioning.

I treated Han Chao exactly the same way. He had an expert cook who would produce delicious Sichuan dishes, and while his ship was in Singapore, I always demanded a banquet, and entertained our friends to be guests aboard it. He had no right to refuse it.

Outraged at first, I got to look forward to Han Chao's visits. I was learning slowly, becoming acclimatised to this warm-hearted, casual society in which people would do anything for you and expect you to do the same for them without question. (But he once brought an Icelandic confrère whose wife accused me of cheating at blackjack after I'd won everyone's money. Now *there* was something for me to sulk about — especially as it was the only time we gambled in our house, just to please them. However, perhaps on reflection it was a little discourteous of me.)

I had to teach D so many many small things all Chinese people know. Always to dress up when visit someone for first time. Always to accept presents with both hands — only foreign devils so impolite to take it with one. If the present is a covered pot with hot food, maybe for a party, never give back empty, always put in something to eat. Also do not give clocks or knives or handkerchiefs as presents because unlucky. If give money, put it in lucky red envelope, but do not use red ink pen to write letter or put it in blue envelope. Red ink means blood, and blue means dead.

'I really not superstitious,' Ping protested brazenly, when I asked her why she insisted on fixing a red collar around the neck of our black dog, 'just believe good and bad luck.' A nice distinction, but I understood. Why take a chance? One did the things one was taught as a child — brushing one's teeth, crossing one's fingers, touching wood, and not walking under ladders — for fear of what might happen if one did not, until they became as involuntary as a tic in the jaw.

On the other hand Ping shunned fortune-tellers and astrologers, and ignored the signs of the Chinese zodiac. As for the annual rites, they passed one by one — Chinese New Year,

Qing Ming, the Feast of the Hungry Ghosts, the Mid-Autumn Festival, the Dragon Boat Festival — without the family praying to the Kitchen God, burning joss sticks to the ancestors, feeding the ghosts, or setting off illegal firecrackers. We observed some Chinese New Year customs — a display of pussywillow and tubs of orange trees, tips in red envelopes for the kids, no quarrelling on the day etc — but mainly we just ate the food prescribed for these occasions, the New Year buns, the raw fish salad, mooncakes at the Mid-Autumn Festival, the Dragon Boat dumplings.

When it came to things that go bump in the night, Ping was open-minded; but then Chinese ghosts and demons often bear little resemblance to our own humourless apparitions, and on the whole have a more comfortable relationship with ordinary people. Some Chinese horror stories may chill the blood, but in others humans befriend ghosts, get drunk and play music with them, 'lay' them in both senses of the word, marry them, beget sons by them, bicker with them, sell them, kill them, and of course scare them to death, so that in the end you scarcely know who's who.

Ping was the same about gods. Unlike millions of Chinese women, she did not pray regularly to Buddha for a winning lottery ticket, and her only reference to the possibility of reincarnation that I can remember was, 'what good thing I did in past life to get a husband who waits for me for breakfast?' But she became tuned in to western custom and accepted the paganism of Christianity — Christmas trees and Santa Claus and mistletoe and wreaths on the door (wreaths to celebrate the birth of a *boy?*) — just as she accepted in tactful silence the Virgin Birth, Christ's miracles, the Resurrection. Despite her work in Hong Kong for the Catholic Church and its rewards, she remained outside it. Playing safe, she treated all religions with respect — 'means I can deal with all the gods' — but like a good Confucian regarded them rather as she regarded ghosts and the malevolence of black cats. 'I don't believe anything,' she said, summing it up, 'but anything is possible.' So when one day I proposed we take a boat trip to the outer islands, she refused. Why?

'I won't go out today.'

'Why not?'

'Friday thirteenth.'

9

FRIDAY the Thirteenth. It symbolised the measureless gulf between our traditional attitudes to life and death, and set us not merely a world, but a universe apart. 'Excuse me, Miss Mellis, but what is Jesus?' I asked a shocked kindergarten teacher at the age of five, for my parents were innocent of religion. I was given a more explicit answer than if I had asked about sex, but it was not until I was a boarder at prep school that I really learned the worst. There, in the friendly neighbourhood village church at Birchington-on-Sea, I first heard of the horrors ahead, of the ultimate boredom of a Heaven full of angels sitting on pink clouds and strumming harps all the time even if I did brush my teeth, and of eternal hellfire and brimstone, with horned demons poking me with tridents like Britannia's if I did not. Confirmed a Christian at 15, I grew up with a minatory voice within me that forever murmured, 'Be good — *or else.*'

Ping knew the story of the Crucifixion and therefore why they said Friday the Thirteenth was unlucky. But that still meant nothing to her. Her inhibition was just a knee-jerk reflex, on a par with not turning a fish over on her plate while her brother was at sea, otherwise his ship would certainly capsize. While my incentive to watch my step has subconsciously sprung from terror of that white-bearded nemesis in the sky and the threat of the life to come, Ping and many of the 'heathen Chinese with the inscrutable face' managed to conduct themselves with propriety without any feelings of guilt or fear of damnation to drive them, for they had no sense of sin to sin with, but only a sense of shame if they misbehaved. The reason was simple. The good Confucian was spared any belief in Heaven or Hell.

Confucius said all discussion about the next life just idle talk and absolute waste of time, not suitable for educated gentleman because cannot possibly know what speaking about. You do not know earth,' he told his students, 'how can you know Heaven?' and refused to talk any more about it. 'Heaven does not speak,' said Mencius. So I don't know God, but God knows me, so why I worry about such things?

Which seems to me a far sounder statement than all the blasphemous claims of pious Christian evangelists that they are better acquainted with the Maker of a billion galaxies than you or I. Listening to them in all their insignificance is like straining to hear the sea in a shell. I can't stand religious bigots anyway — always throwing the Book at you.

The Sage was severely practical, for since there was no identifiable paradise in the sky, man must create it on earth. That implied building a peaceful, happy and harmonious society here below in which the upright individual would play his part by treating his fellow men with benevolence and respect in all circumstances 'as if attending at a ceremony'. But how to become that upright individual he had to work out for himself. Confucius was open-minded, an enemy of dogma. There could be no standard answers to moral problems; in the everyday world Truth was relative, a moving target to be treated as if 'following someone you cannot overtake but fear to lose'. The correct thing to do at any given moment depended on the circumstances.

He led his students along the path of right conduct towards the 'Way' only with broad guidelines — 'Do not do to others what you would not wish others to do to you', always put yourself in the other man's place, be ready to forgive. The rest was up to your conscience, and your first duty was to cultivate it. The disciple of Confucius was urged always to examine his own actions — 'If a man does not constantly ask himself whether what he is doing is right or wrong, I do not know what is to become of him.' He must 'practise how to live', as Ping put it.

When she was not quite sure in her own mind what was the correct course of action, Ping was ready to give way at once. 'Do as you think,' she would say on these occasions, which naturally persuaded me at the outset that marriage to her was going to be a cinch. But more often than not her conscience would decide what was morally right *in the circumstances* with startling speed and decision, and then there was no budging her. I was left to play the role of the wishy-washy on-this-hand-on-the-other-hand Westerner agonising about what ought to be done and dithering for days until she took pity on me and put her foot down, if not the boot in.

Crisis in 1997. A book project had fallen through and we had suddenly lost one-third of our income. We had already sold one house to meet our needs ten years before; should we take out a reverse mortgage on this one? It would solve our problem, but mean that we would have to give up the title deeds to the insurance company, and when we died the boys would inherit only what was left from its sale after the loan and interest had been repaid. I worried away at the problem night after night without saying a word to Ping. She loved her family and her home, and with the fierce determination of a Chinese for whom property is sacred, had badgered me into buying a place of our own from the first, as I have related, instead of fecklessly paying rent year after year — 'a man without a house got his feet in the air like snail without shell'. Not easy to visualise, but one gets the sentiment.

When I finally decided the time had come to put the distasteful idea to her, therefore, I braced myself for the coming squall. For an eternal ten seconds there was a breathless silence, and no birds sang. Then, in place of a stream of protests she broke it with two sharp syllables that killed the problem stone dead on the spot. *'Do it!'* No questions asked. End of argument before it started. So much for my sleepless nights. In theory one should pass on one's meagre wealth to one's progeny, but in practice the time had come for me to retire, yet be independent of them — 'even a horse should not die in harness'. And it was practice that counted.

I had no quarrel with this down-to-earth Confucian philosophy. As it happened I myself had long since ceased to believe that man knew anything whatever about the hereafter or God, and the notion that the silliest, most destructive animal on earth, the one that fouled its nest every day, had been fashioned in his image was the most preposterous blasphemy I had ever heard. So for me, too, salvation depended on weighing the arguments and then acting according to one's conscience. We were beginning to find each other. 'If loyal to yourself,' Ping said to me, 'cannot be afraid anything.' (This above all ...) 'Never allow other people control you.' Faced with vigorous opposition from her family, 'I wrote to my mother in Taiwan and told her I already decided right thing is to marry you, so if I do not, it will be wrong,' she explained simply.

Knowing Ping's idiosyncratic logic and understandably filled with alarm, the family immediately despatched a close friend from Taipei to Hong Kong to dissuade her from her criminal folly and tempt her with a beguiling alternative. This had precisely the wrong effect.

One day when I practising wearing my high-heel shoes, walking round and round the courtyard, unexpectedly the gate opens and entered one of my mother's friends from Taiwan I do not like. I called her 'Turkey', because she had the same skin and voice, a fiery person with a whiplash tongue, rather tough to deal with. 'I only carry out your mother's wishes,' she said, looking at me coldly. 'She want you to go Taiwan.'

'Mother should know I soon get married. I already made up my mind.'

'Marry a barbarian?' she snapped. 'Your mother and brothers beg you if you want to marry must marry a suitable Chinese in Taiwan. You should be a good obedient daughter, remember you are a Liang, have proper name and position in society. How much value you worth in barbarian's mind, even you wear clumsy high-heel shoes just to feed pigeons like market woman? You are well-born and well-educated and have to behave like a lady. You disobey your mother, you are guilty.'

'If I marry someone I did not love, that is guilty, and if I refuse to marry someone I do love, also guilty,' I answered.

At this Turkey was boiling with rage, and screamed, 'The fortune of your family seems truly evil. How dare you do that to your mother? You are like a rat falling into a pot of delicious soup.' Then she left, banging the gate.

Her words gave Ping great pain — a Confucian daughter should above all obey her parents. But not at the expense of her personal integrity, the Sage had added. 'I refuse to live for a bowl of rice,' she called after the woman. It would not be right simply to accept the easy way out of the dead end of her life in Hong Kong by sinking back into the old Kuomintang society.

I was impressed when she told me this. But then she spoiled it all.

Anyway, I don't want to be put in cage in Taiwan be fed every day by mother-in-law and told what to do like a little dog. Don't forget I am not little dog, I am black sheep in my family, full of my own idea, spoiled, really horrible person, have not changed. I want freedom. I must have my own life, rely completely on myself, just as when I became school teacher. Only that way my conscience clear.

Now wait a minute. If that was the case, it did appear a bit of a coincidence that her Confucian conscience had told her to do exactly what she wanted to do, didn't it? Just as it had when she had persuaded herself she could become a nun without believing in God? This time it seemed to be giving moral sanction to a marriage of convenience — her convenience. And Ping had sound pragmatic reasons for finding it the 'correct' decision for her to escape from her world into mine.

So I mean what it amounted to was that all this so-called Confucian morality simply put a halo around expediency, didn't it? Well, didn't it? And I mean in the West we would read it as specious double-think and rank hypocrisy and cunning oriental casuistry and phoney feminine sophistry, and we'd be *damn* right. I mean where did I come in, God's sake? Just how genuine was this so-called undying passion we shared, just how faked were those moments of — well, you know?

D never know all logical arguments why to marry him add up together means nothing. When you are in love, you throw everything else to the wind. In Chinese history there are so many stories of girls mad about literary world immediately fall passionately in love with famous writer, just as western beauties in 19th century adore great heroes. For instance there was one great scholar and writer Sima Xiangru was invited by nobleman to his home. After dinner Sima noticed beautiful daughter of the house hidden behind screen and so played love songs to her on the zheng, the Chinese lute, with deep feeling. The young woman at once so enchanted and ardent she forgot all propriety and ran away with him the same night.

I just so quickly abandoned my family for the romantic journey with my English writer. I became like a sunflower turning to the sun, and I felt there was an inconceivable power holding us together. Shakespeare said poet, lover and madman all no different — brave, serious, strict, 'more stubbornly loyal to their ideal', and praised this kind of 'divine madness'. At this time I seemed to hear a voice crying inside my heart, 'What are you waiting for? Why betray yourself? Why obey feudal ethics and make yourself to be a slave of family custom and convention? Why put on mask to deceive people and yourself? Why fawn on audiences to play virtuous and virginal?'

My spirit could not be locked in any more, love had burst into my heart. I could not refuse temptation, and in split second our blind love rush together too quick, too hot to stop. But not just like that. I knew at the same time our feeling fine and smooth and sweet and true, because this is real thing. So I was loyal to it, and at once felt clean and honest, confident in my decision, true to myself. So, yes, my conscience did told me marry D was right thing to do.

'When you are in love, you forget everything,' Ping repeated when she gave this to me to read. 'Everything. Even propriety, *Li*.' All my secret Anglo-Saxon agonising over Chinese pragmatic morals — or was it Chinese moral pragmatism? — had been a shameful waste of time. What could I say? I grinned at her feebly and gave her a guilty kiss on the cheek, like any unfaithful husband returning from the bed of his lover. Whether she suspected me of suspecting her motives I did not know, but she looked at me solemnly for a moment, and then let me off the hook: 'And of course for me most important of all is we Chinese believe firm round fat bottom like yours means reliable, trustworthy man with solid, comfortable future — just what I was looking for.'

'You mean you married me for my b—?' But at that point I gave up. It is unwise to plunge into the labyrinth of Chinese thinking. It is best to wait at the exit for the results.

For all her love, Ping could not for long forget the *Li* she had mentioned, the character for which originally meant 'ceremony' (act towards others 'as if assisting at a ceremony'), for it is the Confucian word for decorous behaviour and correct conduct.

This, too, had a familiar echo. I was assailed by gilded memories of summer afternoons of my youth when I was instructed in the strict etiquette of school cricket. Never argue with the umpire's decision. When unjustly declared out, walk away from the wicket with a smile. When cheered on scoring 50 runs, behave modestly and do no more than tip your cap towards the pavilion. And when the other fellow hits a six against you, clap and congratulate him — 'well played, sir'. It came to me that this antique code, ridiculous to many now, epitomised the spirit of *Li;* it was 'the done thing', and what was not *Li* was simply, as we said, 'not cricket'. Myself from an external threat of eternal damnation, Ping from an appeal to the 'voice we hear in solitude' within us, we were coming ever closer, seeing shining black eye to fading blue, the mists between East and West dissolving.

Before we met I had seen Confucius as a ponderous, essentially chair-borne old bore as he is usually depicted on silk or in ivory. But I came to understand that this image, too, was a reflection from the distorting mirror of the centuries. For he was keen not only on poetry and music, but on archery and chariot-driving, both of which he practised himself, believing that they were 'character-forming', as my teachers would say of Latin and cricket at school. One could almost picture him today as a sportsman clapping decorously from the Members' Pavilion at Lords (while less enthusiastic about a boxer who bit the ear of his opponent, or a sprinter who stuck out his tongue at a rival as he overtook him to become the world's fastest man).

But in my youth, long before the Chinese started winning gold medals (with or without benefit of steroids) and joined the International Rugby Board, I was ignorant of this, and the very idea of associating the Chinese with sport would have seemed absolutely ridiculous. They were obviously an unhealthy lot — mandarins in long robes with long fingernails protected by ornate sheaths, women tottering about on bound feet, a people who fattened their kids like ducks, and believed that (by some quirk of the anatomy) a big belly gave a man bigger 'face'. And that prejudice appeared to be borne out when Ping and I went for a walk. If I was alone I kept up a brisk infantry pace, but if she came with me I felt as if I were doing a slow march at a military funeral. It figured. She obviously walked for relaxation, not exercise.

In Singapore Dennis walking and suddenly rain pelting down, he never like to find some place to avoid it, but keep his original Great Britain spirit and continue to stride forward. The crowd on roadside applaud lively. Then come home drenched head to foot, like chicken dropped in soup. But usually, I walk leisurely and carefree as I can, let lots of fresh air blow in and with delicate fragrance of flowers, watch butterflies, listen birds singing, look up in sky, the clouds like dogs and cats coming going.

I ask you, what could she know of sport? When I took her to a cricket match her first remark was 'Why those men standing around in the field all doing nothing?' That blasphemy was in character, I thought condescendingly, as former vice-captain of the first eleven at Sevenoaks. But was it?

Soon after our wedding we were invited to the mess of the Jungle Warfare School across the Causeway in Malaya, the lair of young, rock-hard British and Australian toughs inured to the exhausting rigours of night marches in the snake-infested *ulu* and the importunities of communist guerrillas. I wore a safari suit, but Ping, faithful to her rule that you must dress formally when visiting a house for the first time, went in a long and tight cheongsam that seemed hardly to allow for any movement at all without bursting at the seams. After dinner and coffee, one of the bone crushers suggested a game of ping pong. I hastily declined, but Ping, always deferring politely to a host, accepted. I shut my eyes and took a quick swallow. Half an hour later, when she had wiped the floor with two of them in straight sets, we said our thankyous and went home before they could suggest arm-wrestling or pistol-shooting.

Not that it would have mattered, as it happened. It turned out that Ping was also a good pistol and rifle shot, having been coached by one of her military brothers, as well as a powerful 200-metre breaststroke swimmer and a junior ping pong champion of Guangzhou Province (pop. at the time: about the same as California). I had taught pistol-shooting in the army in the course of a shady career, but there were no contests between us. I recoiled from the idea that our marriage might end abruptly with coffee for one, and, for the rest, I was anxious to avoid becoming a ripe subject for a sexist inversion of the old trick question: 'when did you cease beating your husband?'

That could also allude to Ping's real passion — tennis. She would watch Wimbledon on TV into early morning, practise her service for hours on end (patiently banging balls over a net in the garden, collecting them in a bucket, and banging them back again), or dispense with the balls altogether and just go through the motions, an exercise known as 'dancing with my racket'. She played for the Singapore Cricket Club in Thailand, Hong Kong, Taiwan, and Brunei on occasion, and once nearly broke a leg in her enthusiasm on the court, just as she once broke a wrist trying to play ping pong in an incipient typhoon on board a cruise ship taking her to Hong Kong. It was all quite exhausting to watch for a protective male.

She was a competent horsewoman, another area in which I did not shine — I had not fallen off a horse even once, the *sine qua non* of the seasoned rider. But Ping had had a lively introduction to the business, thanks to the impulsive Hua Sheng. Instructed by his elders to be a 'good brother' and take care of his younger siblings Hua Sheng's immediate reaction had been to turn to Han

Chao, and say, 'Let's go! I will teach you to ride.'

Han Chao jumped for joy. I worry they leave me behind, and hung on to his belt. Hua Sheng said, 'You are a little devil! Don't fear thrown off a horse and death? Then come along.' Arrived at a wide cavalry field, both mounted their horses and completely forgot me. I could only content with my lot, running around behind the horses' bottom, until getting tired and lying on the grass, puff and blow and gasp. Finally Hua Sheng came picking me up to his horse's back, telling me how he beat the enemy assault and teaching me to grip the saddle. Suddenly the horse swift galloped forward and he shouted in full tone, 'Kill! Kill! Kill!' In such a moment of excitement, my blood boiling up, I could not help to yell at the top of my voice, like legendary Hua Mulan, who joined the Chinese army to replace her father, or Joan of Arc. Finally two brothers stopped their horses convulsed with laughter. I was so shaken by now, feeling very embarrassed, jumped down to the ground and wanted to cry. When hear this D says if known it never marry such bloodthirsty creature. Later I really learn to ride horse, even fall off and break five teeth need replace. So everything fine.

And then at Hakone in Japan, with Mount Fuji gazing down frostily from afar, she read in a brochure that our hotel had a pool fed by hot springs, and suddenly decided on an early morning swim. I played my usual role when these frenzies seized her and watched from the window of our centrally heated bedroom. As she walked across to a seat by the pool, shed her towel and put on a bathing cap, more and more members of the Japanese hotel staff appeared from nowhere and silently formed a line to watch her, too. She poised on the edge of the pool, took a deep breath, and dived. That breath was nearly her last, and she must have broken a world record reaching the other end and scrambling out in an almost vain effort to catch it again. The pool was not heated after all. It was February. And the water was freezing.

The performance concluded, the Japanese dispersed, nodding with satisfaction. But they may still have had an eye for 'Apprehensive Ice' for warmer reasons than simply enjoying her possible demise, for she was careful to keep her figure. It was fortunate for me, in fact, that she did not take up Chinese martial arts because 'Kung Fu means waist like a bear; I want waist like a bee.' I had to be thankful for small mercies. For in the meanwhile it was gradually being borne in on me that I had married a health nut.

10

IT WAS not simply an obsession with exercise and diet. Ping preferred fish to meat and vegetables to either, but could eat suckling pig or waxed duck with the best. She was a good cook, and if eight people came to dinner would make a point of serving them nine rich dishes. (*'Nine?'* 'Of course, follow Chinese custom, always one more, cannot just give guests enough to eat like in West.') She would dress up dull western fare with plum sauce and chilli and sesame, as I have described, much as a Confucian will dress up an unpalatable truth with comforting words. A good meal left her stomach 'cooing like a pigeon', and there was little she would not try, though on hearing that an Indian family had chopped up an unpopular relative and cooked him in a curry, she did go so far as to say, 'You cannot *do* that.' It was, so to speak, beyond the bounds of good taste.

Confucius also would not approve. He never ate food that was too heavily spiced or not fresh, for one thing: sacrifices of meat and fish for gods or ancestors left on altar three days were uneatable. He linked the health of the people with what they ate and drank, and the Chinese do the same now. Chinese believe that for example the more stronger the toxicity of the venomous snake you eat the better, for the aim was to make use of the snake's poison to eliminate the poison inside human's body. Best was the hundred steps snake so-

named because if it bit you, you could run no more than hundred steps before fall dead. Snake was good for cancer and rheumatoid arthritis and improved women's beauty look, making the skin light and delicate. Snake's gall improved vision and cured inflammation of the trachea. The meat was wholesome, and the blood increased the circulation. In short there was nothing so good for you as a thoroughly vicious snake.

Snake cooked with cat and chicken, called 'the meeting of dragon, tiger, and phoenix', was a marvellous tonic to build up fitness, and stewed dog was good for you too. But not just like that. Since in general the traditional ideas of food were to preserve health, therefore from the Han Dynasty Chinese medical science above all constantly picked out the healing properties of dry fruits and herbs and mixed them with delicious food. This kind of food is called 'medicinal meals'. I have eaten them since childhood, and prepared them for Dennis. You find them all over everywhere.

I was not, therefore, forced to prolong my existence by confining myself solely to an inevitably dreary vegetarian diet dominated by pulses, legumes and brown rice. But I was not to get away with my greed scot-free either. It is said that the reason why the English put mint sauce on their roast lamb is because back in the days when wool was our main export, a perspicacious monarch discouraged the eating of mutton by ruling that it must always be accompanied by bitter herbs. Similarly, 'medicinal meals' meant that if I was to be served a particularly delectable dish from Ping's book of recipes I would also have to drink an improving soup on the side well-calculated to take the fun out of it. This beneficial potage would be made of untranslatable ingredients chosen from the array of bottles to be found at a Chinese apothecary, or unidentified herbs bought behind my back in the Chinese wet market, and would honour to the letter the principle that what does you good must taste pretty foul or it won't work.

And it often did work — for insomnia, night sweats, diuretic difficulties, and the aches and pains of the ageing, when not administered simply 'to make you beautiful'. There were, moreover, rare exceptions to the rule — I have to confess that her nostrums did not always taste uniformly disgusting. There was ginseng tea to fortify, luohan fruit with almonds for the throat, pigs' tails and red bean soup to strengthen the spine, and I was made to tuck dried orange peel into my cheek to curb an excess of mucus, or swallow a multitude of tiny, nameless pellets to cure all forms of stomach upset from acidity to the runs. (These were given to Shutup Charlie when he had a hot nose, apparently on the principle that what was good for me was good for the dog.) Ping also rubbed my scalp with the juice of the aloe plant to give me a healthy head of hair and to stop my wiry eyebrows from 'flying away everywhere'. (One might do worse. Compare Cleopatra's formula: one part mouse, one part horse's teeth, bear grease, deer marrow, reed bark and shredded vine.) These remedies were drawn from a two-volume pharmacopoeia of Chinese alternative medicine, of which Ping was an enthusiastic amateur. The only thing she did not make me do was to play mahjong, which, it was said, demanded quick thinking and therefore staved off senile dementia. One nevertheless hopes for the best.

I so interested Chinese medicine because my father always very busy with revolution, but still practised as herbal doctor, as I said. When he was arrested by the French and put in jail in Hanoi for three years, two of them he was locked up alone by himself without light or air. But after he cured the sick wife of a powerful local millionaire all the other doctors had said hopeless, he was allowed out often every day. In this way he survived so that later I could be born in Beijing to my mother, his second wife.

Ping wanted to emulate her father in all things, and in consequence the East-West confrontation in our household extended to the medicine cabinet. I had been brought up a staunch believer in pill-pushers, in the rational western practice of diagnosing the trouble and then attacking it with the right drugs or surgery. There was no doubt that it often worked, but I constantly found myself on weak ground with Ping when scientists and doctors changed their minds, and dogma was turned upside-down. Drinking and smoking were bad for one, right? But the day came when it was incontestably proved that alcohol, and especially a liberal daily dose of red wine, could reduce the risk of heart attacks. Furthermore, while overindulgence might give one the shakes, demon drink in moderation would stop a tremor, as many a neurosurgeon discovered to his — and his patients' — advantage.

Worse still, later statistics showed that people who smoked heavily for years during their irresponsible youth were less prone to suffer from Alzheimer's or Parkinson's disease when older and wiser. A high-fibre diet prevented cancer of the colon, then it didn't; at one moment, butter was bad for one, the next it was good; eggs were good for one, then bad; then polyunsaturated fat that had been good for one was also pronounced bad and monounsaturated recommended; then salt which had been bad was good, low cholesterol was good one year and was linked to violent death the next, and so it went on, right today, wrong tomorrow, wrong today, right tomorrow.

And not just like that, the way. Western doctors only treat the disease, not the cause why it happens. If there is natural poison in the body they put in artificial poison to fight it. Typical. In general western people always want fight everything face to face, while we in China want find solution to prevent trouble in first place, and seems this principle also the case with illness. Chinese doctors believe cannot wait until sickness develops, but must try to prevent it by putting whole body in harmony, strong enough to fight disease from, inside by itself without drugs. I was told insects always creating new immune strains to protect themselves in this natural way. Of course, because got no western doctors.

When she broke her wrist playing ping pong aboard ship, she went to a Taoist healer on arrival in Hong Kong instead of a local hospital. The wrist never fully recovered from the experience, but that did not shake her. She had a proper respect for western medicine, but continued to avoid it in cases where she thought a Chinese sinseh could cure her, and dodged taking modern drugs whenever she could. Rightly so, it seemed, for the dislike proved to be mutual. She turned out to be allergic to all antibiotics — her head went round and round and her heart pounded until 'my body felt like a Chinese lion dance'.

After our son Dominic was diagnosed as having cancer and operated upon, the oncologists warned us that his case was terminal. Chemotherapy could not save him, and while he might live a little longer, he would suffer more if he undertook it. We therefore turned to Doctor Feng. Doctor Feng came down from Hong Kong looking like nobody's image of a physician. He was a middle-aged, short, solid, round-headed, smiling cherub who wore a T-shirt and a long unlit Filipino cigarette permanently stuck between his lips. His treatment consisted in running two bamboo sticks over Dominic for one or two hours at a stretch for three days on end to restore balance to the 'meridians' of his life force, and prescribing a strict diet that included crushed pearls and bile of buffalo.

Dominic at once began to feel better. He was soon walking two or three kilometres a day and swimming 50 lengths and more in his condominium pool, and after a few weeks started to travel on business — Taiwan, Beijing, Shanghai, Frankfurt. He may have overdone it. Sadly, Feng could not save his patient. He had taken on the case after the western-trained doctors had already given up, and the disease was too widespread. But there could be little doubt that he had stimulated Dominic's immune system into putting up a stiff fight and that his last months had been happier and more comfortable. The specialists had raised no objection when we had brought in this unconventional Chinese herbal practitioner. It 'could do no harm', they said. They were right.

Feng was credited with quite spectacular cures, and any doubts in my mind that there could be a time for Chinese medicine as there was a time for Western medicine ended there. But Ping and I could still disagree about which had done the trick if both systems were tried. When after several frightening months of waiting Ping was given laser treatment for a massive haemorrhage in the right eye, her vision not only returned but actually improved; to the surprise of her ophthalmologist, she no longer had to wear glasses to drive or play tennis. 'Now you see what western science can do,' I remarked smugly. 'No,' retorted Ping. 'My eyes better because drink carrot juice every day.' 'Oh, come on,' I said, the adrenaline beginning to work. 'You just had the laser operation and that fixed it immediately.' 'Laser operation only in one eye, eyesight better in both,' she replied crushingly, and winked to prove it.

So I took to drinking carrot juice every day myself, just to be companionable, and two years later my chuffed ophthalmologist told me that my eyesight had inexplicably improved and, like Ping, I need not wear glasses for driving any more. So where did that leave us? I remembered the wartime ruse whereby we spread the rumour that RAF night-fighter pilots were enhancing their eyesight by eating carrots daily ('bags of vitamin A, old boy') to conceal the fact that they owed their new and uncanny ability to spot the enemy in the dark to a new secret weapon — radar. Could it be that all the time we hadn't had radar after all, only carrots?

Ping's idea that the carrots had restored good vision to both eyes harmonised with the holistic view of the Chinese school of medicine that the body was all one. But from that stemmed a wider challenge to my beliefs. I had been born into a world of Aristotelian reason and analysis in which everything was categorised, classified and labelled. But Ping had been born into a world of two great native philosophies — Confucianism and Taoism — and the Taoists specifically condemned man for dissecting the world and giving the pieces 'ten thousand names'. In doing so he had artificially divided the indivisible, for the oneness of the body reflected in microcosm the Oneness of the entire Universe. He should have left well alone.

Taoists believe the Cosmos is all one piece, and man must not meddle with it. And can see today what happens when meddle — nature unbalanced, world getting hotter, rainforests disappear like ghosts, fish in sea not enough. Why? All unnecessary action upsets the universal order, they say. Do not try to change things — they will look after themselves. For man to be in harmony with nature, he must move with it, not fight against it. If a drunk man falls out of a chariot, he will not hurt himself, just because he does not try to stop himself. So do not disturb things by dissecting them, they say; it is enough that 'they are so without knowing why'.

If you confront the traditions of the Taoist sages Laozi and Zhuangzi with those of Aristotle and Descartes, you might think that Ping and I lived in two different versions of the same planet, one the breathing original, the other an anatomical chart of it with little red lines and numbers identifying the different parts. My mind automatically analysed everything it saw, hers simply accepted it as part of the cosmic unity. And while she used words to talk, like everyone else she could certainly be vague about the 'ten thousand names'. Although she assiduously cultivated her garden, for example, she never knew what most of the trees, shrubs or flowers in it were called. What I might (just might) identify as a *jacaranda evalifolia* she would describe as 'that tree with the blue flowers opposite, today no wind, so tail won't wag'.

She simply loved it for what it was, something indivisible from herself.

If there is some superfluous money, I spent it on the garden. I believed in happy marriage home should be full of free and easy atmosphere and flowing style, and if the couple found the view of the garden pleasing, could relax under the moon, chatting, drinking, and listen the crickets chanting. Who need names?

She belonged to a universe in which to translate everything into 21 consonants and five vowels was as foolish as analysing love into psychological complexes or cerebral biochemistry. And her view of the world-as-one seemed subconsciously to colour her speech, for she instinctively found expression in the pathetic fallacy, where I, as a reporter with only six column inches in hand, might stick to plain statement in which trees were trees, flowers were just flowers, and life was man versus the rest. 'I am part of the garden,' she would say, and you, you are just part of me.' Flowers were given 'injections' (pesticide), and when fed fertiliser 'put their heads up', they got 'drunk' when doused with the heel of a bottle of red wine, looked 'comfortable and happy' when talked to and cared for, but 'cried' if not watered — 'so sweet'. As I have said, she hated artificial arrangements that violated nature, and proudly claimed that in her backyard 'all the plants do as they like'.

It was, inevitably the same with animals. 'Sukey is working' (the cat is snoozing in her study), 'Charlie is in the garden on business' (no need to explain further), 'Charlie gets up late because he knows Sunday and no postman to bark.' (She had not heard of Chesterton's dog Quoodle who could *smell* the Sabbath). She always sees things from the point of view of the animal: 'Sukey see me naked first time gave me funny look, means 'What happened your fur?' The dog won't eat a piece of banana 'because it too cheap for him.' Having said I smell like Banner, she sprays him with perfume, but not me. Not only does she feed her stomach medicine to the dog, but she proposes trying the dog's vitaminised skin lotion on herself — 'coat so glossy, maybe do my hair good'. (At this point I step in.) Shutup Charlie has a 'strict dress code' — always barks at people wearing loud colours. Even a wriggling tropical fish is 'musical'.

The only time I saw Ping frown on favours accorded to man's best friend was when we went to lunch one day at Eden Hall, the residence in Singapore of Lord Selkirk, the British Commissioner-General for Southeast Asia. We were only eight in the august dining room, not counting the four dogs. It said much for the softhearted Lady Selkirk that the dogs were all strays she had picked up, but as they ran around and under the table hoping for titbits, Ping learned that as no one had known their names, if any, when they were found, her hostess had called them after the most renowned of the Chinese dynasties — Han, Tang, Sung and Ming. That did not amuse her, as will emerge.

The stereotype of the Englishman is a great animal lover, although he may mercilessly hound foxes and hares and deer to their death and massacre thousands of more or less edible birds in season, and his forefathers revelled in travelling far to shoot tigers and rhino and buck in other people's countries, and before that in organising dogfights, cockfights, and bear-baiting at home. It was safe to say that, unlike the Chinese Buddhists of Hong Kong, he would not bother to chant prayers for seven days to appease the souls of a million or so chickens slaughtered to prevent the spread of 'bird flu'. But no one thinks the worse of him for that.

The stereotype of the Chinese, on the other hand, is widely known for his cruelty to animals in spite of this concern for their afterlife, and some live up to the cliché. In Singapore he may give his overfed toddler a puppy to play with, but when it grows bigger and the kid yells for a Tamagotchi instead, simply throw the unfortunate pooch out of his car in some distant street and drive off quickly. However, a stereotype is only a stereotype, and the Chinese lady next door may feed stray cats and fast-breeder pigeons in the face of government frowns as defiantly as any old dear in London. 'Singapore people grow so many birds,' Ping once commented approvingly.

According to the director, visitors to the Singapore Zoo have been known to wake sleeping animals by throwing bricks at them (after all, they have paid good money to see them in action, haven't they?), stub lighted cigarettes on the pachyderms, and fling broken bottles into the hippo pool, leaving beasts with bruises, burns, and bleeding feet. But other doting Singaporeans will almost kill the inmates with kindness, bringing with them baskets loaded with deleterious junk food they normally fatten their children on. As the Confucians say, there are no fixed rules. One could hardly better the story of the Chinese mother and her two teenage daughters in Hong Kong who in 1998 were hospitalised in a critical condition after giving mouth-to-mouth resuscitation to their dog — it had vomited and fainted while being shampooed with a toxic anti-tick solvent. The dog it was that died, but still...

As a child Ping tore her dolls apart and kept animals instead, including dogs, cats, a monkey, a rabbit, a bird, a white mouse that tirelessly worked a treadmill, and a squirrel that lived in her back pocket and was a permanent part of her *toilette*. She loved them all. Hence my present to her of the kitten Christmas, of Sukey, Rusty, Banner, two Morgans and Shutup Charlie. She laughed with delight at the wild life in the garden — the occasional monitor lizard, the leaping tree frogs, the scolding tree shrews. When a shrew was caught in a rat trap, she insisted it had to be released into the jungle. With disastrous results. For shrews have the disagreeable defensive mechanism usually associated with skunks, and once in the car it produced an appalling stench that lasted for days, although Ping sprayed it with perfume as she had sprayed Banner when she realised he smelt like me.

I got used to this sort of thing. Returning home from covering some squalid event in Vietnam or Indonesia I would find a new addition to the family — a parrot, or a monkey, or another kitten. Despatched to get a dog licence for Rusty on one occasion, she forgot the licence but came home with an insufferable pomeranian that was fortuitously run over not long afterwards. (I was in Cambodia and had an alibi.) As for actually eating dogs as so many Chinese do, Ping had strong views on the subject.

I know dog's meat is valuable for health care, and after eating it the blood circulation became smooth, whole body felt nice and warm. But make me sick. Because dog always be loyal to human being, and between them was a true friendship. How could people eat their own friend? During Cultural Revolution under Mao when no food to feed dog or cat, once a dog appeared immediately was killed on the spot with authority of law as hated plaything of capitalists, and publicly operated shops sold the dog's meat at a low price. How horrible a deplorable social phenomenon like that!

When our first Alsatian died at the age of 14, I was out and she phoned me. 'He has gone back to Heaven,' she said simply, and that 'back' gave the words an almost unbearable poignancy. Only Ping could have put it like that. Although she derided popular superstition, she allowed the maid to line the box he was to be buried in at the bottom of the garden with 'Bank of Hell' notes, which Chinese burn when seeing off their loved ones so that they will not arrive at the gates of Paradise broke, and if necessary can bribe their way in. For long she would not contemplate getting another dog, but after much cajoling I at last persuaded her at least to look at a litter of Alsatians advertised in the *Straits Times*. 'Now do please choose one,' I urged timidly once she was faced with the gambolling pups. 'Which would you like?' She shook her head sadly. There was a long silence. Then she straightened and pointed. All right, if you really want me to, I'll have that one,' she said reluctantly. Pause for a sigh — and then a sudden smile and a swing of the finger — *'and that one!'*

By the time they were twin monsters of seven, I was already 68. I had retired from the *Observer* and was working part-time on modest book contracts, the boys had long since gone, and we decided to capitalise on our property and move into a smaller place. We therefore prepared to sell our bungalow with its half-acre of garden, and I braced myself for some stiff bargaining with our best bet for a buyer, a knowing old Chinese who had brought with him a bodyguard, a geomancer from Hong Kong, and a daughter-in-law with a face like painted glass to look the place over. I would stand out for a minimum of 1.2 million dollars, I decided. That would pay for a condominium townhouse and leave us with a comfortable balance in the bank.

Ping was heartbroken, because — animal-loving Englishman or no — I had said that we would have to find new homes for the dogs, as there would not be room for them where we were going. When I explained to the old man why she looked so downcast, he snapped at the chance like a chameleon. 'No problem. We will keep them here for you. They will be in their old home, and you can come and see them any time you like.' And as her face lifted, he added swiftly, 'I'll give you 1.12 million.' 'Right!' cried Ping at once, decisive as usual, and before I could move shook hands with him as the Chinese will to seal a contract. From one second to another, we were $80,000 out of pocket. He was delighted with his bargain, of course, and told me as I stared at him speechlessly that he would add a second storey to the house, put in a swimming pool, extend the...

It was September 1987. Three weeks later the stock markets of the world crashed. The bungalow remained empty and neglected for years, no second storey or swimming pool was added, and not surprisingly the buyer broke his word and did not take the dogs. He had lost out, we had sold just in time, lucky to get the price, and the money was safe in the bank. If I had held out for my 1.2 million, we could have ended up with no sale and no buyers in sight. Ping had done the right thing, and since it was too late to find new homes for the dogs, she could now insist on keeping them in our new place, despite the overcrowding. Like a good Taoist, she had got what she wanted by not striving for it, but letting it come to her. Elated, she would hold their heads, look them in the eye, and say 'You *are* ...' The uncompleted sentence was like the Sanskrit *Tat tvam asi* of the Hindus, 'Thou art *that*' — part of the same nameless, undefinable essence, the indescribable Oneness of all things. At such moments, saddled with my divisive *Cogito, ergo sum* and not understanding how you could have a sentence without an object anyway, I would feel as if I belonged to a different species.

Sometimes the pathetic fallacy extended to the inanimate. Although modest in her demands, Ping acquired mountains of clothes over the years because she was reluctant to part with them; they were like old friends, and when she found after losing weight that she could fit into one outmoded favourite, she said it was the dress that 'had got younger every day'. A fresh set of tyres for our secondhand Singer 'felt like new shoes'; but it 'only listens to you', she complained to me when it wouldn't start for her.

To the ancient Taoist philosophers the car would be an artificial creation, against nature and therefore automatically in the wrong. Ping, of course, did not carry things that far. But her relationship with gadgetry was sometimes uneasy. When we were first married she assured me she had driven in China, and I put her behind the wheel of the Hillman to give her a refresher course before she took her driving test. She listened patiently to my explanation of the gears, started up confidently, put her foot on the accelerator, and took me on a hair-raising race through the narrow roads (as they then were) to the east coast of Singapore while I sat hanging on to my seat and shouting, unheard either by her or my Maker. She knew all about the accelerator, all right, but had forgotten where the footbrake was. Yet she was to develop into an almost neurotic front-seat back-seat driver — 'I only feel old in the car,' she says nowadays. It is her turn.

Her compromise between Taoist teaching and artificial man-made contrivances was expressed in three words: keep it simple. A washing machine or a tumble-dryer or an electric cooker was chosen for its lack of controls — 'look, this one very good.' 'You mean only $425?' 'No, only three buttons.' Flashing coloured lights and fingertip controls would only mean more breakdowns either on her side or the gadget's. Leave them to the wives of Singapore yuppies. She would have nothing to do with most modern gimmicks from credit cards to answering machines, let alone the Internet or e-mail and similar horrors of progress, and she once described the clamour from hip-pocket handphones and pagers disdainfully as 'too much noise from too many bottoms'.

She consented to use an old IBM-convertible personal computer of mine for elementary purposes, but my Compaq Presario, in front of which I sat alone for much of the day, she jealously dubbed my 'concubine', and considered its ability to entertain me with music and simple games like some sort of electronic geisha in poor taste. The more natural the means, the better. She constantly reminded me of the old Chinese joke about the man who drew the outline of his feet on a piece of paper before going to the shoemaker, forgot to take it with him, and said he would go home to fetch it. 'What do you want it for?' protested the cobbler. 'You've got your own feet here, haven't you? Isn't that good enough.'

I always feel the more things you have, the more you want, and the more miserable is the life. After certain point they are simply what D calls 'dead loss'. I know I very difficult person to choose presents for. 'Don't buy me anything,' I tell him, and when 26 December, day after Christmas, I am very happy because no need to open more. Especially I hate expensive gifts like jewellery that just become responsibility afraid to lose, and when once I finally agreed he could buy me new dinner set I told him 'give me plates I can break.'

For the ancient Taoists the secret of happiness was also to renounce all artificial striving and only take what came along. Ambition to get to the top could lead only to disaster, for when we stood on tiptoe we stood unsteady, a brimming glass was easily spilled, and the tallest tree was the first to be chopped down. And if possessions were a deadweight, so was position. 'Wealth, rank and arrogance add up to ruin as surely as two and two make four,' said Laozi, and Zhuangzi echoed him. Zhuangzi was fishing when he was approached by court officials who invited him to become the Chief Minister of Chu. He declined the honour with the words, 'I would rather be a live tortoise wagging its tail in the mud, than a dead one venerated in a gold casket in the king's ancestral shrine.'

We appreciate Zhuangzi hold aloof from the world. Today for same reason we don't admire Nietzsche, and Faust's Mephistopheles never appeared in our study. My mother said 'wise people are frightened to get famous as wise pigs are frightened to get fat.' If someone does not seek for luxurious living, naturally no need to carry the load of fame and gain, feel much comfortable. Peace is the highest limit of fortune, your face to the world, nothing to fight for.

Confucianism and Taoism may sometimes appear diametrically opposed, but the pragmatic Chinese can accommodate both as complementary *yang* and *yin*, positive and negative. There are many reasons why a Chinese may fall back on the consolation of Taoist 'non-action' after an active career. It may be because he has suffered a political defeat or a professional failure — 'When there is wind, the dragon soars; when there is none, he goes underground,' quotes Ping. Or it may be because the Sages have ruled that one should serve a good society, but withdraw from a bad one. But very often it is a question of age. Having worked conscientiously for most of his life to bring honour to his family, to be 'a crane among chickens', a Confucian may reach for his slippers with a sigh of relief and embrace a doctrine which teaches him that it is virtuous to do nothing. When at the age of 77 I suddenly lost a prestigious book contract, as I have described, I was downcast, but Ping was jubilant. 'You work too hard,' she said. 'Why you work for somebody else at your age? Now you are yourself, free, so why worry? You getting old. I don't want you famous. I want you just be a — a *remarkable nobody.* That is happiness. Now is time you wag your tail in the mud.' So we took out the reverse mortgage.

I began to see it her way. Taoist quietism is hardly compatible with the usual image of the unscrupulous Chinese businessman cheating his way to his first ten million, let alone the stressed-out Singapore yuppie with his eye on the chairman's chair. But it is there, in ambush in the race memory, just waiting for their hair to turn grey. In theory Taoism was certainly not compatible with my fidgety western instinct to be dissatisfied, to want a bigger byline for longer articles and greater recognition, to want to beat the competition and murder the subs when they cut my copy down to size, to worship progress and perfection, and — like some policy-maker in Washington — to want to change everything to suit myself except myself.

I had always been in a rush, my jerky movements reflecting the fretful rat race of the foreign correspondent in contrast to Ping's harmonious, slow-motion dance of life which was like an unending exercise in *taiji*. But for me the day of the deadline was now long past. On thinking it over, and having already made my peace with Confucianism, I found myself drawn more and more to Taoism.

And not just because there was a lot to be said for reaching for the carpet slippers.

11

PERHAPS my Taoist revulsion from things artificial developed because, like Joan of Arc of blessed memory, I began to hear voices in my head telling me what to do. And not just in Singapore. In 1996 I even listened to one 7,000 miles away in London, when I laboriously punched 31 numbers and two asterisks into a telephone keyboard in order to talk to Ping at home, only to be told in reproving if dulcet tones, The-number-you-have-dialled-is-incorrect. Please-try-again.' But there are many such. Another will say consolingly, 'The-person-you-have-called-is-unavailable-if-you-wish-to-record-a-message-press-one.' I press one, and I get 'The mailbox-of-the-officer-you-wish-to-speak-to-is-full-if-you-wish-to-speak-to-another-person-press-2-for-general-information-on-information-press-3-for-faxed-proforma-documentation-press-4-for-computerised-printout-applications-press-5-for-enquiries-on-the-state-of-your-application-press-6-to-speak-to-our-customer-service-officer-press-zero.' I press zero and get 'Greensleeves'. After four minutes of this, I try something else and another of my disembodied voices says, All-our-operators-are-engaged-at-present-please-hold-on-and-we-will-get-back-to-you-as-soon-as-we-can.' This is followed by 30 seconds of Vivaldi, followed by 'all-our-operators-are-engaged-at-present ...' Then more Vivaldi, followed by 'all-our-operators' ... Vivaldi, 'all-our ...',

Vivaldi, 'all-our ...', Vivaldi, 'all-our...' That recital goes on for five minutes after which I am abruptly cut off by the engaged signal. 'For God's sake,' I cry, alone in the automated wilderness, 'please, *please* let there be another human being somewhere for me to talk to.' If I phone God will I get — 'for remission of sins, press one, for recovery from illness, press two ...? (Fortunately, no — not yet, anyway.)

I am meanwhile a martyr to my temperamental computer. It has me fruitlessly cursing it, but it never gets mad at me. It just gets even. The same with the printer. I try printing out a hard copy. 'Paper-jam,' says the printer unctuously. I correct the fault. 'Paper-jam.' I correct again. 'Paper-jam-paper-jam-paper-jam-paper-jam-paper-jam ... Close-printer.' I examine the printer. The printer is closed. 'Close-printer.' I open it and slam the lid again. 'Close-printer ...'

At the checkout counter of the local supermarket I tot up the bill in my head, say 'seventy-three dollars fifty', and put down the cash. The girl ignores me and I stand by, fists clenched and eyes on the ceiling, as she punches a string of figures into two different machines. Three minutes later one of them registers $73.50. She looks at me in wonder, mouth open. 'How did you know?' she asks. She can no longer count. The calculator has taken over. My ultimate fear was that Ping might be tempted by an offer of a cheap handphone and my peace and privacy would then vanish forever. But of course it was groundless. 'It would get rusty,' she said. We were on the same net. Zhuangzi would have approved. My favourite headline in the *Straits Times* (2 May 1997) was 'Police have kept crime rate in check *in spite of progress*'.

As for artificial striving, I was no longer in danger of toppling over from standing on tiptoe, and began to realise that probably I never had been. When young I wanted to make my mark, but as a famous writer rather than a tycoon, and in World War II as a decorated hero rather than a general — I saw myself much admired, with a bloody bandage around my head on some forlorn battlefront. I got the bloody bandage but without the admiration — a train I was foolish enough to take was bracketed in York station by German night-bombers and then blown into a burning wreck. I was not decorated by King George VI for my pains, but, as I recollect, had to fill out a report proving my head wound had not been self-inflicted. And the blood ruined my new trench coat.

I twice declined promotion because it would have entailed a humdrum posting, preferring what was interesting — to be up front as field security officer of a crack infantry division, to serve with a mission in Russian-occupied Hungary — and in consequence remained an obscure captain for five years, which might well have been a wartime record. (I told Ping I felt embarrassed in front of her brothers — 'Why worry?' she came back. 'You are a captain among generals.') In peace as in war, I remained true to form. For 27 of my years as a foreign correspondent I chose to remain holed up happily in the Far East, a news backwater between wars and revolutions and half a world away from office politics in London. I should have been angling for transfers to other regions to gain all-round experience — perhaps to key posts like Washington and Moscow — with the aim of making it one day to the foreign editor's desk. I paid for that.

So it appears in retrospect that I was a cinch for the two main Chinese philosophies before I knew anything about them, which made it easier for them to exert their influence over me across some 25 centuries when I did. It seems a long time, and I sometimes wondered if I were some kind of one-off freak. The 'Thoughts of Mao Zedong', stamped into the minds of the workaholic 'blue ants' of Communist China, had ostensibly obliterated all memory of the old doctrines, and left them with nothing in their heads but revolutionary slogans. And at first glance only ludicrously distorted traces remained in the stereotype of the Singapore Chinese, with his relentless materialistic drive to achieve the five Cs, his Lego dream home embodying three clashing styles of architecture but innocent of books, his 'Taoist' and 'Confucian' temples with their gaudy images, at which the hopeful clutched their lottery tickets and prayed in exchange for promises, promises.

But beneath the surface the subconscious accretions of Chinese culture and the race memory were still at work. 'Confucian ethics' were the East's moral challenge to the West, a subject of lively debate among intellectuals that carried a considerable clout. In Singapore its influence could be clearly seen in the policies of the government, with its mandarinal elitism, its emphasis on education, thrift, hard work, and achievement, on filial piety, on incorruptibility, and on putting society before the individual. A Chinese Chinese from a very different background, Ping was steeped in her traditions just as I was steeped in mine. Although a sceptical dropout, I would never be able to shake off my Christian sense of sin, and she would never shake off her father's Confucian counsel. As she repeated when I reminded her recently what she had told me 40 years ago:

If you look in your heart and know you right, you never scared. Build up yourself to be yourself never depend on other people, never worry they help you or hurt you, doesn't care what kind circumstances. You are you. My mother say, if dogs bark at you, don't bark back. If people speaking against you, don't see them or hear them. Be like big piece stone.

But — Apprehensive by name, apprehensive by nature. To my chagrin, I began to think that in practice Ping no longer followed her Confucian parents' advice. Theoretically cool, calm, and collected, she showed a dismaying tendency to flap, to cry before she was hurt. 'I beg you, don't mend ceiling light, leave to the electrician, may be electric shock, then fall off ladder.' (I'm only changing a bulb and I'm standing on the second step.) 'I beg you, don't go walking in park, can be rain soon, you don't know.' (The sky is blue from end to end.) 'I beg you, don't go quarrel these people. Can be gangster. Can make trouble.' (He's a five-foot-nothing government dentist and I'm only going to ask him to move his car.) 'I beg you, go to see doctor, cut can be poison.' (It's only a scratch.) 'I beg you, go now, otherwise late.' (It's still two hours before my appointment.) Had I married a broken reed (not knowing it was one that bends in order to spring back later)? 'Why are you always so nervous about everything before it happens,' I asked her, filled with growing foreboding.

Not nervous, just common sense. If D Chinese, no problem. But he doesn't understand. Wise person always apprehensive, always expect worst, never take chances if no need. Confucius says 'cautious seldom err'. But D is too impatient to take risk. Stupid. Already enough trouble in world you cannot avoid. So when can avoid it why not? But D exactly opposite. He doesn't care about avoiding trouble when can. No. He only gets worried and excited in case where he cannot stop something bad will happen anyway. Which also stupid. Because if it does happen, means must happen, cannot change, so have to accept.

Disentangled, this meant that if trouble came despite all your efforts to avoid it, it was obviously inevitable; and therefore to be faced with dignity, as the Chinese had faced it for millennia. But while Ping did all she could to forestall disaster, I would pooh-pooh her fears, tempt fate, and then curse when I got my comeuppance — I got drenched in the park ('like chicken dropped in the soup'), the cut turned septic, I was late for my appointment. Ping was no wimp. She had been through the riches-to-rags mill, and her anxiety before a calamity was matched by her patience and fortitude after it had struck. 'Have to accept,' she would repeat whenever I shook my fists at Heaven.

She did not say 'I beg you' not to go when I took a 500-ton rust bucket to Sumatra without a valid visa to join the incompetent rebels fighting against President Sukarno, or flew to Vietnam after the first Vietcong ambushes, or to Borneo to cover the armed Indonesian guerrilla infiltration into the jungles of Sarawak, however little she liked these adventures. On the contrary, she would somewhat disconcertingly 'beg' me to get to the airport three hours before takeoff so as not to miss my plane to mayhem.

She did not flap when faced with a cancer operation (hers), beyond saying 'how silly to die in such a beautiful world' as we drove past the Botanic Gardens to the hospital, nor when faced with a second one (mine) as she sat in a hospital corridor, lonely and ignored, waiting for the verdict while the doctors did one scan after another. She only exploded when she discovered that they were taking so much time to tell her the worst, not because the case was so serious, but because the radiologist had gone out to lunch. All these things had to happen and so be faced with composure. Even on my meeting with Rupert Bond on rue Catinat in Saigon which lit the 42-year fuse of our future lives in 1955 she said with fine resignation, 'it had to happen.'

Although Chinese people usually very cautious they still great gamblers, but keep calm whether end up with million dollars or broke, because believe in long run no such thing as win or lose in the life, cannot tell when bad luck will turn out to be good luck or good luck turn out to be bad luck. So must accept. Chinese have old story about a man who lost a mare. Neighbours say 'bad luck'. But after few days mare came back leading a wild horse. Congratulations, say neighbours. But the man's son try to ride the horse which immediately threw him down and break his leg. Bad luck, say neighbours. But next year there was a war, all young men in the village must go to fight except cripple, and so all killed except him. Congratulations? Depend what happen next.

I was ready to accept the dual *yang-yin* nature of luck, all the more so because the story of two distinguished namesakes of mine bore it out. In 1665 the population of the City of London was decimated by the Great Plague. The following year the Lord Mayor, Sir Thomas Bludworth, was called to his bedroom window one night to observe a blaze that had broken out in Pudding Lane. 'Pish,' he said contemptuously, annoyed at being woken from his sleep just for this. 'A woman might piss it out.' Not quite, for it was the beginning of the Great Fire of London that ended at Pie Corner in which almost the entire city was burned down.

However, not only had the fire driven out the rats that brought the plague, but it had got rid of all the old, narrow, stinking, vermin-infested streets and wooden buildings that had housed them. The City was then rebuilt in brick and stone, and beautified by the work of the great architect Sir Christopher Wren, who designed not only a new St Paul's Cathedral but more than 50 other churches.

Nor was there ever another plague in London. Bludworth was dismissed by the great diarist Samuel Pepys as 'a silly man', but I am proud to bear the name of this lazy and incompetent buffoon whose stupidity had turned so much bad luck into so much good.

And then there was James Bloodworth, who was deported from England for life for some petty misdemeanour, and sailed with the First Fleet to Australia as a convict in 1787. Bad luck. But he was a brickmaker and mason by trade, and since the early settlement that was to be the great city of Sydney was then 'forest-clad, unkempt, uncanny and unknown', his value was without price. By the time he died he had built Government House, a citadel, a parsonage, a judge's residence, a brewery, a printing house, several warehouses and a playhouse, and the Governor gave orders for him to be buried with full military honours. If he had not been deported, he would have died in obscurity, probably after rotting for the rest of his life in some vile London jail.

As for ourselves, in 1958 I bought a book of tickets for an Automobile Association Christmas lottery for ten dollars, but somehow had the bad luck to mislay it. I therefore bought another book of ten tickets, and it was one of these that won the second prize — $6,500. Returning home after collecting my cheque, I immediately spotted the first book of tickets lying on the window sill opposite my desk, where it had been all the time. Now if I had not had the bad luck to lose it earlier, and the good luck not to find it ... As it was, it changed our fortunes. Added to my pitiful savings as a correspondent with a small swindle sheet, it prompted Ping to demand that we buy a house with a mortgage. We found a snip, and never looked back. Over the years property values soared. We bought and sold, each time pocketing the difference in price, and despite the odd setbacks we suffered we now live in comfortable retirement in the home of Ping's choice. The $6,500 had been the foundation of our future.

It was a good thing that Ping's philosophical attitude enabled her to ignore the slings and arrows of life with Confucian aplomb, for being a Chinese married to an Englishman was no joyride in the early days. When we went out together the cruder Chinese would automatically assume she was a cabaret pick-up, hawkers would shout indelicate innuendoes at her in freestyle Cantonese, waiters snigger behind their hands, shopkeepers freeze her with a glance (the tart might ask for a commission on what I bought). In Taipei a taxi-driver who took her for a whore with an American client attacked her with a tyre-lever, only thinking twice about it after I gave him a backhander with a clenched fist on the carotid, and in Singapore another stopped his cab and refused to take us further, yelling as yet unprintable epithets. (He was not to know, of course, that it was our 20th wedding anniversary.) At the Imperial Hotel in Tokyo a flunkey stopped us as we came through the door late at night and said I could not take a Japanese woman to my room. (*Japanese?* Ping restrained me.)

Mixed company could be a special problem on occasion. At parties where she was not well-known crusty old Singapore hands would paradoxically treat her with courtesy and smiling respect, but many newcomers to Asia, impatient with her Pinglish, might snub her, talk over her head, or turn their backs on her while I swithered with frustrated fury and insulted anyone I could buttonhole. But that was not true of all. There were those kind souls who automatically assumed she was a halfwit, and on being introduced treated her accordingly, yelling infantile banalities at her at point-blank range in words of one syllable. And at the other end of the scale were the intellectuals who could not be bothered or were too dense to make allowances for her linguistic limitations, and in unstoppable voices would rattle off their unsolicited opinions in polysyllabic jargon whose meaning mercifully eluded her. However, we were usually surrounded by fellow correspondents and diplomatic or political friends with whom Ping was popular and at ease, and she was particularly happy when giving her own parties.

Once D came back from covering stories abroad I often arranged dinners at home, and especially during the time D was vice-president and president of the Foreign Correspondents Association we had many interesting people, journalists, well-informed sources, writers, musicians, artists, godknowwhat, and many spoke freely and cheerfully, making a vivid scene. There were people like Foil Tsong, the famous pianist, who made me happy telling me that when he gave a performance his mind always thinking about the great Chinese poet Li Po, and our friend Raja, that time Foreign Minister often just back from talking at UN or important international conference and spoke about politics, and P.S. Raman who discussed mainly culinary art with me, and when Singapore's ambassador to Moscow himself cooked all Indian dishes for whole banquet for VIP guests. Then there was Sergei Svirin, intelligent fellow with bright and cheerful disposition, spoke excellent Mandarin. He was correspondent of Tass news agency from Moscow, but when I asked who owned the biggest and most luxurious car of those parked outside our gate, he surprise me by saying 'it is mine'. Very interesting and odd, that moment communism and capitalism seemed no different. And I can never forget Tony and Sheila Colton, our close friends who were so helpful to us for so many years; Tony had been a British civil servant in colonial days, then an executive on Times Publishing, and spoke fluent Hokkien.

But when we were invited out I could never tell how an encounter was going to work, and whether a knowledge of Chinese in fact helped. At one cacophonic thrash I was at first relieved and grateful when an Englishman addressed Ping in adequate Chinese and they fell into conversation. I should not have ignored the warning signs — the supercilious, carrying voice and permanently raised eyebrows with which he had graced Wadham College in his time — for they soon parted company after he tried to show off his Cantonese by correcting hers, and then proceeded to give her a lecture on her own dialect.

But knowledge of things Chinese could work the other way. At another dinner party I was horrified to see Ping placed next to a senior British atomic scientist on a visit from Oxford. What on earth would they have to say to each other? Feeling even more guilty than usual for dragging her into this situation, I glanced across the table furtively from time to time, but was soon astonished to see them engrossed in conversation and ignoring their food. The usually taciturn Ping was in full spate. What had happened?

The professor had asked a few polite questions which had quickly led to talk about China in her father's day, for to her surprise he revealed that he had been born in Manchuria. Ping knew it well, since Hua Sheng had later been a provincial governor there, and she somehow came to mention in passing a notable incident that had occurred in Mukden the year she was born in Beijing. This concerned the 'Grand Marshal' Chang Tso-lin, a foul-mouthed, opium-smoking warlord of dubious origins who was at the time master of Manchuria.

Japanese made use of him to help them plan to nibble away Chinese territory. Consequently they treated Chang very kindly but at the same time threatened him by force too. That made him angry, and once he shouted with a mighty roar, 'I would rather surrender my weapons to the southern revolutionary army of KMT, and don't want your Japanese help to preserve my little empire.' As a result, Japan disappointed and laid a mine under his train to kill him. He was enemy of KMT, but his death changed people's idea of him and he became a national hero.

A former bandit who played by rules which he made up as he went along, Chang planned in 1927 to take advantage of the revolutionary turmoil to his south by adding all North China to his Manchurian fief. But when he had left his capital once before with his troops, mandarins offended by his rough and ready manner of going about things had plotted against him behind his back. He therefore summoned them to the courtyard of his palace before setting off this time, ringed them with trigger-happy soldiery, and addressed them in a sustained bawl. Ping did not quote him, but according to one unexpurgated account, he did not mince his words:

'Do you know what's happening beyond the Pass? Fuck your mother, it's just like a whorehouse. So I'm off there tomorrow. You know there are good pickings to be had down there? Well, they're going to be ours. But, fuck your mother, last time I went through the Pass I heard that you all started mucking about on the quiet back here. I won't have any mucking around this time, and I dare you to try anything on. I've got guns all over me. Fuck it, do you think I'm scared of anyone? That's it.' On which note he strode out of the courtyard.

'But I was there,' exclaimed the distinguished English boffin. 'I was actually in the courtyard with my father. I remember it well even now. You bring it all back. I was seven at the time. My father was ... Well, well, fancy you ...' And they were off. It was just one year later that Chang Tso-lin was blown up in his armoured train. He had already served his purpose. I was eternally grateful to him.

The Chinese connection nevertheless only fitted where it touched; hardly any westerner and few English-educated Chinese could talk about the good old days of the twenties in China, let alone the thirty or forty centuries that had gone before them. Too many of these gatherings to which I had to take Ping would suddenly open a cultural crevasse between us. We might have come to know enough of each other's background to be at home with each other at home, but a roomful of Anglo-Saxons shouting to be heard on every subject from the absurdities of political correctness to the latest soccer scores in a hemisphere to which she had never been left her stranded and silent.

Worse still were the earnest discussions of upmarket chatterboxes on modern art, ballet, the theatre in London and New York or Sydney, or on the latest books she had not read by contemporary authors she had not heard of, to which she was obliged to listen, orange juice in hand, 'like big piece stone'. Their disdain for her was all the harder to bear, for in Chinese terms these were her domains, the rich fields of literature and painting and opera of which the barbarians knew nothing; they had no more heard of

Qi Bai-shi than had she of Andy Warhol and his cans of Campbell soup. It was another humiliation to be set beside her giddy descent from boom in China to bust in Hong Kong.

She had her own back, however. She had escaped loneliness amid all the pragmatic English-educated go-getters of Singapore by being welcomed into a select coterie of liberal and left-wing emigres from China — mainly journalists, writers and teachers. Remembered with affection as a fireball of student activity that at times had drawn the baleful eye of authority at Zhong Shan University, she was also in touch with a diaspora of former professors and fellow students across the world, and when she visited Canada and the United States was dined and feted by the influential Cantonese community everywhere she went — Miami, San Francisco, Los Angeles, Vancouver, Toronto — and that did her morale no harm.

It did my morale no harm either, since I was not with her. But her friends also came to Singapore sometimes, and I might find myself in my turn grinning uncomprehendingly in the company of Chinese writers and painters, or former school principals and teachers of the arts, all happily swapping references in rapid-fire Chinese and dropping names from a Who's Who that went back 3,000 years or so. I should have known what would happen. Almost the only thing Ping brought with her as a dowry when we married was a large carved sandalwood chest full of nothing but books.

So we both preferred to have people to dine at home, where Ping could escape into the kitchen from the babble of English on the terrace, or I could hide in my study when the swift tide of Chinese flowed over my head. And, as I have said, that applied even within the Chinese Tower of Babel that was our family. With the exception of Dominic's wife, they had all spent some years in England, and our lingua francas were English and Cantonese.

But this still meant that at one moment Ping might be baffled by their parochial British allusions and run for cover, and at the next it would be my turn, a poor wight of a Caucasian married to ten Chinese (including three grandchildren) without a polite word of Cantonese to his name.

We bridged the gap simply by not trying to. I did not attempt to turn Ping into an Englishwoman, she did not attempt to turn me into a Chinese. Our union was more like a federation, we gave each other 'space', and we were all the closer for it. Our marriage and all that we shared formed the core of our life, but beyond its fringes we each enjoyed cultural autonomy, a separate existence into which the other did not penetrate like some tactless spouse suspecting infidelity. Apart from fulfilling our social obligations, I did not go to Ping's binges, and she did not go to mine. And just as I did not tour the United States and Canada with her, she did not for 33 years come to England with me. 'You hold my leg, I hold yours, no good,' as she put it. Not a bad principle on which to base relations between Washington and Beijing. Exploit what you share, but do not impose on each other what you do not.

In theory it is sad if there is a distance between the married couple's two lives, for then they would not understand each other well. But if on the contrary husband and wife hold together all the time, they will become estranged. I believed with D that an ideal home should preserve a space for personal needs, so each enjoys what suits his own temperament and interest. We have separate studies in our house like animals defend their own territory, where for example I could feel at ease listening to Peking Opera, and Dennis to Prokofiev. Even if sometimes we did conflict with each other, I could retire and see the whole thing in a clear light. So the studies helped us to keep a good and humorous mood between us.

And for the married couple to take a separate short holiday is a wonderful arrangement, because distance always makes the view more beautiful and mystical. It is when you stand on the river bank and look at the other side, the land draped in a veil of mist, lamplight faintly visible and trees swaying, that the scenery is most touching. So when D went to England without me, or I went to America or Canada alone, distance across wide ocean created incomparable feeling between us. We couldn't help making long calls to each other, talk bursting with tender sentiment, because during separate tours sweet memories would reappear.

Just so. 'Distance lends enchantment to the view', and so 'absence makes the heart grow fonder'. Moreover, separation provided a golden opportunity for one to pursue a little of one's own fancies. When I went West for five weeks in 1996, Ping at once rang up some of her chums and told them to come to Singapore — the Mouse was away, and the cats could play — and they flew in from four countries for a nonstop spree of gossiping and mahjong and shopping and dining out together at noisy Chinese restaurants. I would have given much to see these six old ladies on the loose, 'but it must have run away with quite a bit of cash,' I suggested on my return. And what were you doing playing mahjong? I thought you were the one Chinese in the world who disapproved of gambling?'

It is true. My father taught me difference between right and wrong, and gambling of course wrong. But when I play mahjong I know it is wrong so it is all right. I don't rush to make money immediately push in pocket straightaway like usual gamblers. Instead, we play intellectual kind mahjong which aim for elegant combinations of tiles, not win lots of cash. And not just like that. We put money we lose into a pool and go out to spend it eating together. That way we are not playing for money but for food, and I am happy to lose because means I give good dinner to my friends.

'You only pool what you lose?' I asked, after digesting this carefully and avoiding her eye. 'But what about the winnings?'

Silence. Then: 'Ye-e-es, what happened the *winnings?*' Ping echoed in wonderment, suddenly turned to a 'big piece stone' again as if to match my poker face. I knew it would work, if not for long. Finance was not her strong suit. But, luckily for me, not only her Chinese cultural life but also her personal budget were part of her autonomy, and therefore not my worry. That, presumably, is how successful federations survive.

12

LIFE had given Ping a schizoid money sense, the free-spending urge of the well-heeled miss wedded uneasily to the penny-pinching of the poor refugee. 'How much did you pay for it?' I asked when she rushed out at the last moment with Nalini and bought a wedding ring for the ceremony. 'Seven dollars.' But as a bargain-hunter writh no head for figures whose first instinct was to buy while the going was good, she could in theory have proved a costly wife — except that for that very reason she avoided temptation by rationing herself like a reformed chocoholic; she never carried more than a limited amount of money in her handbag, forswore credit cards, and firmly refused even to learn how to use an automatic teller machine. However, as the Taoists would be quick to point out, this discipline — like all disciplines — flouted nature. She would return home from a local shopping expedition after sticking religiously to her budget but with no bread, let alone butter, having run out of money at the last minute after buying a cut-price blouse before she could get around to them. ('Only thirty dollars. Can you believe?')

A bargain was always a good buy because it meant saving money by spending it, which served both her warring instincts to be prodigal yet parsimonious. She was far from mean, but she hated 'inappropriate' expense. When in 1987 we moved into a smaller home she was happy to give away a lorry-load of good furniture to a charity rather than sell it to the highest bidder, but indignant when the charity made her pay for the hire of the lorry. That was just dollars down the drain.

It was for similar reasons that she shied away from gambling: that simply was not the way to be relieved of one's mad money. Her mahjong was indifferent because she rarely played it. In the eighties we went to Hong Kong on the *Orient Princess*, a cruise ship almost as schizophrenic as Ping's attitude to cash. Chartered from China by a Sino-American group in colonial Hong Kong, it had two captains, one to run the ship, the second a political commissar to keep the first and all his crew ideologically pure. And there was no doubt that this appointment was a wise precaution of the Chinese Communist Party. For the main attraction aboard was an almost nonstop capitalist casino run by two cigar-smoking American experts from the Caribbean in white linen suits and panama hats straight out of O. Henry. The political commissar was not overtly concerned with the passengers, but Ping took on his role as far as I was concerned, and I remained unpolluted, gently restrained from trying to turn an honest penny at the tables. However, when we rather disastrously ran out of cash in Japan on another occasion and I put us back in the black with an extraordinary winning streak at roulette, she did not demur. In the circumstances, the gamble had proved 'appropriate'.

'Appropriate' spending meant buying the best quality food, the best tennis rackets, plants, books, kitchen equipment; it meant paying for my lone visits to the UK to see family and friends, and a Nissan Sportswagon beyond our budget because it could comfortably accommodate the dogs ('I'll take that one — and that one'). It also meant buying the right clothes for all occasions, for Confucius had been a stickler for etiquette and that was a matter of *Li*. The superior person must not only behave with decorum and propriety but be dressed for it, and Ping was meticulous about what she wore, whether she was playing tennis (whites only) or meeting the Queen. 'No, not that tie,' she would say of some skittish cravat I had furtively acquired in Honolulu. 'Remember you are Bloodworth.' The ostentatious and gaudy were out. The 'remarkable nobody' must obey the rule that correct dress was inconspicuous — 'That way your shadow is lighter,' she said. I did not object. After all, I had been taught the same thing in England when young, unbelievable though it may sound today. But the gap between sartorial East and West could still suddenly widen, especially in the very early days.

When Dennis first returned to Hong Kong from China that time, of course I put on my high heel shoes and wore a special new dress made by fine cashmere hair, the coat and skirt both colour in pink. I want to surprise him, show my deep feeling for him, see him smile. But I was shocked by his face when he gazed fixedly at the new dress. There was a frown between his eyebrows, he was silent and upset, a pair of ice eyes radiated sadness and confusion. Although autumn I felt the sweat oozing on my forehead and back, and I wanted to stamp my feet and scream. Instead I said coldly, 'Could I have done something wrong? What harm of this dress? It was mode of best material I cannot afford, it is special to welcome you.' 'The colour of pink never suit Chinese,' he said briefly. 'Am I ugly then?' I asked almost with tears. He smiled suddenly. 'You are looking extremely well, smart, elegant as long as I forget that damned pink,' he said, holding me very lovingly, 'and what a pair beautiful shoes!' I had a queer feeling I never been so close to him before, and my heart gave a cheer.

But she never wore pink again, not even when a friend gave her a pink blouse 40 years later. It was now against the dress code.

For all the frivolities of the 'fun' generation, the adult Chinese can still be conventional and conform strictly to accepted practice, and it behoves foreigners to be on their best behaviour on solemn occasions when dealing with them, whether they are attending a wedding or arguing the toss at the White House. Even then, they may be at risk in spite of themselves. Chinese tend to go by appearances, so that not only unsuitable clothes, but a high-pitched voice, an evasive manner, a mobile 'monkey' face or an unfortunate nose (though not a round, fat posterior) can quickly draw an invisible frown. As one sardonic commentator remarked, 'They like everyone to be like everyone else.'

Anything in the wrong place may jar. Singaporeans have a childish streak, and may paint a block of flats all the kindergarten colours of the rainbow — sky blue, pink and yellow — and stuff the sill beneath the rear windows of their cars with a toyshopful of dolls and cuddlies. Ping is highly critical of this conduct, has the whole house painted white, and keeps her four teddy bears strictly confined to our bedroom. And she has strong feelings about ostentation.

I hate show and extravagance, women dress up like Christmas tree, the earrings too excited. Everything too much is no good. Should wear good clothes that make the people feel comfortable. When I hear a colleague at Radio Television Singapore got 24 pairs trousers I said to D godsake how many bottoms he got? Showing all the famous Italian labels outside on handbag and shoes and dark glasses to prove how much money you got just bad taste. D said Chinese dragon without money is just worm. I told him no but worm wearing diamonds is snake.

She would make up only slightly, dismissing most cosmetics as 'all those dirty things' that turned a face into a forgery. We were a long way from the bridal doll in the palanquin, and I was relieved. It always seemed to me that if the object was to attract men, the girls had got it all wrong. The warpaint on a brightly coloured bird or butterfly was often designed to scare off predators, rather than dazzle prospective mates, and the warpaint on women could have the same effect. A polished mask was hard and cold and sexless, and warmth lay in crow's-feet and dimples and little lines around the mouth. Too much mauve shadow looked as if the wearer had very understandably been handed a couple of black eyes. We agreed. Ping's mother had told her, 'You just have to accept whether you are beautiful or not,' adding by way of consolation, 'you are not too ugly'.

Ping was equally unimpressed by vulgar displays of rank or riches because she had been there herself, and it pained her to sit in exorbitant restaurants surrounded by flunkeys swishing the silver covers off some repellent morsel of nouvelle cuisine, impudently demanding that she 'enjoy' it, and ordering her to 'have a nice day' at 10:30 in the evening as she left hungry. We were 'eating their uniforms', and the thought of the bill made her shudder. Memories of the corrupt KMT and their showy ways of gaining face would surface. Who had our generous host cheated to be able to afford to pay for this?

She had no side. She committed an unforgivable solecism aboard one ship by declining an invitation to sit at the captain's table; it was in keeping with her self-effacing nature. Dominic threw a banquet for me in the Pinetree Club in Singapore for my 70th birthday, and a band played to an empty dance floor as the 130-odd guests concentrated on the delicious Chinese dinner and champagne, pausing only when Raja made a neat speech telling me I was getting on a bit. On Ping's 70th birthday all she wished was for the two of us to lunch at a modest little restaurant. This proved to be full, so we ended up eating noodles on the terrace of a Chinese coffeeshop. For our silver wedding she declined a banquet in a smart restaurant and just wanted the two of us to dine *à deux* in the old dining room of the Cockpit Hotel where we had held our marriage reception. When we got there, it was closed and we were told that it was due to be torn down the next day. It was as if the God of Wealth were taking his revenge on her. When offered a first-class airline ticket to Hong Kong she found 'the food too much and my feet too far away. I think I born economy class.'

Her clothes had to be good but somehow cheat the price tag, and to this end she would ruthlessly scan fashion magazines for an idea, haunt the sales for the right material, and then pass both to her 'little woman' around the corner, an inexpensive treasure who would put the two together for a few dollars. Or she would pick up bargains at the nearby shopping plaza, and get the seamstress to alter them, though that was not always necessary as she was stock size. When a local department store went broke and prices were cut by up to 50 per cent, she came home from the fray without the bread or butter but with eight bras. Remembering the 24 pairs of bespoke trousers, I nearly said, 'God's sake how many …?' But of course I knew.

The salesgirls were her secret agents, knew her size and taste, and when they spotted an incoming bargain would quietly put it aside for her. 'Why you so kind?' she asked one once. 'Because you always so polite, lah,' came the reply, 'always say "thank you".' 'But don't the other customers?' 'No, you try to show them something special, they just look at you, think you cheat them.' It was the same when she bought fish and poultry. The stall owners would set the biggest sole and the fattest ducks aside for her. She was known as 'queen of the market', not because she spent a fortune there, but because she dressed properly and was unfailingly friendly. It was not an affectation or even a strategy. She liked simple, natural, hardworking people rather better than any sharp-elbowed climber with a degree and a mortgage on a villa with a marble floor and a plastic chandelier like a shower of crocodile tears.

I been one of them in Hong Kong and they always more sincere and warmhearted and ready to give, because we all in same boat going nowhere. We had nothing to win or lose in money or the position in the life, and so of course also much happier. They got one dollar, give you fifty cents. Millionaire cannot give half million, just found school, hospital. Not the same.

She herself was always putting me to shame. 'We've been asked to give Chinese New Year tips to the condominium staff,' I would say, and suggest a conservative figure for fear of a lesson on the evils of western extravagance. 'Not enough,' would be the invariable reply. 'Maybe give twice.' I would double it, and we were quits.

We say in England not only that 'it's the poor what 'elps the poor', but that charity begins at home, and this is very much in line with Chinese thinking that family and friends come first. Ping and I found ourselves at one in preferring to bring comfort to the less fortunate around us rather than throw money at impersonal benevolent funds. I realised this early on when we acquired a cat. The cat needed sand, and when I was away covering a military coup in Thailand in 1958, Ping drove the car across the island to Changi beach to steal some. She now knew where the brakes on the Hillman were, and so arrived there safely. It was late afternoon, and the beach was empty. But from a lone fishing shack near the sands she heard moaning, and on pushing her way inside it found a very sick-looking and very pregnant fisherwoman and no one else about. Ping asked the woman what she felt, whether she wanted to go to hospital immediately. The woman said she was all right, the baby was not due for two months, and her husband was coming back soon. After staying with her a little, Ping drove home in the failing light.

But I cannot eat my dinner or sleep when I go to bed. I worry about the woman so much, even she say she is okay. Some time after midnight I cannot bear any more so got up and took some housekeeping money in case needed and drove back to Changi in dark. I found the little house, the husband back all right, but the woman feeling worse. So although she say not necessary I drove them to the hospital, the man show me each turning how to go, but when we there the staff say cannot give empty bed for the woman in third class wards because baby not due. So I angry, told them no such thing, they must take the woman, don't care what ward, and I will pay. So finally they did, and baby born that night.

Ping had given the couple our address and telephone number, and urged them to contact her if they needed help. Two months later she heard a ring at the door, and when she opened it a woman fell on her knees before her as if she were the Goddess of Mercy. It was the mother, with her husband. A horrified Ping quickly pulled her to her feet and invited them in for tea. Until then, I had not been told a word about all this. 'You were a hero,' I said, knowing she would think 'heroine' was a drug. For a moment I was in fact terrified that I had married a saint. Hero? She looked at me in astonishment. 'But in the end I didn't have to pay anything,' she objected.

Three years later she was nonetheless rewarded. She woke up one morning almost unable to breathe. Overnight a huge goitre had developed in her throat and was half-blocking her air passage. This time I was in Taiwan covering the visit of President Eisenhower. Almost suffocating, she rushed to the bank as soon as it opened to draw money for whatever lay ahead, only to have her cheque rejected at the counter. The bank had credited my latest draft from the *Observer* to the wrong account. Unable to argue, she drove straight on to the Singapore General Hospital, where the staff refused her admission as she lacked the necessary deposit.

But then her luck changed. A leading Singapore surgeon called Yahya Cohen happened to be passing, saw her condition, asked what was going on, and said at once, 'Damn the money and the paperwork. I'll take responsibility for her. Get her into surgery at once.' For Singapore the emergency operation on this explosive tumour was a first, and a complete success. Yahya had saved her life. 'You see, I knew who she was because I had read your articles and recognised the name,' he told me later. A nice excuse for his humanity — I suppose there is something to be said for not being called Tan, Lim, Lee or Smith. But I knew Ping had got her just reward, and now the books balanced.

Ping had turned her back on both the KMT and the communists, but when it came to people as people she treated everyone the same from the bottom to the top of the social ladder, irrespective of age, job, or politics. It was natural for her to save their 'face', and we never misunderstood each other over this fundamental Chinese principle because, as it happened, it came instinctively to me.

When she taught at the nearby school in Oxley Road, I would come back tired from a press conference at City Hall to find the flat aflutter with about thirty bouncing girls in white uniforms, all chattering away happily so that the sitting room was — as Ping would say — 'like a cage birds'. These were her students, whom she had invited home for tea, every one of them ardently pro-communist, and all delighted with their new anti-communist teacher. Her popularity prompted the school principal, who was short of staff, to heap more and more subjects on to her, so that she found herself teaching everything she knew nothing about from needlework to geography. Her great *tour de force* was to leave the island of Sulawesi (area 72,000-odd square miles against England's 50,000) completely out of her lessons on Indonesia as if it did not exist.

I was overjoyed when the principal of the Singapore Girls Vocational High School took me on, because as I said Dennis spend most of time away from home I could not stand idle. So I absolutely surrender to her order. I am so happy to guide the grow up girls in Chinese literature, whatever is alive in Chinese classical writing. Even in playtime most of them cluster together around me like bees to discuss about Chinese traditional concepts. But when the school suddenly short of teachers, and the principal urged me to meet emergency by teaching those subjects I knew nothing about, I made a mess of the job, I deeply felt compunction, I could not allow myself to harm the young girls, and decided to resign.

It made no difference whether she was talking to a teenage domestic or an affluent businesswoman — and in Singapore's highly mobile society they could be the same person, given a little time. In 1995 I arrived home one afternoon to find a lively party of well-dressed women in the courtyard, swapping news, sipping tea, and laughing more often than not. Ping was entertaining Ah Yok and Xiu Lan, our two teenage maids of the mid-seventies. They had come to call on 'Auntie', the boss who had treated them as her own daughters twenty years before and seen them safely married off. In those days they had earned $120 and $90 a month respectively, and came from tin-roofed cement-floored homes where they had slept up to a dozen to a room. But times had changed, as little Xiu Lan's latest purchase proved. She had just bought a flat in a new housing estate for $600,000. By now she could probably buy us up before breakfast. They were both pushing forty. But Ping was still 'Auntie'.

Their arrival on our domestic scene had marked the end of the era of the traditional Chinese amah in her black trousers and white tunic. I had mixed feelings about these good ladies, who would rule the house with an iron rod if given half a chance, so that while I was excluded from the kitchen by Ping, she could find herself excluded from it in her turn if she was not careful. What worried me was the mental baggage they brought with them to justify their tyranny, a small, jealously-guarded bundle containing a rigid daily work routine which must never vary, and a head full of startling ignorance apart from the space taken up by a jumble of Chinese superstitions and weird but incontrovertible beliefs.

Ah Yee was convinced not only that white men lived off roast chicken and jelly, but that if they did not put ice in their drinks they would die young. Ah Fu warned Ping that she should have nothing to do with a Catholic priest who called because 'that kind don't believe in God', and when an American professor in beard and jeans turned up at the gate, shouted to her 'there's a beggar here who won't go away'. Ah Gan (notable for driving nails into doors to hang things on), said that since she could type Ping could go out and make a fortune — why bother with me? Ah Yoke (not Ah Yok) told a delivery boy that not only Snoopy but all beagles played tennis, and seeing Ping dressed for a game for the first time protested, 'But you have no number on the back!' This was followed by, 'Ah, yes, I see. Clever. Then they can't tell which side you are on.'

Yet many Chinese treated their amahs as members of the family, and Ping would listen to all their wisdom woman to woman. She was showing her Confucian respect for the individual as another human being. So after we had mentioned the name of Lee Kuan Yew to two Singapore workers during an early election campaign, and one had replied, 'You mean the tall thin one or the short fat one?' I asked her whether all this democratic chumminess of hers meant she believed everyone in China itself should have the vote.

'Of course not,' she scoffed.

'Not? But why?'

'Why? Because one-man-one-vote *most* unfair.'

13

ONE MAN one vote *unfair? Of course?* That piece of instant blasphemy above all reminded me that Ping and I touched fingers from different dimensions. But there was more to come.

Look. Chinese society like pyramid. Hundred clever men at top million stupid people at bottom, know nothing. Give them vote like giving four-year-old child piece gold. He doesn't understand what it is, he doesn't care, he is not interested. You promise him piece candy for it, he give it to you; offer him money, he sell it to you. This means if one man one vote, power go to those who lie and cheat and bribe the most ignorant people the best. So of course unfair.

Democracy as fools conned by knaves? And Ping was certainly not speaking only for herself. More than three hundred years before Christ, Zhuangzi had described how a monkey trainer had persuaded his charges to accept a daily ration of acorns. When he told them, 'you will get three acorns in the morning and four at night', the monkeys were furious, but when he relented and said, 'all right, it will be four in the morning and three at night', they were delighted. One wonders if they, too, would have believed that all beagles played tennis. Very probably, if it was put to them in a nice way.

No Chinese had ever suggested that every peasant should have a say in running the country. But then no more had Plato in that cradle of democracy, Athens. It did not mean that China's recorded history was a discreditable tale of 30-odd centuries of despotic rule. But I could be forgiven for thinking so. I had been brought up in a country where the *Encyclopaedia Britannica* could devote eight pages of small print to democracy without mentioning China once. However, as I began to see the world through the mirror of Ping's eyes, I realised I had got things back to front. While in England we were taught that the West had bestowed the benison of this one true political faith on the benighted subjects of the Son of Heaven, it was the Chinese who had not only got there first, but — although only more than 2,000 years later — bestowed the benison of Confucian 'democracy' on the West during the Age of Enlightenment in the 17th and 18th centuries.

There is more to democracy — 'democrazy' as one Chinese wit put the practice — than marking a cross on a piece of paper every few years. Confucius himself took the first step towards it by preaching that only education, and not blue blood, could qualify a man to administer a harmonious and happy society. And that man should be chosen regardless of his origins, for the best and brightest could come from a pigsty just as well as from a palace. It was an eminently democratic proposition. 'All men are born equal in evil,' added the great Confucian scholar Xunzi sardonically, 'therefore all have the chance to become sages through education.' Education was the key. While every man should be treated with respect and benevolence, learning or the lack of it should decide his place on the social grid: 'If all stood on the same level there could be no government.'

According feudal saying dragon bears dragon, phoenix bears phoenix, but son of mouse only knows how to dig hole. In old tradition ordinary Chinese people know nothing, only look to good leader who will give them good government. So suddenly give one vote to every peasant no sense. First they must be educated how to use it, not just dig holes. Take time.

But although the ordinary Chinese might wish to be well-governed rather than govern themselves, they had their own way of protecting their rights. 'Heaven sees and hears as the people see and hear,' runs an ancient Chinese warning that could be regarded as the first law of democracy. Xunzi stressed that government is for the people, not the ruler — and the main concern of the ruler must be their happiness, said Confucius. When asked which was the most important to a state — food, weapons, or the trust of the millions — he replied that it could dispense with food and weapons, but without that trust 'it cannot stand'.

At the time few of the hereditary overlords of China would even turn a head to listen to this nonsense, but the days of their hegemony were now numbered. The great Confucian Mencius emphasised that the ruler drew his right to rule from the 'Mandate of Heaven'. If he was cruel and profligate and subsequently fell from power, it was because the Mandate had been withdrawn. But since 'Heaven sees as the people see', this was mere celestial gloss on the reality that in the last analysis the people were the masters, and since they did not have the vote, they would express their disapproval by adopting the far more exhilarating alternative to general elections — bloody revolution. In consequence the story of imperial China is one of long periods of peace and quiet punctuated by violent insurrection or at least a popular *coup d'etat* (when not by a foreign invasion). Any successful uprising was thus automatically sanctified by (for want of a better word) God.

Its leader was likely to be a man of the people himself, and it was the ignorance of the first rebel to overthrow an emperor that was to give the Confucians their big chance. That hardly seemed likely at the outset. Founder of the great Han Dynasty in 206 BC, Han Gaozi had started life as a sly, vulgar peasant, and early showed his contempt for the scholars around him at court by pissing into the tall hat of one of them. As for the Classics, who needed such stuff? When a dignitary quoted the *Book of Poetry* at him one day, his only rejoinder was a dismissive 'I won the Empire on horseback, not by reading books.'

'Yes,' the other retorted boldly, 'but can you rule it from horseback?'

Han Gaozi, who was no fool, thought it over and later selected the best of the scholars to advise him and administer his empire. That was to lead in time to the emergence in the Tang Dynasty of China's most democratic institution, a civil service open to all. The mandarinate was a vast bureaucratic system of government by educated officials who (as Confucius had originally suggested) were drawn from all classes: any village hopeful could aspire to become a mandarin by taking the successive examinations that began at the local level and led up to the final test for the highest office in the capital itself. This meant that the cowherd could dream of becoming Grand Secretary of China, just as (somewhat later) any American farmboy could dream of becoming President of the United States.

Improbable as it may seem, not only is there a link between the two, but for some Americans it might seem too close for comfort, did they but know of it. In the 17th and 18th centuries Europe was still ruled by spendthrift aristocrats and effete royal families whose dynastic quarrels and futile wars almost incessantly plagued the continent. As for the attitude of these sinfully overdressed dandies towards the common people, it was summed up by Marie Antoinette's reputed remark when told the French poor were starving for lack of bread: 'Let them eat cake.'

It is not surprising, therefore, that radical thinkers of the Enlightenment, whose advanced ideas were to contribute to both the American and French Revolutions, should have read with reverence reports from Jesuit missionaries that painted distant China a Utopia of order and harmony and justice, administered by scholar-officials dedicated to the happiness of the people. Even the sceptical Voltaire declared fulsomely that 'the mind of man could not imagine a better government' and 'the constitution of their empire is in truth the best that there is in the world,' evolved as it was from wisdom acquired in China 4,000 years ago 'when we did not know how to read.'

The Enlightenment opened western minds to new visions of democracy and clean administration, and its debt to Confucianism is undeniable. When the British Parliament was debating measures to create a civil service recruited through examinations, not family or favour, it was described as the 'Chinese principle', and when Congress was similarly engaged 3,000 miles further west, Emerson remarked, 'China has preceded us, as well as England and France.' Preceded them in fact by about 1,000 years. More convincing still, men who disapproved of such disparate institutions as the French Revolution and the British bureaucracy were quick to blame these pernicious egalitarian ideas on the wretched Chinese.

However, those who find the debt distasteful may comfort themselves with the thought that intellectual giants are always the first to have the wool pulled over their eyes — it took Bernard Shaw to call Stalin's police state 'a really free country' and Sir Herbert Read to speak of 'the happiness and contentment of the peasants' in Mao's regimented 'people's communes'. Human nature being what it is (human nature), the reality was that by the 19th century the Celestial Empire had degenerated into a state as flimsy as rotting silk, administered by greedy and corrupt mandarins and eunuchs under the alien Qing Dynasty of the Manchus. Falling easy prey to outsiders with the ships and guns, it was to be callously torn into strips and shared out among the western powers, and later occupied by the Japanese before it was freed — not by its own liberating heroes, but the American atom bomb. How were the mighty fallen.

Western people do not understand. The Emperor of China was the master of the world. He was Son of Heaven, ruler of the one great superior culture of the Universe nothing can compare, so that all barbarian kings must come to him to go down on the knees at Imperial Palace and give tribute. And now look what happen! So the Chinese people very proud and cannot bear loss of face since that time, of course very bitter, very angry, cannot bear shame, very jealous about their respect as nation and sovereignty of all China's territory including Taiwan and Tibet, even very small islands in South China Sea.

This was the inexorable history that had shaped Ping's prejudices, just as the history that had shaped mine consisted of a chequered tale of good and evil that had led, among other things, to Magna Carta and the Mother of Parliaments, and the sometimes disreputable rise and sometimes honourable fall of the British Empire. The secret of harmony between us was to observe the *yang-yin* principle of the two opposing halves that make one whole, for us to learn not to differ but to dovetail by being sensitive to each other's feelings. On my side, for example, it was important to see how deeply wounding it was to Ping that the titles of the great dynasties that rang like bronze bells down 2,000 years of Chinese civilisation — Han, Tang, Sung, Ming — should have become the names of four stray dogs.

I had looked forward to a most interesting and civilised meeting when we got an invitation to lunch with Lord Selkirk. After all, he was English aristocrat and highest ranking British figure in Southeast Asia at the time when British army, navy and air force all defending Malaysia against Indonesian military 'Konfrontasi'. And indeed his conversation so cheerful and amusing, and Lady Selkirk talking to us so friendly that I enjoyed such unconstrained atmosphere, until I discovered a peculiar arrangement.

There were four stray dogs that Lady Selkirk had given a home to lying underneath the table and she told me she had named each one after a Chinese dynasty. Immediately my mind distracted, and especially I thought about contemptuous foreign aggression in China and national humiliation of last hundred year, making mischief in me and creating a sense of inferiority. I was suffering and quiet. I had to behave well and polite, but others thought I was just dull almost stupid, nobody knew my heart was crying, my head full of questions which my soul repeating sadly.

To comfort me local friends afterwards told me names mean nothing to the English — 'what's in a name?' they say. People got names like Crabbe or even Ramsbotham but don't feel disgrace or funny, and give titles of dynasties to dogs have no meaning to insult China. Most people in England looked upon the dog as their children, and if no other family probably could write down in their will giving their heritage to it. On other hand more than 100 years ago when General Gordon gave Li Hong Zhang, China's most distinguished admiral and ambassador, a rare pedigree puppy from England as sign of friendship and esteem, Li had it cooked and ate it. What Gordon think?

So I was wondering over the problem for a long time until a thought from Confucius swept in, 'Is not a gentleman after all one who will not take offence when others fail to appreciate him?', and my mind calmed down gradually. But there is always room for misunderstanding between East and West. For when we behave in tolerant way and accept their blows like that, they simply think we are cowards. But what could we do except to bear it?

The incident exemplifies the sensitivity of the contact between the two alien cultures. But the Americans, faced with a wounded dragon of uncertain temper, too often seem intent on confronting it first and asking questions afterwards. President Clinton stands firm on 'engagement' with Beijing against a vociferous opposition in Congress but rudely tells his guest, President Jiang Zemin, that in the matter of human rights China is 'on the wrong side of history'. The response to this sort of thing is predictably touchy. Any attempt by the US to pass judgement on the lack of democracy and freedom in China is inevitably seen as an insufferable affront and blatant interference in their private affairs. 'We tend to forget,' said Henry Kissinger drily in 1997, 'that they managed to get along for 5,000 years without advice from the United States.' 'Sometimes Americans too much like human beings, often behave very young,' says Ping.

To a people whose very different tradition goes back to the open-minded Confucius, the hidebound thinking of the redneck lobby in Washington who believe the world should conform rigidly to American values and institutions irrespective of local circumstances, is as ludicrous as it is sinister. Zhuangzi reputedly said, 'Men claim that Mao Chiang and Lady Li were beautiful, but if fish saw them they would dive to the bottom of the stream, if birds saw them they would fly away, and if deer saw them they would break into a run. Of these four, who knows how to fix the standard of beauty for the world?' Only God.

And from what I read in history — or was it on TV? — God gave the Ten Commandments to Moses, not George Washington. Democracy is like beauty, everyone got their own idea. So who has right to fix the standard? I hate dictatorship, but now some Americans even want to dictate democracy. They forget what it is for — happiness of the people. And to make the people happy every country has to find their own way. The same for freedom.

I sympathised. Freedom? Take Singapore — an island of 600-odd square kilometres in which some 3 million Chinese, Malays, Indians, Eurasians, Buddhists, Christians, Muslims, Hindus lived eyeball to eyeball. How could the government allow unbridled freedom of speech, press and information in this confined space in which it only needed a mischievous rumour that a Chinese had thrown pork bones into a mosque to spark a bloody race riot by the Muslim Malays? As it was, there had not been one for more than 30 years. Free speech can easily be a licence for racial and religious baiting, as Dr Mahathir Mohamad of Malaysia proved when in 1997, like a runner-up to Hitler, he insinuated that his economic problems as Prime Minister were due to the evil machinations of international Jewry.

Maybe in Singapore freedom not perfect, but have order and peace. So many western-educated local people may complain but they actually don't want to change government. Why? Because no race quarrels, everyone walk safe at night, not much crime, nobody without home must sleep in doorway, no beggar in street, no terrorism, nobody shoot politicians, not too much drugs, no guns for kids to kill kids, family usually hold together. Americans got no such human rights. Mrs Albright say if human rights okay everywhere means 'Americans are safer'. Must mean safer than in America. So how can they criticise? Yet every year American government put out report on human rights record not only of Singapore but 194 countries, each one different.

Singapore has so many rule and regulation to maintain public order it became famous as 'fine city' because people fined for all kinds of wrong behaviour. But not just to punish guilty, also teach everyone abide by the law. People complain, but majority still happy. Maybe not ideal democracy, but when opposition blindly criticise without other constructive idea of their own, just throw society into confusion, that also is not ideal democracy. Maybe people think I am doggie of Singapore government. I won't care. I grew up with corruption and violence and misery and poverty in China. I seen the alternative.

Right or wrong, this is the sort of sharp riposte the more rough and ready among America's spokesmen have an uncanny knack of evoking. And what applies to a country because it is small and vulnerable like Singapore may apply to a big one like China because its people are as yet less sophisticated.

Of course. People must be educate to freedom as they must be educate to democracy. If give it too early is like that four-year-old kid with the gold. Allow him run around free in the street and soon killed by bus. Have to grow up first. Cannot give him rights without responsibility, like Americans. Needs time. Even in England women only can vote since 1918 something.

Stung at last, I protested, 'you complain about the Americans, but you Chinese are always boasting about your Confucian ethics and your wonderful Confucian society, too. Yet China and Taiwan are both riddled with corruption and crime — in China they even cheat the sick in the hospitals, and in Taiwan secret societies have got an iron grip on politics. People go on in the *Straits Times* here about 'Asian Values', but there are no such values, just as there is no such place as Asia — what are Syria and Japan supposed to have in common, for example? What is so Confucian about Chinese Olympic swimmers taking anabolic steroids?' 'All right,' replied Ping, unconcerned despite this unpardonable dig at her prowess in the pool. 'But we do not give 194 countries grades for their Confucian ethics and then fine them if they don't get a pass mark. *Bloody* cheek.'

Shocked silence for the rest of breakfast after that lapse from Confucian propriety. But I agreed with Ping that democracy had to grow like a tree in its native soil and climate; it could not be exported from Detroit as standard parts for local assembly.

Taoists say 'ten thousand names' divide the world. Democracy, Communism, Capitalism just names, can be made to mean anything, not important. What is important is if government good or bad. In time as Chinese Communist Party old fellows die and new generation who know Europe and America come up, so-called 'Communist' China will change as Eastern Europe, even Russia, already changed, become more democratic. But of course in Chinese way.

Mao Zedong ensured that his communist revolution would be a success by mounting it 'with Chinese characteristics', as they would say today, ignoring Marxist-Leninist orthodoxy and basing it on China's vast peasantry instead of its small proletariat. That made sense. Fifty years later Chinese leaders ignored the dogma practised in the USSR that glasnost should accompany perestroika, that political reform was indispensable to economic reform. The USSR fell apart, but a China under Deng Xiaoping that had adopted a socialist market economy 'with Chinese characteristics' moved forward to the next century.

As democracy evolves in China it, too, will doubtless be 'with Chinese characteristics' that will flout the orthodox Anglo-Saxon ideal. And the same will be true of civil rights. But, says Ping, at least Beijing will not concede the freedom for all to carry a gun, for muggers to sue their victims, for the media to invent news and publish lies that ruin people's lives, for publishers to peddle 'how-to' paperbacks to teach complicated people in simple language how to make an atom bomb or poison gas or be a successful hit man (a satisfied customer carried out three cold-blooded murders inspired by that one), for a convict to charge the prison authorities with violating his civil rights because his ice cream has melted before he could eat it — and all in the sacred name of the amended American Constitution. There will be no freedom for criminals to abuse freedom.

It is a simple matter of priorities. The down-to-earth Chinese would always put social order before individual freedom. They feel that you cannot have both in an imperfect world, and they have had enough of disorder for too long. Take freedom too far and it becomes a licence for gangsters, says Ping, while law-abiding men are not troubled by the restrictive laws they agree to abide by. And anyway for the most part freedom as conceived in the West is a luxury that is low on the list of the people's needs in developing countries, coming well below a square meal and a square deal, a roof, food, jobs, running water, schools, hospitals, security, just government. For them America's fancier freedoms are Marie Antoinette's cake. But at least Marie Antoinette did not try to ram the cake down the peasants' throats, says Ping. *Bloody* cheek.

14

WHAT dismayed Ping about all this parading of American ideals was that there was no war on to justify it. 'All war is based on deception,' the great Chinese strategist Sunzi had laid down in the 4th century BC. So, Ping explained matter-of-factly, to prove you were fighting for a righteous cause you naturally had to shout high-sounding slogans proclaiming glorious objectives that were the exact opposite of the truth. These would excuse all the unspeakable things you did, while cloaking in a heroic flag what you were really after which was, of course, naked power. When a brutal, opium-smoking warlord like Marshal Chang Tso-lin planned a murderous attack on North China in search of loot, his waving banners announced to no one's surprise that he was acting 'for the salvation of the country.' When the Japanese inflicted their idiosyncratic atrocities on the peoples of the East it was naturally to 'liberate Asia from western colonialism'.

During the Cold War the communists explained their ruthless conspiracy to establish an iron dictatorship everywhere as 'a revolution to free the enslaved masses'. So of course when the Americans bombed and/or napalmed the hell out of the Vietnamese peasants and their neighbours, and backed a succession of fascist dictators in Saigon whose feared secret police were trained by the CIA, it was all 'in defence of democracy and freedom'.

'But what you're accusing them of is barefaced hypocrisy,' I protested, dutifully shocked. I explained the word. Ping looked at me in astonishment.

Of course hypocrisy. So okay. Everyone understands. Just words. Nobody fooled. But now not even Cold War. So if politicians in Washington still want American-style freedom and democracy be law for everyone, maybe is not hypocrisy but dogma and so exactly different matter altogether. I hope I wrong. Because dogma means end of common sense, makes men crazy, blind, especially not practical, so you cannot deal with them.

Dogma. I thought of the Crusaders butchering their way through Eastern Europe in the name of gentle Jesus meek and mild. But I rallied. 'So what you're saying is you don't believe in ideals at all? That you are a complete cynic?' I said, sticking my chin out. Ping wanted to know what a cynic was and I explained. 'But naturally,' she replied, 'must always think the worst, then never disappointed. Be a pessimist means be happy.' At this I added with some malice that the word came from the Greek for dog. She was delighted. 'Of course, dog is right, does not trust what he sees, only what he smells.' Forget dreams, face reality, life is the art of the possible.

Usually Chinese are practical people, have no patience with all your 'isms', ideals, dogma, truth, godknowwhat carved in big piece stone, just make trouble. They believe East and West should better work together, even ideas different. D agrees, says carrot is mightier than stick. Soviet system collapsed under friendly American influence, not American atom bombs. In China Stalinist 'Thoughts of Mao Zedong' already given way to capitalist 'Thoughts of Deng Xiaoping' in same way. Chinese leaders always hate to deal with your honest American presidents like preachers full of principles still want quarrel; they feel truly comfortable with hard head practical unscrupulous leaders who just want peace, and of course for us big hero is President Nixon, who was first to recognise China and visit Mao in Beijing.

'Hero? Nixon? But Nixon was an unprincipled villain, a man entirely without scruples.' 'Exactly. So we can understand each other, come to sensible agreement to mutual advantage, then wonderful historic moment for China and America, open new relations between Beijing and Washington and whole world happier.' Kissinger had said something like 'learning to live with people whose actions you disapprove is part of growing up'. The Chinese have a lot of time for Kissinger, too.

'But Nixon ... Well, what about Watergate? You heard about Watergate? Nixon was exposed as a totally unscrupulous cold-blooded political twister. And not for the first time ...'

But the Chinese are short on moral indignation and Ping was not impressed — 'You must expect the worst of people and look at the best.' The Mao responsible for the misery of the 'people's communes' was the same Mao who liberated China, the Deng Xiaoping responsible for the Tiananmen massacre was the same Deng who led the Chinese into a new era of promise and reform. The Nixon that lied and cheated over Watergate was the same Nixon that got the Americans out of the Vietnam War and held out a hand to China. The JFK whose sexual profligacy shocked a nation was the same man who outstared Khrushchev in the Cuban crisis. The Clinton of the Monica Lewinsky scandal was the same man who presided over America's booming economy, who first abandoned Washington's eight-year campaign at the UN to condemn China's human rights record, and who won applause from the Chinese by admitting straightforwardly, 'I am going to China for one reason: to advance America's interests' ('and his own,' added Ping predictably). No flowery flimflam about undying friendship that would have had everyone yawning.

So who cares about all these women anyway? Is nobody's business only their wives. Most important for country is good leader, and clever man with high spirit who is likely to be good leader of course also more likely to show high spirit in the private life. Even Guang Gong, greatest hero in Chinese history of Three Kingdoms time, win so many battles and adored by million million Chinese even now, was also famous for chase after women. Nobody say one word. If you want the butterfly, you must accept the caterpillar. In China Clinton scandal never can happen. No such thing. Childish. According old Chinese saying 'men are not saints, how can be free from faults?' Even an angel must have half day off to be a devil.

I remember how, when I had tried to insult the bombastic American columnist William Safire by comparing his literary style to Mao's, local Chinese insulted him far more effectively by strongly objecting to my comparing Mao's literary style to Safire's. Mao might have been a wilful tyrant whose whims killed innocent millions, but to them he was still the Mao who could justly announce in 1949, 'The Chinese people have stood up.' All successful political leaders were liars and rogues by definition, said Ping placidly. Of course they had to be. If they were not, how could they succeed? Was Churchill the cherub he looked?

No good to be idealistic. Everything good or bad all part of the same world, and when things go right I am happy, but when things go wrong D fed up because expected should go right. We discuss about it, and I tell him that life naturally muddy 'clear water no fish', as we say, but he curses like hell, shout into mirror, wave fist, always filled indignation and outrage against horrible news in newspaper every day, stupid, cheating, rude people, Charlie barking, big bills, flat tyre, godknowwhat. If amah stupid he gets mad, forgets if more smart won't be amah. It seems to me western idealist always intolerant and miserable, while Chinese 'cynic' tolerant and happy.

She had reason to think that way. She would always rather forgive than fight, as Confucius had taught, and while I might have the patience of an irritated warthog, hers had a halo around it. I was reminded of this only yesterday. It was our wedding anniversary. We had rubbed along together, English idealist and Chinese 'cynic', for more than four decades. Forty-two years ago we had set out on a honeymoon which justified Ping's pessimism — the old bore who kept me up drinking on the first night, the acute sunburn that had me shrinking from my bride, the car top that tore off in a jungle 'infested with communist terrorists' as the tabloids might erroneously have described it. And I still remembered Ping's smiling acceptance of all that went wrong (along with her joy with what went right). For this day, therefore, I planned a cosy little anniversary lunch at her favourite Italian restaurant, perhaps with a single rose in a silver vase and candles and a carafe — or two — of the best Chianti, soft music, and the whole afternoon before us.

Parking was always a bit of a problem at the Al Forno and we had not been there for some time, so we set off early, dressed for the occasion. I drove confidently into an empty slot in what seemed the familiar car park and it was only when we walked out to the front of the building that I discovered we were in the wrong block. Uneasy, for I remembered that there had been a 'Residents Only' sign on the wall, I sat Ping down in all her finery under a bus shelter, returned to the car, and drove it into the block next door, only to be met with a red notice saying 'Unauthorised Vehicles Will Be Clamped'. Cursing my luck and beginning to sweat, I walked around to the front again, to find Ping waiting for me with the news that the Al Forno was not to be found. It had evidently moved away. We seemed to be unlucky on these occasions, I thought, remembering the fiasco on her birthday.

Gritting my teeth and with Ping trailing behind me in the heat, I called at four shops in succession to ask if I might borrow a telephone book so that I could check the new address, only to be told that none of them had a telephone book. Before I could explode, however, an obliging young woman in the last of the four asked me what exactly I wanted to look up, and when I said the Al Forno restaurant, at once gave me detailed directions to its new location 'just down the road.' I subsided and we collected the car, which had not been clamped, and drove along to where the girl had said the restaurant now was — 'go over the red light and it's just past the gas station' — to find ourselves facing the vast blank wall of a gigantic shopping plaza that might have been a high-security prison.

Could it be somewhere in there, then? I had no choice but to press on, and after searching for the entrance to the block drove up the dark spiral of its multistorey car park, foolishly comforting myself with the recollection that we had actually been here in the distant past and might remember our way around once inside the mall itself. But once inside we discovered that the entire interior had been torn out and remodelled, and we were in a monstrous glittering labyrinth without a ball of string. There was no information desk in the lobby, and no indicator listing the Al Forno among the bright-lit Chinese restaurants, boutiques, hair stylists, snackbars, cafes, bookshops, body-shops, art studios and other superfluous establishments that followed us with glassy stares as we wound our way around the dizzying atrium, up and down half a dozen escalators and through tier after tier of galleries and corridors that spread out in all directions at every level like dead ends in a maze.

After half an hour of aimless wandering while hunger gnawed ('didn't we pass this place about ten minutes ago?'), Ping was still following me gamely in her high heels and the long white skirt she had donned for the occasion, as we pushed our way through uncaring mobs of T-shirted teenagers and office workers bent solely on a Big Mac or a bowl of noodles, forlornly asking for help at every turn, only to be told that no one had heard of the Al Forno. At last, dehydrated and almost exhausted, we saw a Pizza Hut, and made a dash to join the long queue for one of its precious plastic-topped tables, all of which were of course taken.

Amid the clatter of the simple buffet, we finally celebrated by swallowing a wedge of pizza with a cup of tea before setting off again to find our way back to the car park without the faintest idea how to get there. We discovered the car by a miracle after wearily searching for it on the wrong level, only to realise that we had to feed our parking ticket into an enigmatic payment machine for which we had no change left. Finally, a contemptuous Malay parking assistant saw us off the premises, and we breathed fresh air. I clasped Ping's hand, almost speechless with frustration and chagrin, and tried to think of something to say, having successfully turned this day of all days into a nightmare.

No woman I ever met would have allowed herself to be dragged through that ordeal without nagging my head off and finally sitting on the floor, bursting into tears, and refusing to move one more step. But Ping spoke first. 'Well,' she said gently, pressing my hand, 'it's sometimes nice to find out just how stupid we are, isn't it? And, after all, it *was* an Italian restaurant.' She looked at her watch and kissed me on the cheek, 'and look — how wonderful, we have now been married for exactly ten minutes!' In the circumstances I did the only thing I decently could on our wedding anniversary. I fell in love with her all over again.

15

'FIGHTS are the best part of married life,' said Thornton Wilder. The rest was only 'so-so'. But if marriage was a form of warfare (as many of its walking-wounded might ruefully insist), ours would be one long cat-and-dog dustup, for we would be fighting by quite different rules. While I came from a Europe imbued with the principles of the great German strategist Karl von Clausewitz, whose genius inspired the futile face-to-face butchery in Flanders during World War I, Ping came from a China imbued with the subtle, almost feline principles of Sunzi that inspired the hit-and-run guerrilla armies of Mao Zedong and Ho Chi Minh in China and Vietnam. True to western tradition in all matters, Clausewitz believed in bloody confrontation, one final 'Great Battle', a big bang for which generals should build up their forces and unflinchingly throw them straight at each other. (The soldiers could do the flinching.) Sunzi, on the other hand, believed that one should above all avoid a head-on collision, and that 'to subdue the enemy without a fight is the acme of skill'. Clausewitz despised the use of deceit and stratagem 'as the last resort of the weak and small', while, as we have noted, Sunzi preached that 'all war is based on deception'.

Be elusive, flexible, take no chances, only stand and fight if you are the stronger; if you are the weaker, run away to fight another day. Lead the enemy a dance, choose your ground, and when ready to attack, feign confusion, draw him on, and strike suddenly from behind — *downhill.*

'You mean you resist by taking the line of least resistance,' I said. 'How typical — dodgy sly very oriental, practically immoral.'

'Of course,' replied Ping smugly, 'but that is why American eagle fly into Vietnam ready kill everyone end up like chicken dropped in soup.'

If wedlock could be equated with war, the 'Great Battle' of Clausewitz would be that final screaming showdown between man and wife after a long buildup of grudges that leads to the messier kind of divorce in the West. But the only direct confrontation I can remember with Ping occurred during our first year when she learned that I still exchanged letters every Christmas with my ex-wife and an ex-girlfriend from the carefree years of World War II. Madly jealous of these white rivals from my dim past (long since happily married), she reacted by throwing a fine fit of hysterics, sobbing and beating my chest with her fists and threatening to 'go back to Hong Kong and become a nun'. It looked as if we might be in for a nasty crisis — until she gave the game away by overdoing the histrionics.

Sunzi had said if your position is weak, use deception to pretend you are strong, and Chinese armies finding themselves outnumbered would create a systematic hullabaloo, beating drums and yelling defiance at the enemy, blowing discordant trumpets, waving a sea of intimidating flags, and doubling the number of their camp fires at night (under cover of which they might safely sneak away). True to this doctrine, the Chinese instinctively throw themselves into an orgy of righteous indignation whenever they know they are in the wrong, their object being to shift the blame for everything onto the other side. The only trouble is that when they are called upon to act out the role of the injured party, they can be absolute hams, and what should seem to be a demonstration of genuine outrage is revealed as so much hot air. This happens particularly when they themselves do not expect to be believed — they are just going through the motions. Ping saw that the script called for a show of anger, and duly produced it. But she knew she was on weak ground, that her jealousy, though real, was totally unjustified, and that in consequence her explosion of sound and fury was too exaggerated to be credible.

So the crisis evaporated almost before it threatened — 'but it's nice to have some noise sometimes,' Ping said with an unrepentant grin at the end of the performance, 'it makes a change.' The show was over, the curtain came down, and we went back to our daily lives. When I taxed her with being unConfucian, she was not to be provoked. 'But I am only on the way to the "Way",' she protested. (She nevertheless remained jealous for years, but time healed all, and the day finally came when she even suggested that the ex-girlfriend come to stay with us — after the lady had turned 83.)

I half suspected that what riled her was that I had not hidden my continued contact with these ghosts from the past.

Married people in West so often quarrel and go to divorce because believe life must be transparent and have to know exactly everything about each other. But Chinese believe be open and frank only makes trouble. They feel not comfortable, just like when Washington asks Asian countries to open their account books up, and want to know every small thing about each other's business. If everyone tell truth about everything, and nobody speak lie to save face, of course cannot live in this world five minutes. As a matter of fact D and I did not lie to each other, but also did not speak every private thought or ask be told it. Too many questions not polite. If we trust each other, so naturally must accept everything. What is there more to know?

In consequence there was no buildup to a confrontation à la Clausewitz, and marriage to Ping was more like guerrilla war à la Sunzi. Ping could not be drawn into a stand-up fight, but would retreat into silence, leaving me hitting the empty air. The most she would mumble would be 'Okay, I am wrong' (while rather disconcertingly pointing a finger at me at the same time, as if to add 'but we know the real truth of the matter, don't we?'). She could be frankly critical — offended, her 'elder brother' once said 'you should have married Henry VIII; he would have chopped off your head for saying that', and when I remarked that I was surprised he knew something of English history, she replied, 'Of course we all do, because the British do so many bad things for China.' But she seemed pathologically incapable of sustaining a row. 'I cannot angry,' she said, explaining why she remained tongue-tied. 'Perhaps because when I was kid, my nanny would hand me a mirror every time I got mad and say "look at your ugly face". Anyway, I don't know the swear words.'

Home should be full of humour, peaceful as Paradise. To quarrel uncivilised. How can lady or gentleman behave like ferocious barking dog? I will never believe any question big enough to risk harmony of our marriage, and absolutely refuse to take stupid chances with our happiness just to win some small point, but always give way to D at the time, 'sacrificing a finger to save the hand' as we Chinese say. Because what is the life for?

One my favourite heroes in Chinese history is the famous Chinese general Han Xin. One night he be caught by bandits, and they order him crawl down between the legs of their leader. He did not argue, but immediately did what he was told with the gang shouting and laughing and insulting all round him. Don't care about face and feel no shame. He had to win a war, more important things to do than risk the life fighting stupid bandits, perhaps be killed just when his country need him so much. (Anyway, they could all be massacre later when more time.)

When she could have nailed me for being completely in the wrong, Ping did not push me into a corner to do so. When I blew my top over the state of the world or an unironed shirt, she would be solicitous instead of impatient — 'I worry you only hurt yourself,' she would say, and cook up some vile calmative which would effectively silence me. My sometimes barbarian habits were accepted without comment. She would like me to have stopped smoking 40 a day, but did not bully me about it. She scarcely touched liquor ('As long as I am writing, I don't need drink; I already drunk'), but she had nothing against my routine of two vodkas at happy hour, my glass of red wine at dinner, and three thimbles of postprandial Scotch — 'Why you should not enjoy something? You don't go to nightclubs or gamble or buy girls, you don't sing karaoke or play golf.' She would only drink a modest glass of Wincarnis, which I had always regarded as a tonic wine much recommended by doctors for dear old ladies. (I discovered only recently that it was 17 per cent alcohol.)

In old days D drank quite lots, but not really drunk. I remember forty years ago one quiet evening an old friend of D who was brigadier in Australian army appeared on our doorway unexpectedly. He had a natural manner, was clever and a good talker, the voice very gentle and soft. So with a drink in their hands they chatted cheerfully on wide range of subjects. When the time already midnight, I had to say good-night. Next morning it was surprised me that they both still sat on the same chairs as last night, even the position not a bit changed, only there were two more empty bottles on the table. They could not avoid a bit tipsy but still with refilled manner. So of course I said nothing. Why quarrel?

Then in early Autumn 1962 I brought D to visit General Zhang Fagui, who was my father's old friend started in 1918. Zhang had performed many meritorious deeds in the Revolution but relations with Chiang Kai-shek never got along well, so despite support from abroad and being considerable figure once his power and position vanished like soap bubble, and he retired to Hong Kong. Indignant and facing life dissatisfied, he and his wife drank heavily, and when they gave us a banquet they raised their glasses in the direction of D again and again. I was very worried he might get drunk, and indeed when went back to the hotel he fell in bed and slept like dead log, while I awake most of the night because so anxious about him.

When I woke up next morning already noon and Dennis stand in front of bed, shaved, dressed, glowing with health and in high spirits said to me mockingly, 'Ridiculous! Awake so late? Did you get so drunk last night?' But, again, I did not say one word — especially as although I drank nothing I was the one truly felt muddy-headed. And in the end I never had to wait for right moment to speak face-to-face about D drinking, for later he cut it down himself to very strict limits, only pouring first vodka at 6:30 PM happy hour.

If she hated discord, Ping had a horror of violence. One night three drivers parked their lorries illegally just outside our house, and we got into an argument that quickly threatened to lead to a fight. But as I raised my fist at one of them when he shook a large lump of wood at me, Ping rushed out of the gate shouting 'No, no, don't hit him,' and seized my arms, momentarily pinning them behind my back. Taking advantage of the opening provided by this unexpected ally, the thug struck me soundly on the head and I bled like a pig, as I had on York Station when it was bombed during the war. Ping then dragged me back through our gates and bolted them, and we called the police. But the three men were stupid enough to continue prowling around outside. In consequence a patrol car arrived before they could decide to break in or back off, and they were caught — almost literally — red-handed. The usual accusations and counter-accusations followed, and the police might have decided there was nothing to choose between us and shrugged the incident off as a non-seizable offence. Ah, but then there was the blood...

'Why did you pin my arms?' I asked Ping dazedly, after the officers had taken over and we had agreed to file a complaint. 'I can't bear you fighting, so I tried stop you,' she said simply, 'and now you see how it worked out I was absolutely right.' Stunned for a second time that evening, I was left speechless by this irrefutable logic, and made for the bathroom to wash off the blood — now that it had served its purpose.

An angel? A *boring* angel (if you will forgive the tautology)? After all, Thornton Wilder had said the fights were the best part of marriage, and we had none. On the other hand it might be thought that since Ping believed everything should come second to peace and quiet, to the harmony and happiness that Confucius preached as the object of life, I had it made. However, this is not Heaven but — as they say — an imperfect world, and that would be to ignore the influence on Ping of Taoism.

As we have seen, the Taoists believe in non-action, in moving passively with the natural flow of life, not struggling against the current of destiny, but seizing the opportunities it offers when the right moment comes. That was the doctrine that inspired the guerrilla strategy of Sunzi, who advocated dodging confrontation with the enemy until all the factors were in your favour, and then hitting him with everything you had. Timing was all, and Ping was faithful to that principle. If, therefore, she had given way over some question without an argument, I could not congratulate myself on my victory, but resign myself to a day of reckoning once the ground was on her side.

She was not going to get into a futile running fight with my addiction to nicotine, since it would only have driven me deeper into it — 'never try to change what you cannot'. But in 1962

I caught TB, and that gave her her chance to 'fight downhill', relentlessly pushing me into giving up smoking when she had the doctors and x-rays and my own blue funk as her allies. It was almost as if moving with the flow of nature meant that destiny would do the dirty work for her in the end in return. As she put a strip of plaster on my bloody head after my altercation with the three lorry drivers, I remembered that other occasion in Taipei when the taxi-driver had attacked her with a tyre-lever and a stream of filth, and she had stopped me from hitting him after I had struck the first blow. 'Don't fight,' she had shouted, to my astonishment. But she had shouted with good reason. The timing was wrong, as it was for Han Xin. A crowd had gathered that might prove hostile. And there was more to it than that. Ping had not forgotten that we were on our way to dine *à quatre* with the Mayor of Taipei and his wife, and when they looked displeased that we arrived late, she at once told them what had happened. Within the hour the taxi-driver was in a cell.

Wait patiently and then seize the day. She had accepted with unhappy resignation and wifely meekness my decision that we find other homes for our two Alsatians when we moved from our bungalow into a condominium. But once it turned out that she had saved the situation by impulsively accepting a lower price for the bungalow just before the stock market crashed, her moment had come. While the property market dropped dead, we could laugh all the way to the bank, and when she demanded that we keep the dogs despite the overcrowding I — as she would have put it — 'could not say *one word*'.

Very often the opportunity for her to strike came when I had to cover some lunacy elsewhere in the region, and I would return in trepidation as to what I might find. After we had made a little money with my first book, Ping of the green fingers suggested we could now spend some of it on the garden, as it was looking a bit too ragged at the edges even for her. This was when we lived in our first bungalow in Shelford Road, which had more than an acre of terraced land for her to care for, and we had been talking about it for some time. But when I objected that we should first pay off the mortgage on the property and maybe get a new secondhand car, she nodded submissively. It was one of those occasions when she would peaceably admit 'I am wrong' — and point at me.

I took off for Saigon a little uneasily, having left her enough cash in the bank for her needs, and returned late at night only three weeks later. Ping let me know that she could not meet me at the airport, so I caught a cab home. But the cabbie did not seem to know the way, which was not unusual in Singapore, where many taxi-drivers were Malaysians from across the Causeway. We suddenly appeared to be going past the Botanic Gardens with its illuminated trees, which meant he must have overshot my turning, although I did not remember our having crossed Dunearn Road. I tried to redirect him, but five minutes later we were passing the same spot, and only at the third try did I get it right.

Ping greeted me at the gate, took my hand, and walked me around the side of the house to the terrace, from where the three levels of garden descended. I had been wrong about the Botanic Gardens; the illuminations were here. All the trees were floodlit — coconut palms, durian, guava, madras thorn — but then so was an ornate Chinese archway with a roof of upcurled tiles that had not been there before, a new ornamental goldfish pond on the second terrace with a fifteen-foot-high fountain, and a rustic bar with a palm-thatched roof for alfresco boozing on fine nights. It was riveting, a garden of light.

Ping had bided her time and seized her chance to spend some of the money from my book on 'improving' it, never mind about the mortgage and the new secondhand car. I had meanwhile been told no more than I needed to know, which was, of course, precisely nothing. 'And cheap,' murmured Ping. 'Not up to $3,000.' Obviously an 'appropriate' expense. I was duly riveted. 'I hope you had enough money left over for bread and butter,' I said at last, once I had got my breath back. It was the best I could manage.

She celebrated her victory with a party.

Lots of laughter and happiness, because when dinner over all guests spent the tune outdoors, resting on the terrace. I switched off the light inside the house, and because the house on a hill with three levels of garden, below the spotlights under the huge old trees obviously giving marvellous views, beautiful and peaceful. And the fountain spurting water into the air in all directions, the moisture with various colours reflected light reminded me of a broken section of rainbow. The party went on till moon had already sunk, the scenery enchanting shrouded in morning mist, the guests forget to go home. Those were memorable years thanks my beautiful garden.

If weaker than the enemy, do not confront him, but creep up on him slowly from behind. When much later I faced Ping with the idea of moving into a condominium, she mourned not only the loss of her dogs, but of her land. 'Cannot be without garden,' she protested unhappily. 'What happen all my flowers?' However, moving with the flow of destiny, which at that moment was showing her the cold face of financial logic, she did not strive against it, but bowed to it, contemplating the little courtyard that was all our new townhouse had to offer for a show of potted plants with no more than a sigh of resignation. But her guerrilla instinct soon told her the ground was in her favour; she was only retreating today — *force majeure* — to advance tomorrow.

The fourth side of the courtyard around which the townhouse was built opened onto the common land of the condominium, and beyond that a displeasing view of a 19-storey block of flats. Outside our fence nothing grew to screen us from this but one ageing bottlebrush tree and a row of five pots of dispirited bougainvillea. But coming home one day from a lunch appointment I noticed that the pots had been moved about three yards further away from the fence, and two small Thai bamboos planted in the space behind them. 'I just been to market garden and put them there,' Ping explained casually. 'But that's the common property of the estate,' I objected, 'it's not your garden. You can't start planting things out there, or you'll have the Management Council on our necks. It's against the bylaws, and the bylaws have the force of Singapore law.'

It was no use. The Chinese have scant respect for the law except when breaking it costs money. But she did not provoke the powers-that-be by suddenly taking over the land beyond our fence and promptly filling it with illegal plants. She first encouraged me to become a member of the Management Council, and then chairman of the Landscape Subcommittee. She then became a member of the subcommittee herself, and having protected her back, so to speak, proceeded to Phase Two. This involved shifting the five pots of bougainvillea even further out, like the forward pickets of a stealthily advancing army, and when no one raised any objection after two or three weeks, adding three young sealingwax palms to the Thai bamboos behind them; and after another pause to make sure she had not alarmed the enemy, moving the bougainvillea forward again and marshalling two powder-puff plants, a mickey mouse shrub and an alamanda bush into position behind these...

That was eight years ago. Now the bougainvillea are already on the other side of the main path of the condominium, thick stands of 25-foot yellow and sealingwax palms shut off the rest of the condominium from the courtyard, and the entire area of common property around the house is a controlled jungle of trees and tall bamboos and flowering shrubs — firecracker, cat's whisker, hibiscus, ixora and a dozen other species whose names Ping is the last to know — through which a stone path she has laid herself winds its way to our back gate.

The whole is maintained by the condominium gardener who moonlights for her at weekends, watering the plants from a tap that Ping illegally moved to a convenient position at the outset of the operation. The Management Council (on the advice of the Landscape Subcommittee) has long since accepted the principle that subsidiary owners might add plants to the common property of the condominium as long as they enhanced it, Ping has her garden, and our privacy is complete.

Because right time always will come, I very unhappy when everything go wrong just because the people too impatient and will not wait for it. The student leaders of democracy movement that explode like a bomb in Tiananmen Square in 1989 make a terrible mistake. They do not understand cannot at that time challenge the Communist Party face to face when it got all the power and must hold up its authority, don't care what. So of course for Deng Xiaoping only answer to keep control must be stamp on the revolution. How else? Students should know nothing can be done from outside yet. First had to win some leaders over to democracy idea, make the Party soft or split from the inside, godknowwhat. But students misled by western ideals most do not even understand.

And not just like that. Same with Hong Kong's last governor Patten. Policy all wrong to try to make Hong Kong democratic in last moment before British return it to China. Of course Beijing angry, wait change everything back. If British start to give Hong Kong democracy a piece a piece last 40 years, Chinese cannot say one word.

Softly, softly catchee monkee? I do not know who first said that, but what immediately strikes me about this excellent piece of advice is that it is, significantly, couched in Chinese pidgin. And after more than 40 years of guerrilla wedlock I have an uneasy feeling I know who, in our case, is the monkey.

16

IT WAS as instinctive for Ping to fight her way through life on the principles of Sunzi as it was for me to duck a well-aimed brick. But the Chinese can hardly be blamed for treating existence itself as an unending guerrilla war against misery.

Chinese so proud having such ancient civilisation, but of course means we suffer from human nature much longer time than other races. For 5,000 years Chinese people have been robbed, raped, killed by armies when got in the way of the battle, their crops trod down or stolen, their cattle cut up for the barbecue, their farms burned down. They been cheated and beaten by officials, ruined by heavy taxes just invented by mandarins to make money, or fallen in hands of greedy moneylenders, and their land still taken away by landowners because cannot pay rent, actually forced to sell children to eat, or else even happened eat own children.

On more grand scale millions torn from their homes to work as slaves to build Great Wall or Grand Canal suchlike, and as if this not good enough, they get big floods and famine and fire and drought by nature century by century, their harvests ruined and their families wiped out generation by generation. And not all old history. Mao Zedong 'Great Leap Forward' and 'Great Cultural Revolution' ruin the country completely and kill 16, maybe 20 million people quite recently.

True to their tradition, the Chinese did not confront misery head-on with the dire ravings and imprecations that rise so readily to my lips when adversity strikes unfairly (which, it goes without saying, it always does). They absorbed it, just as for centuries they absorbed the waves of uncouth invaders that periodically overran their country — Hun, Mongol, Manchu — as Ping absorbed me. The shrug of acceptance, not the closed fist of defiance, was the usual answer to misfortune; it was best defeated by meeting it with indifference, leaving it hitting empty air, as Sunzi advised. Ping might be devastated by the ruin of her family's fortunes, the death of her sisters, the prospect of endless penury in Hong Kong, but it was not going to show on her face. Her tears were silent, like rain seen through a window, and meanwhile life must go on. These things were unavoidable, 'the predestined enemies that always meet in a narrow alley'.

I soon discovered that the secret of Ping's equanimity was that, as she had said in a more literal context, she deliberately 'saw the flowers but not the pots', her eye focusing unerringly on the one bright spot of happiness amid the most depressing clutter of mishaps, and ignoring the rest. And nothing epitomised this more than the disastrous Great Rhino Hunt up Slim River.

It was our misfortune in 1962 to run into a wild life enthusiast named Milton who had just located at least one rare Sumatran rhino in the swamp jungle bordering Slim River in North Malaya. With the forlorn object of persuading an indifferent Malayan Government to declare the area a nature reserve, he had accordingly made plans to photograph the beast, and to this end had laid a trap for it, he told us one slightly inebriated evening. At one point about 200 yards through the jungle from the river bank, he explained, there was a small palm-thatched rattan hut on stilts, used periodically by aborigines when they tapped the surrounding trees for gum. Two nights before we met Milton had put a bag of salt under the floor of this hut and kept watch over it, and, sure enough, he had 'practically been able to scratch the back of the rhino through the boards when he came to steal it'. He was going to do the same again, but this time take pictures. Would we join him?

My British sporting instinct baulked at this paltry deceit to be practised on a poor dumb animal, but little did I know who was to have the last laugh. Ping was enchanted, and Milton radiated confidence. A huge, hairy, muscular creature, he seemed to justify the name 'orang utan' — 'man of the forest' — far more than those somewhat pensive old fellows one was accustomed to see hanging from the trees of North Borneo. He drove us in a jeep to our base camp, and wasting no time piled us into a narrow pirogue, whose native boatman gave us a gap-toothed grin as we set off up — or down — river. An hour or two later the boatman landed us on a small isolated beach near the hut, and puttered off back the way he had come, promising to return for us three days later.

We stood on the spit of sand, watching him disappear around a bend, the only other human in a suddenly silent and faintly sinister stretch of jungle on a dead black river. In front of us lay a narrow track that led through thick foliage, but to one side the saltwater had seeped into the roots of the trees, killing them and leaving a great tangle of gaunt, gleaming skeletons like a standing charnel house, through which the sun ... but abruptly there was no sun; it had been ruthlessly obliterated from one second to another by a pitch-black cloud that covered the entire horizon. The next moment there was an ear-splitting crash of thunder, and lightning zig-zagged wickedly through the forest of bones, from which a great flock of green parrots suddenly flew upwards with an eerie psychotic shriek like some monstrous emanation from an ancient graveyard.

'Come on,' said Milton, hoisting the wooden case that was to serve us as a field kitchen on his brawny back, 'the hut's just through there. We've just got time to reach it before the storm breaks.' We hadn't got time. The rain came down on us in one solid sheet as we turned the corner to where the hut should have been, to find it had fallen flat on its face. The rhino had got there first; it had evidently come for the salt during the night, casually shouldered aside one of the stilts that supported the hut, and brought the whole rotten, termite-ridden structure to the ground. We were alone with the rain.

Soaked through already, we set about building a *basha* with our one inadequate tarpaulin and cannibalised bits of plank and palm thatch bound together with split rattan. We then stretched out our inflatable lilos under this flimsy shelter and tried to sleep amid the crepitation of the brittle trees as they crumbled to the ground around us. But there was to be little sleep, for lilos are so designed that the longitudinal seams that join the different sections act as runnels for water, which coursed down from our exposed feet to settle in pools beneath us.

Three days to go, with an occasional break in the clouds and steaming sunlit mornings when the gibbons barked ironically among the trees as we tried to cook breakfast. But that was not enough. For the damp and dripping Ping, now cast in the role of housewife, this brought one humiliation after another.

Milton have 'kitchen box' special for cooking in jungle, but I don't know where everything kept in it, knives, forks, plates, godknowwhat, and cannot find. Also I don't know to light kerosene burner with wet matches, or clean knives and forks in dirty sand, or split creepers with parang for make rope. And although when we meet Milton look like ape don't mind the rough life, now begin behave like old maid with stupid servant, always nagging me never stop complain, always angry me, push me one side, put forks and knives in proper place himself, say I am 'no damn good for anything'. And just the same when I don't know simple things about jungle like be careful not to tread on snakes in case hurt them.

Watching the great tarantulas of his hands as they moved prissily among his beloved campware while he upbraided Ping, I was ready to break his thick neck twice over — once would not have been enough. But Ping wisely waved me down so that I survived to tell the tale, and since nothing lasts, the day unbelievably came when our pirogue arrived to return us to base camp. Once there we wasted no time, but bundled into the jeep and rolled back down the tracks to civilisation, Milton muttering it was late and driving like a madman, Ping discreetly seated in the back. Suddenly an impudent mother quail leading three chicks crossed the road in line ahead just in front of us, taking her time, as they will. Ping squealed in horror, but there was no need. Milton jammed on his brakes, leaned around the windscreen, and said 'come on, mum,' in a soft companionable voice, 'we haven't got all day, you know.'

Poor Ping. She had been expecting a jungle safari in glorious Technicolor, and all she had got was rain and discomfort and the inedible muck Milton called rations, and then on top of it all the insufferable ape himself, chivvying her at every turn. 'You didn't say a word at the time but you must have hated his guts,' I said when we recalled the whole business a few weeks ago.

'Hated him?' protested Ping. 'But I *loved* him.'

'*Loved* him,' I said disbelievingly. 'Loved Milton? But the man made your life an absolute misery.'

'I know,' she said, 'but you see, it was the quails. You remember the quails? He was so gentle with the quails. Such a huge big fellow. It was beautiful.'

The quails. 'Little things please little minds', they say disdainfully, and as usual when people are disdainful, they are wrong. For Ping the simpler the source of one's joy, the easier it was to keep the bloody-minded world at bay, leaving the pretentious to their misery. She took endless pleasure in her flowers and plants and evil-smelling fertiliser, the sudden appearance of a first precocious bud ('bloody cheek'), in her special relationship with Shutup Charlie ('how did you keep him so quiet when you were waiting in the car; he usually barks his head off?' 'I told him the story of Little Red Riding Hood; he loved it, never took his eyes off me'), in tinkering ineffectually with her long-suffering piano, in her collection of teddy bears that would never let her down. 'Why were you so long in the kitchen?' 'I was looking at my new wok.' She laughed at zany sitcoms, clutching my hand tightly in a sort of ecstasy when Mr Bean got his comeuppance, she loved movies with happy endings, and would watch only those played by handsome actors and beautiful stars out of some early Hollywood heaven.

Enough trouble in this world. Why I watch ugly gangsters and poor women in horrible trouble and children crying, everyone shooting each other and exploding cars, and the bad people with so many guns burning houses, and bombs ticking like the clock on TV? Only an idiot still need more misery when finished work and can sit comfortably watching amusing dream.

It sometimes seemed that action TV was out to get its own back on her, for if she sat down to watch it only for a moment, a peaceful sequence of talking heads had an uncanny knack of bursting into an uproar of AK-47s and Uzis and flaring flamethrowers, bodies jerking like dolls in all directions. But she was quick with the remote and would fire back ruthlessly, obliterating the villains. Her idea of violence was one of those kung-fu films in which, inexplicably, nobody ever seemed to get hurt.

The stock response of a Chinese to a menacing world is to keep his head down. The first rule of survival is stay out of trouble, never get mixed up in anything dangerous or unprofitable. It is not your business. Discretion is the better part of valour. Leave heroics to heroes whom you can admire from a safe distance. You have a family to think about, and if you haven't you ought to. 'Better a dog in times of peace than a man in times of unrest,' they say.

A nation of moral cowards? 'There are 36 stratagems and the best is to run away,' says a famous Chinese misquotation. However, the Chinese do not run away to escape challenges, but rather in order to confront them better at the right moment. The name of the game is always survival — survival after those 5,000 gruelling years.

As far as coping with misery is concerned the Chinese are not cowards, but tough adversaries. In 1962 Ping's mother fell seriously ill in Taiwan, and one night shortly afterwards Ping received a call from Radio Television Singapore saying that a telegram had arrived for her from Taipei, and she had better collect it. We rushed down to the office, and a clerk handed Ping a slip of paper. Had her mother died? Ping took it from him slowly, started to read the string of Chinese characters, and suddenly stopped short. 'But I can't understand this,' she whispered, 'it is in code. Please, for God's sake, what does it say?'

The man shrugged. 'Sorry,' he said. 'I can't help you. You see, we don't have the Taiwanese telegraphic code in Singapore, so we can't decipher this for you.' It was late at night. There was nothing to be done until morning. Ten hours to wait and no phone connection. We took the useless piece of paper home. It was, I suppose, the worst moment of my life. I cannot speak for Ping. But she sensed the truth. Her mother had died. Her face was carved in ice.

Inside I was heartbroken. My mother never had even one bit easy time. Among the chaos caused by war she made strenuous effort to bring us up, also the whole group grandchildren. Now, all at once, she fell into a faint and lost consciousness forever. How could I repay her kindness now? But useless to show grief. Can only deeply regret for always.

When Dominic died, Ping's eyes were again dry, empty, frozen, and all she said was, 'I be all right, but do excuse me, just now I prefer alone.' She pressed my hand gently. I knew there was nothing I could do but keep away.

Dominic was born in miserable time while our family faced a dead end, growing up in poverty. He was a sensible child, usually exemplary student in school, with will of steel to work hard for brilliant future. And not just like that. People often said, 'mother's heart and child's beat as one'. It was true. Dominic always understood me perfectly without being told, and listen me even when elegant grown man, natural and unrestrained, rich in talent, his career just then achieving results, like a musical performance reaching a peak. Then in a flash all strings broken, sound stops abruptly. It stabbed me to the heart, just cannot believe.

For these blows of fate there was no answer, but when there was an answer, Ping struck back hard and promptly. In 1969 Singapore suffered one of the worst floods of all time, our garden became a lake and our bungalow an island marooned above it as the rain poured relentlessly down. And then it happened. The second terrace below the house began to slither down the slope into the third, the top terrace started to crumble into the second, and when its tiled surface cracked, it revealed that it was no more than a thin crust resting on a huge hole that stretched right back under the house. I was away. Ping was left to cope, and quickly marshalled an army of red-hatted women construction workers to fill the yawning cave below us with cement, shore up the slopes, and build a five-foot retaining wall right across the garden to stop the rot. The situation was saved. But Ping had not finished with fate: it was a few weeks after that that I came home one night to find the entire garden floodlit and a 15-foot fountain rising derisively where before the landslide had threatened to topple the whole house into the rain-soaked valley below. Ping had got her own back.

Derisively — and derision lies behind much of the cruel humour of the Chinese. At one moment he will laugh uproariously at the evil that befalls the wretched victim of some banana-skin comedy precisely because he sometimes feels like the wretched victim of a banana-skin comedy himself. But at the next, for the same reason, he will cheer on the underdog, the weak and the small who make fools of the mighty, the pompous, the pretentious, all those who are stupid enough to take life seriously. One of his great heroes is Yanzi, diminutive diplomat of the state of Ch'i and master of the swift backhander. When Yanzi was sent on a mission to the powerful state of Chu, his hosts, contemptuous of his lack of inches, tried to humiliate him by building a little wicket for him to enter the city by. 'Of course,' said Yanzi, unperturbed, 'in a dog's country one enters by the dog gate.' They opened the main portal for him without more ado.

There is nothing like turning the tables on fate. Essentially, the Chinese tend to believe they are all part of the same bad joke, and the effect is not all negative, for it can mean that good Confucians will conspire to cheat Misery of her fun. When the three thugs were caught by the police with my blood on their hands, so to speak, nothing came of the affair in the end.

For to my disgust, our neighbour Mrs Wong arrived to see Ping the next day with tears in her eyes, begging her to ask me not to press charges as one of the men was a relative. Ping agreed at once, and there were happy faces all round. 'You have to forgive, after all they are all one of us,' she explained, a trifle ungrammatically. It was just one more chance to take the mickey out of misfortune.

17

BUT THERE is more than one way of cocking a snook at destiny, as the funeral of Mr Yip Hon in Hong Kong in May 1997 demonstrated. Instead of burning the paper comforts one might reasonably expect the dead to need in Paradise — Mercedes car, 31-inch television, million-dollar notes on the Bank of Hell, and so on — his grieving family formally incinerated a baccarat table and two card dealers (in flimsy effigy) to accompany him in the afterlife. For Mr Yip Hon was a popular casino mogul, and, as we have noted, the Chinese are notorious gamblers, well known for being addicted in their spare time to risking all on the turn of a card (Ping's family betted with rice harvests).

This seems out of character with your prudent, look-before-you-leap, cautious-seldom-err Confucian, but it is in the nature of things that *yin* is always complemented by *yang*, and it has been the very submissive patience of the Chinese when under harsh imperial yoke over the centuries that has led to violent and very unConfucian revolution when that patience was exhausted. For the westerner the prudent side of their make-up may evoke the image of a canny Swiss banker in his Zurich counting-house, but to me the *yang* side is more like that of an excitable Sicilian, perhaps with a knife in his belt. Farfetched? Possibly. But it is not without interest that it is the Sicilians and the Chinese who share the distinction of having given us the two most renowned criminal organisations in the world. It was a patriotic uprising by Sicilians against their hated French masters that eventually led to the emergence of the modern Mafia, and a patriotic uprising by Chinese against their hated Manchu masters that led to the emergence of the modern Triads.

Despite their reputation for Confucian caution, the real Swiss banker would be horrified by the business methods of the Chinese and the lurid history of their commerce — the bold adventurers who sailed into Southeast Asia, risking not only massacre by infuriated Siamese and Malays, many of them little better than pirates, but also the imperial edict that treated them as criminals if they went outside Chinese home waters, so that instead of returning to China to have their heads lopped off on the orders of the nearest mandarin, they often turned pirate themselves. When they did not, they settled down among the native peoples of the subcontinent and proceeded to form exclusively Chinese trading networks right across it that would largely dominate the regional economy at the expense of the locals. Not quite the thing, as the banker might well say, pursing his thin lips, not quite *Zurich*.

But he should not be surprised. Behind the impassive mask of the conventional Chinese there often lurks a bold, passionate, impetuous, highly emotional, intensely romantic human, with all the characteristics of the inflammable Latin. This is the Chinese that has given China much of its great art, its poetry and paintings, its legends of swashbuckling heroes, 'the men of the rivers and lakes' as depicted in the great novel, *Shui Hu Zhuan*, with its brotherhood of 108 bandits still beloved of millions. And, of course, its Triads. This is not the Singaporean who shames one by asking for 7-Up when offered even a beer, but the Chinese with 4,205 years of wine-making behind him (roughly speaking).

Since then the relation between wine and Chinese civilisation very close. It is true some always associate wine — Chinese wine is hard liquor — with erotic life, full of error, alcohol as evil spirit linked to sexual desire and corruption, like the magic combination of champagne and perfumed women in the West, and such misunderstanding hard to clear up until today. But it is not true to Chinese culture tradition, and when Cao Cao, the heroic villain of The Three Kingdoms' era, banned wine in the third century, linking it with profligacy, a distinguished Confucianist whose house always full of guests and bottles retorted sarcastically, 'Now that liquor and sex ruin the country, women also are guilty of a crime, so why don't ban marriage?' Cao Cao killed him, but the ban fell flat; wine was a good friend, said our forefathers, all heroes were heavy drinkers, and drinking increased, especially among men of letters, for Chinese believe wine and poetry go together — I drink ten litres and can write a hundred verses.' One famous writer made his name by reputedly staying dead drunk for 40 days, while another laid down in his will that when he died his ashes should be mixed with clay and made into a wine jar.

And although I don't drink much and would easy get drunk on half glass wine.

I enjoy an atmosphere of liquor and strong tea in the companionship of writers to discuss pleasantly about life and literature in impassioned mood, not drunk but slightly tipsy and unrestrained and natural, the plates all in disorder after a feast.

Couplets written on paper and stuck up on two sides of front doors at New Year and on ceremonial occasions express our deep lyrical feelings about liquor: 'Up in the sky the aroma of wine ascending, flying birds on sniffing become phoenixes; down on earth the lees of the wine descending, swimming fish on tasting become dragons.' And 'The wind blowing nearby, a thousand families become drunk; the rain ceasing, the open bottle yields fragrance for ten miles.' The Chinese applaud when they hear that the King of England conferred titles on all five families that produce the most famous Scotch whisky for performing immortal feats for British Empire.

The Sicilian in the Chinese also makes him a man of unpredictable outbursts. Hua Sheng, the master of half Manchuria, breaks down in tears when complaining to Ping of the sorry state of their country. (One could hardly see Field Marshal Montgomery doing the same.) Her elder brother, the hero of the victory at Changsha, forgets everything and spews a box of chocolates across the loaded dining table in his excitement to demonstrate a tennis service. Totally different incidents, yet both in keeping, along with Ping's sudden, ephemeral enthusiasms: for Balinese dancing (one lesson), Yoga (one lesson), picket ball (four games), America's Funniest Home Videos (three-and-a-half episodes), and her impulse shopping — her decisions at different times to buy the Shelford Road bungalow sight unseen without having the money, two Alsatians instead of none, and thirty Indonesian muu-muus in one fell swoop to give away as presents — 'just imagine, only ten dollars'. (But thirty?) Not to mention to marry a barbarian on spec and stick with him for 40 years and more.

The old tycoon who bought our Windsor Park bungalow by promising to keep the dogs was another case in point. He rushed in, looked around, admired the view and the pictures on the walls with arms raised, assumed wrongly that there was a 999 lease (it was freehold), talked and laughed compulsively, flattered Ping ('exceptional woman'), asked nothing about title deeds, property tax, noise, drains, neighbours, cracks in the walls, no nonsense about a survey, just shake-hands-on-it-among-friends — and Ping met his mood halfway by instantly holding out hers and accepting a drop of $80,000 in the reserve price.

Combine these two different sides of the Chinese character and you do not, of course, get either a stolid Swiss bourgeois or an excitable Latin cat on hot bricks (or tin roof) 24 hours a day. Nothing so reliable. You are likely to get something far more disconcerting — a mixture that will mean months of soothing Confucian calm and common sense as inert as a terrorist's block of Semtex, followed by a sudden explosion of stubborn and seemingly senseless fury detonated by some completely unsuspected trigger. And this is no artful dodge of Sunzi. It is Sunzi thrown to the winds, along with all logic.

Scene: Our old married couple, who understand each other so well by now, are discovered sitting at the breakfast table in amicable discussion about writing their memoirs.

D: Look, supposing we put that story about X into Chapter 16.

Ping (smiling lovingly, hand on my wrist): What story, Mouse?

D: You know, the one about ...

Ping (the smile vanishes and a frown takes its place): But you cannot tell that story.

D: But why not? It fits in so well with —

Ping (minatory finger poised): I promised her I never tell anyone that story. Just tell you, which anyway not allowed. Definitely cannot.

D: But she's dead, it was fifty years ago, and all the others are in their eighties and living on the other side of the world.

Ping: Maybe dead, but what they all going to think? I promised. No, cannot print it. You print it I will not write the book with you. Finished.

D (quickly capitulating): Okay, okay, then we won't include it. It was only a suggestion. It's not that important.

(But I am too late. She is in a groove.)

Ping (a blind, almost mad, look in her eye): No, now I decided, won't write the book. Throw away what already I written.

D (terrified): No, no, listen. I said I won't put it in, and I won't, and that's that. We'll leave it out. Does that satisfy you? Now, please let's talk about something else.

Ping (rising from table, almost in tears): Nothing more to talk. You already said you want to put it in book? So okay, you go ahead. I won't write one more word.

D: But I just told you that I agree with you, we should forget the whole thing, I promise we will leave it out, so why still say you won't write any more? You're so keen on the book.

Ping: Because you want put in that story so no book.

D (unwisely): But of course if there is no book the story won't be in it anyway.

Ping: Exactly. So that way I keep my promise.

(Ping stalks out leaving D to contemplate the remains of her fish porridge.)

My 'suggestion' was an act of folly. I should have realised I was on forbidden ground, that I had stepped on a booby trap. In consequence I had to fight for Ping's reason as well as mine before we finally settled our nonexistent differences on the subject. But if I learn slowly, so do others. For example many diplomatic negotiators in the West tend to work on the fixed principle that as the Chinese are a bunch of pragmatic moneygrubbers, they will not sacrifice their interests for an ideal, and in the last analysis can always be brought to heel with the threat of material loss — the vast American export market, membership of the World Trade Organisation, Normal Trading Status for another year, and the rest of the carrots that enable the US to wield the big stick.

But there are issues over which the calculating Swiss banker will give way to the emotional Sicilian patriot at the flip of a coin, and all pragmatic considerations will be swept away on a tide of righteous indignation. The Chinese are intensely nationalistic and when their government allowed them to blow off steam in manageable — if not managed — demonstrations to vent their fury over the American bombing of the Chinese Embassy in Belgrade in 1999, it knew what it was doing (even if the Americans didn't). To the Americans, Chinese suspicion that it was a deliberate attack 'defied all logic', whereas to the Chinese this assumption itself defied all logic. The CIA didn't know where the Chinese Embassy — a prime intelligence target — was located? They hadn't even looked at an up-to-date tourist map of Belgrade? Or consulted a telephone book? As for warnings that their sharp reaction would harm their commercial interests…

Western people have to learn although Chinese very practical, even so not possible to settle down every problem with them with some kind smart business deal, maybe bribe or blackmail, because some things cannot even discuss about. For example Washington offer to give Beijing the moon if Chinese give Taiwan independence will only make Chinese people mad and very excited, speak only about insult and national honour. And not just like that. Every year friends of Dalai Lama make so much noise must give freedom to Tibet. Just waste the time. Maybe one day give more autonomy, but ask for absolutely full independence for Tibet is like China ask Americans give back Texas to Mexico. China is China, all one piece. In nineteenth century foreign powers divide our country between them to swallow up like chopped up Hainanese chicken. Today Chinese do not sell their country a piece a piece. Not any more.

It is dangerous even to fly kites in such cases. The Chinese are down to earth, and if you throw out an airy hypothesis, however absurd, just to see how they will take it, they are liable to assume it is a firm proposal and jump on it hard. Being a severely practical people, as Ping said, they are literal-minded. If you say something, you have to mean it. They have no more time for 'just supposing' than they have for vague theories and abstract 'isms'. They think in concrete. As Ping once put it succinctly, 'my mother did not fight the revolution for your democracy, but to end foot-binding'. She lived in a real world that could not afford high-flown western waffle. Her reasons were down-to-earth.

When the time I taught in Chinese high school, my students a group of girls age 18 to 21, and once they came to visit me in holiday time for tea, and atmosphere relaxed, I asked them why they all pro-communist and praise communism so much and want to go to China. They said most important two reasons was that in Communist China they could seeking their own spiritual freedom of love and also hoped to do more advanced studies because in Singapore then have no Chinese-language university. What do they mean, freedom of love? We all spoke Mandarin, but these girls' families originally belong to different parts of South China, so at home in Singapore they spoke their own dialect — Hokkien, Chaozhou, Hainanese, Cantonese, Hakka, and their parents always tell them strictly can only many into another family spoke the same dialect. Of course they never listen, and if love someone definitely would not hesitate to elope with their boyfriend to China, where everyone spoke Mandarin and doesn't care what dialect. That was it. Nobody speak one word about Mao or Marx or revolution or glorious socialist society.

Say 'Suppose we were to ...' to Ping in this real world and she will take it you mean here and now. 'I thought we might take a holiday in Malaysia.' 'How can? We have Gopal coming to dinner on Saturday and anyway I have to go to the hairdresser.' 'No, look, I didn't mean immediately, I meant sometime later this year, or perhaps ...' To her, postulating is 'singing instead of talking'. 'You' means 'you', not the abstract 'one', and you do well to remember it. 'If you go to see your doctor these days, you have to wait ...' 'But I am not seeing my doctor. Why should I? Nothing wrong.'

Talking to her is sometimes an art in itself, painfully learned like everything worthwhile. But quite often it is simply a question of adjusting to the present tense.

Ping has a good sense of humour (despite her short affair with 'America's Funniest Home Videos' — that slip was due to the antics of the dogs, not the humans), but her literal mind makes telling her jokes she may not see a hazardous business. 'But I don't understand. It does not make sense. If the shaggy dog was not shaggy enough ...' And that goes for ill-omened cracks like 'Cheer up, soon be dead,' as my mother used to say to me as a child when I cried. This sort of thing used to lead to arduous explanations, but nowadays misunderstandings are rare, not only because we have learned to decipher each other, but because we each have come to see on these occasions that the other is not actually a halfwit, but just using different software.

That is not true of East and West yet, and it is hazardous for visiting dignitaries to sharpen their wits on the Chinese unless they are deliberately looking for trouble. When my cousin Valerie Hope, who was research assistant to the Lord Mayor of London that year, asked me what advice she should give him just before he paid an official visit to Beijing, I replied 'tell him not to try to be funny; leave it to the Chinese to make the jokes'. He did, and they all got on famously. Nothing turns a Swiss into a Sicilian more quickly than the wrong wisecrack taken at face value.

But that only applies to mundane matters. To see a Chinese standing lost in fanciful thought and completely deaf to the din around him in a crowded household of brass-lunged womenfolk and screaming toddlers is to realise how completely he can separate his material from his spiritual world. Ping's literal-mindedness belongs only to the unremitting facts of life, as the hardheaded Chinese have faced it for centuries. It is matched by the other realm of the Chinese mind, in which the word 'suppose' truly belongs, along with a love of dreaming, of a soaring, often poetic imagination, a desire to get away from it all, a yearning beyond the squalor of daily existence. Ping might be maddeningly matter-of-fact in the first context, but she is the same Ping who wrote, '*I was torn by conflicting thoughts, lonely, void, perplexed and uneasy. I thought I had to find a way out to laugh again a little — even bitterly or crazily, I did not mind...*'

At one extreme the dreamers have been unbridled speculators, the Taoists clouding the whole business of scientific analysis with wild theories for which they had not a shred of proof, alchemists and not chemists. But at the other the Chinese have shown an almost wooden lack of imagination and a craven fear of innovation. And what if the second comes to dominate the first, and the Sicilian becomes the Swiss, so to speak? This is what happened to the very foundations of Chinese culture itself.

More than 2,000 years ago a freethinking Confucius said, 'If I lift one corner of a subject, and my student cannot uncover the other three for himself, I do not repeat the lesson.' Yet Chinese education was to degenerate over the centuries into a mindless system of rote learning. Confucius had encouraged his students above all to think for themselves. Now their 'Confucian' teachers were telling them that thinking for themselves was above all the last thing they should do, for that way lay heresy.

Imagination was stultified. Creativity died. China lost out to the West, where a new, up-to-date 'liberal' system of education was now gaining popularity whereby children were largely left to work things out for themselves, as Confucius had recommended. The only trouble, it seemed, was that many of the children were liable to end up by being unable to read, write or do simple sums competently in a country where a British minister could confidently assert on television that seven times eight made 54. With a Confucian mother and an English father and living in Singapore, halfway house between their two cultures, the question looming in our minds when we adopted them was: which way did the other think the boys should go?

18

HAD PING been a diehard 'Confucian', this could have led to a clash of civilisations. But fortunately she was not. The conventional image of Confucius empathised his alleged conviction that salvation lay in reviving the good old days and ways of ancient kings who had notionally ruled China a thousand or two years before his own degenerate times. Fallible man must not look forward, therefore, but ever backward for his model. No detail of bygone ceremony could be skipped, and traditional flouted.

His philosophy was said to have been derived from the Five Classics, antique works which were a record of the past, and over the centuries that inspired a rigid system of education based solely on these and on the Four Books of the Sage's own teachings as the only sources of wisdom. They were required reading for students preparing to take the imperial examinations for the mandarinate, who were even advised to learn them by heart. Any straying to other works was anathema. To question them or the words of the teacher expounding them only led to 'confusion and error'. In consequence most aspiring scholars were not concerned with acquiring knowledge, but with mugging up these texts and passing the exams by writing orthodox essays on them which in no way varied from the approved dogma.

Medieval? But the tradition survived. In 1999 a Japanese commentator could still remark, "Schools now are only about memory.' And until recently Singapore students were still learning their lessons by rote, slavishly following their books, never questioning their teacher or their texts even when they did not understand them, on no account saying anything controversial, but silently noting down and then memorising what they had been taught. Like their forebears, they swotted solely in order to pass exams.

In competition with western children, in consequence, they easily scored top marks in tests where knowing facts and formulas by heart paid off, which was supposed to prove that 'Asian values' were superior to those of the benighted Occident. But the western minds were fallible just because they were flexible and free, while the Asian minds were often as rigid as computers. They outperform their peers around the world in mathematics and science, but just set them a different kind of test and you will see them panic and fumble,' as one Singapore professor put it. The imagination and the ability to think, to improvise, had atrophied. All that was left was a genius for echoing others. No wonder, when in 1987 a boy who wrote 2 weeks x 7 days = 14 days would be marked wrong; it should have been 7 days x 2 weeks = 14 days, the official solution.

In 1995, according to the *Straits Times*, an official report described the average graduate employee in Singapore as 'lacking in creativity and initiative, awkward, being uncertain and vague, and unable to work independently, preferring to be spoon-fed and hand-held by his supervisors'. In the nineteen-nineties the government became alarmed, a new campaign was launched, an educational institution with a strange title was opened — 'The Singapore Centre for Teaching Thinking'. By the end of the millennium entry into universities did not depend solely on examination marks; students had to pass a 'reasoning test'. Confucius – the real Confucius – was having the last laugh, after all.

For the truth was that Confucius did not emphasise the study of books, rarely mentioning them except for the *Book of Poetry*, and even of this he said, 'If a person can recite the 300 odes, but does not know how to act on an official mission, what is the practical use of all that study?' And he specifically warned against fussy observance of the last detail of a ritual or ceremony as empty posturing if it lacked sincerity. He was an innovator who drew ideas from antiquity, but did not try to revive it, hardly ever quoted ancient precedent to support a course of action, and made little mention of the emperors of the 'golden age'. He had been totally betrayed.

This is Ping's Confucius, not the dummy she dubs 'that dead fellow' and whose alleged pronouncements on the past she dismisses as 'rubbish'.

Education is not to teach facts but to correct people's nature, guide their mind – otherwise they go to the bad way, especially if clever. When they were young I try to teach the boys before they leave me to study hard to be Confucian gentleman – means not dead study books but how to think for themselves, to know right from wrong, to build up their own character, face to the life. That is the Confucius way.

I told them must always to be loyal to themselves, never cheat or lie or pretend to themselves or other people. Whatever they do must do it honestly. They must learn how to act, dress, speak, behave, to control their nature, be simple, be polite, give way to others, forgive. That is happiness. Don't be greedy, don't grab it, don't make business just to make money, and if bad people promise to make you rich, look at it as a floating cloud, otherwise will lose all sense. Instead that, study to be useful member of the society, for example be a doctor or engineer, but also love literature and music.

I was not strict with the boys, never sit down give them long lecture, say don't do this, don't do that. I did not raise them to be a mouse. Like Confucius I get my lessons from the real life, so when some incident happen or boys behave badly I take the chance to point it out what they have to learn from it, and how to use what they learned. They had to study to the limit, but then I let them free, let them work everything out for themselves, follow their own nature. When John came crying to me said did not want to be doctor or engineer, I told him in that case of course not, trust yourself, if not doctor or engineer so only means you have not yet found your genius; find out, and you will be very good. But whatever you do, you must take the responsibility, earn your living, guard your health to keep your mind sharp. John drew well, for example, and D dreamed he might be famous cartoonist. I say nothing.

I had no quarrel with all this. In the event John became an accountant. It was doubtless a good thing. My influence on the boys' choice of careers was negligible anyway, although Ping claimed I tricked Dominic into wanting to become an engineer by buying them a model railway that filled the garage and won his undying devotion. Ping said it made her methods look like those of a 'horrible yakking old teacher' by contrast. I plead innocent. I liked model railways and was simply stumped for what to give them for Christmas – but then a Chinese will always look for an underlying motive (usually bad), a 'hidden agenda' as people insist on saying these days.

In fact, she had her own triumph when her 'yakking' at one point inspired Bosco with a wish to become a surgeon. We knew all about this when he brought home a box of frogs to dissect. The frogs escaped, and by the time he had brought home another box and they had all escaped in turn, the garden was hopping with vociferous batrachia as if we had been suddenly inflicted with the plagues of Egypt. This achieved, Bosco changed his mind and decided to become a chemist instead on the strength of his 'A' levels. Fair enough.

The immediate problem when they arrived in Singapore had been to find the boys places in a good school, but this was rapidly solved thanks to the intervention of a kind acquaintance commonly known as "Turk", a soi-disant Irish American Catholic with an expired Canadian passport who had converted to Islam and ran guns for the murderous Darul Islam movement in North Sumatra. Despite his apostasy, Turk was able to plead the boys' case with a friendly Irish father at Singapore's premier Catholic school, citing the fact that they had been at the Salesian convent in Macau, and to my surprise the school agreed at once to take them, apparently on his recommendation. (Unfortunately not all his activities were so beneficent. Having been deported from Singapore as an undesirable alien, he was found knifed in a Mexico City hotel bedroom.)

So for the most part I was able to loll back in my well-appointed study (one Hermes portable and a telephone with a foreign editor at the other end) and let the Singapore English-language educational system in the shape of St Joseph's Institution imbue the boys with the right Christian ethics and take them through the hoops of 'O' and 'A' level exams. For Ping had agreed all along that they should not go through the Chinese-language stream since it led to a dead end, while English would mean their studies, as Confucius had advised, could be turned to good practical account.

But although the boys learned Chinese in the school as secondary language, I was not satisfied, because I always want they should have deep knowledge of their own Chinese heritage. So I taught them about Chinese culture, and even when small I encouraged them read Chinese books for themselves, sitting on the floor of bookshops while I look around. I really hope to give them my great love for Chinese literature, and they follow my idea, so that finally each one became

Chairman of the Chinese Language and Literature Circle in their school one after the other, and so had to keep up their knowledge and interest. I did not want them to be like that kind English-educated Chinese in Singapore, know nothing.

Ping loved teaching because 'only kids listen'. And she had a captive audience. For the keystone of the Sage's vision of a harmonious society was the principle of filial piety, the duty and obedience owed by the son to the father, by the younger brother to the elder, by the daughter to the mother, and so on down the hierarchy. Filial piety was at the heart of a closed circle of loyalty and mutual obligation that embraced the extended family, kinsmen and clan, and intimate friends who were regarded as 'brothers' and 'sisters'. Confucius believed that the good son would become the good citizen, and that the example of the family would eventually forge a grid of harmonious relations between all men in an ideal society in which all would know their place but all would be equal in respect of their rights. Needless to say, it never happened.

His success was uneven, as his words were forgotten or distorted by time. In 1997 a Chinese in Hong Kong disobeyed them to the extent of hacking off his mother's head with a cleaver and throwing it out of a fourth-floor window, which was regarded as a scandalous lapse of propriety. On the other hand the following year a filial son in Singapore beat his elder brother to death for being disrespectful to his mother, posing an interesting Confucian conundrum. However, among most Chinese the tradition was still honoured without mayhem. Quite the reverse. I knew a doctor who was called in by the son of a septuagenarian millionaire to confirm that a concubine of his father was pregnant. 'Yes,' said the doctor, 'but who is responsible?' 'My father, of course,' said the son. 'But your father is nearly eighty, has had two strokes, and is bedridden,' protested the doctor. 'Well, so I helped him a little,' said the son. The doctor stared at him in disbelief. 'You mean you held him ... while he ...?' 'Of course,' said the young man. 'Who else? After all I am the *eldest* son.'

Nothing like these events has occurred in our family, I am happy to say, though Ping is very strict about family obligations. While I slumber on, she herself will get up at four in the morning to see off a second cousin once removed who has been staying with us and has to catch a plane at dawn, and even today she sends money to a distant relative who looked after her nanny in her old age, considering her a 'sister' without knowing precisely who she is in the scheme of things.

She reaps her reward. When she went around the United States for the first time, she stayed with Han Chao and Kwai San, who now lived in Florida. But after that it was an exercise in coordinated 'niece-hopping', for she was fielded on arrival at every airport by her local niece, driven to her home, entertained and dined in the best restaurants and taken around the sights for a few days, and then put on a plane to be met at the other end of her flight by the next niece. She had six of them, conveniently spread out from sea to shining sea, plus a nephew at Nasa. She was 'auntie', their father's younger sister, and nothing was good enough for her.

After a broken childhood and a barren first marriage in the tradition of hit-and-miss family relations in Europe, I found myself not only the possessor of three instant sons, but at the head of a hierarchy governed by a rigid code of loyalties. Children in the West, where care of the old was often left to the State, might or might not cherish their parents and brother might or might not feel affection for brother according to taste, but the Chinese had no choice. When an aunt asked our rebarbative teenage granddaughter whether she loved her grandpa and grandma she replied coolly 'got to'.

There was harmony within the family, for in principle there

could be no arguing back. Ping acted the autocratic matriarch even when the boys were pushing fifty. When young they did not address each other by name but rank — 'Big Brother', 'Second Brother', 'Third Brother', and Dominic, who called me 'Dad' while the others called me 'Father', kept them strictly in line. Asked when we adopted them whether they would not rather be known by their original surname 'Chen', given their Chinese faces, they opted firmly for 'Bloodworth'. It became a symbol of their allegiance. 'Don't do that, remember you are Bloodworth,' Ping would say when they broke the rules, which of course they frequently did. They were proud of the name, and even more so when it began to appear on successive book jackets. Pointing at my long-suffering typewriter, Dominic boasted to a visiting friend, 'one tap, one dollar'. If only his arithmetic had been accurate.

As a son, Dominic was a stickler for tradition. On one of my birthdays he tried to organise a full-scale Lion Dance on our terrace in my honour, with all the gaudy colour and prancing and deafening drums and clashing cymbals that greet the arrival of a distinguished guest in Singapore. (He failed to command support among his colleagues, perhaps because he was only the back legs of the lion and had not graduated to the front.) When he married, Ping and I sat side by side like royalty while he and his bride knelt before us and solemnly offered us the ceremonial cup of tea that custom demands.

Did I belong? I began to feel like a prizewinning zebra in a horse show. I was living 'like a Pasha', as a friend used to say. Admittedly, life had its minor snags. As a pundit of all things Anglo-Saxon I was expected to be omniscient, and to field questions like 'what is 'epistemology', Dad? The theory of knowledge? But what does *that* mean?' 'Father, what's the difference between a pirate and a buccaneer?' All right, but try this: 'Father, what exactly do you mean by "now then"? When is it?'

Otherwise, however, I was enveloped by a family in which love was expressed in acts — and no gift could be rejected, no expense repaid. Patience personified, Bosco shopped around for the best computer and printer for me, set them up, taught me for tedious hours how to use them, and would at once drive over if I was in trouble with them no matter at what inconvenience to himself. When I went to England to see family and friends, John and Ivy would meet me with their car at Heathrow airport at the crack of dawn, drive me to their much-burgled home, insist I bed down for a rest no matter how wide awake I was, and pamper me until I took my next perilous step into the city of my birth a day or two later.

When I left the country, they would drive me to the airport to catch my flight to Singapore, where I would be met by Bosco and Alice as well as Ping. They were all hard-working wage-earners, but they would drop everything. Of course the same devotion might be shown in the West — the record is full of accounts of English spinsters who sacrificed their entire lives looking after their mothers, for example — but the point is that here, love aside, it was taken for granted.

The boys showered me with solicitous advice on everything from buying a second-hand car to the latest dubious cure for arthritis. I dared not express my dearest wash for they might at once rush out and buy me a bottle or even a case, and then refuse payment. But at the root of this behaviour lay a fundamental difference between us: for the Chinese, the basic building block of society was the family; for an Englishman, it was the individual. And that did not always make for a smooth relationship. Thoughtful as always, one or other of my daughters-in-law would arrive unannounced at our house with something they thought I ought to have, irrespective of whether I wanted it or not. Jealous of my freedom to make my own choices and run my own life,

I might resent it, and that could sometimes lead to a ridiculous misunderstanding.

When Alice brought along a S3,000 queen-size ionising mattress and dumped it on our double bed one evening without even phoning to say she was coining, my sense of privacy was outraged. What did she mean by thrusting it on me, by this peremptory interference with my life? Who said I wanted to sleep on the thing? Had I asked her to buy it? Did she expect me to pay for it? I would decide if I needed one myself in my own good time, thank you very much, etc, etc. It was only afterwards that I discovered that I was not expected to pay for it (a key factor, of course), that it was her own, that out of the goodness of her heart (and Bosco's) she was lending it to us because Ping was tired and unwell and she thought it might do her some good; not only that, but if it seemed to do us good, the boys and their wives planned to club together to buy us one as a present. 'It's nothing,' said Alice. 'We're all one family, aren't we?' As usual, I was sorry too late. One always is, of course.

When I turned 80, the family insisted on organising an elaborate thrash in a private room in a smart downtown club for me, and I was driven to it screaming and kicking despite all my quite genuine protestations that I only wanted a quiet evening with Ping. 'You do not understand; you have to accept,' Ping said. And it turned out to be a terrific party. When the exchequer ran thin after I resigned from the *Observer*, Dominic led the boys in a plea to allow them to contribute to our income every month — the most natural thing in the world in a good Chinese family — and although neither Bosco nor John was flush at the time, they readily chipped in. In my ignorance I protested to Ping that we could not take this, we weren't broke yet, but she replied flatly, 'You cannot refuse.' Our role was to take, never to say no. I finally slipped out of the arrangement when we sold Windsor

Park to buy our Faber Garden townhouse, and I could persuade them that the profit on the deal meant we were no longer on the verge of starvation.

But of course obligations cut both ways, and if they would do anything for me, it was naturally incumbent on me to do anything for them. It was not always easy for someone accustomed to Anglo-Saxon niceties. Could I arrange a small private dinner at my home at which Dominic, now a trader, could meet Dr Goh Keng Swee, then Deputy Prime Minister, to talk about doing business in China? We-ell. Could I ask the Minister for Foreign Affairs to find out why Bosco's security clearance (he was joining the Singapore Civil Service) was taking so long? Ye-es.

But then the day came when Alice asked me to ask the British High Commissioner in Singapore to give a 'friend' of hers whom I did not even know a quick visa to Britain ahead of the queue — she needed it tomorrow, not next week. Alice would do anything for me at the drop of a hint, and naturally thought that I could take advantage of this connection to fix it for her with a phone call. I was suddenly caught between English and Chinese custom, and I will not forget her blank look of total incomprehension when I said no.

19

ALICE with her twelve years in England, her training at Westminster Hospital, her one year of research at Charing Cross Hospital, Fellow of the Institute of Medical Laboratory Sciences, assistant head of laboratory at Brook Hospital in Woolwich, then director of laboratory at the American Hospital in Singapore; Alice, with her excellent English and her sweet rendering of 'The Last Rose of Summer', who married Bosco at Sidcup in Kent. Our Alice. I had forgotten that she was also Alice the Chaozhou from Hong Kong, raised on very different traditions and values from mine, and therefore after 25 years we could still suddenly find ourselves strangers staring at each other in disbelief. It was natural enough. People must always see each other through their own blinker-visioned eyes — who else's? — and in consequence get a distorted picture. An American's subjective image of the Chinese and a Chinese' subjective image of the Americans might well leave both of them wondering who the hell the other was talking about.

When I married Ping in 1957, what was my image of the people I was marrying into, and had it got anything to do with the real Chinese? I had first been to China in 1955, and was to go again in 1958 during the Great Leap Forward. I was enchanted. What a field for clichés! The Chinese were like blue ants, all dressed alike in unisex 'Mao suits', all beginning every sentence with the words 'Thanks-to-Chairman-Mao-and-the-Chinese-Communist Party' (we have more food, better housing, secure jobs, medical services, free schools, flush toilets, etc, etc), rattled off piously as a priest pronounces a routine benediction. Wherever you went the cadres would tell the same tales of their new paradise in precisely the same words, like mindless clones of each other who had memorised their texts in the best Chinese tradition, so that you felt you were travelling through the country only for the change of scenery. They seemed solely interested in work and political meetings, not in food, and scoffed down their bowl of rice at midday in minutes before dashing off to some Mao study session at which they echoed each other, sang choruses in praise of the Chairman, and no voice was raised in dissent.

The peasants and workers were all happy, they said, and to prove it were full of horror stories about the bad old days before Mao had come to save them. Cadres were scrupulously honest. They refused all tips as if money really was filthy lucre, and accepted no gifts. You could not even throw anything away. If you left a clapped-out pair of old slippers behind in your hotel room before travelling — say, from Beijing to Xian — they would inevitably catch up with you at the other end just when you were congratulating yourself on having finally got rid of them.

During the Great Leap Forward men and women without exception vied with one another to make more and more plastics or tractors or steel or grow more and more grain, overworking themselves and their machines and the soil to a point of exhaustion, concerned only with doubling and trebling their production figures for the greater good of Mao's China. In short, they were diligent, frugal, dedicated, obedient, meticulously law-abiding, selflessly committed to the service of the state without thought of personal gain, a society from which greed and crime had been banished.

This was the China and these were the Chinese as they appeared to any alien eye privileged to observe them at that time, and distinguished foreign academicians taken on guided tours of the country duly waxed ecstatic about them. But they were waxing ecstatic about a painted veil behind which were failed crops and fudged production figures, dissatisfied peasants and discontented workers playing their parts in the communist charade simply in order to survive. Certainly there was a minority of loyal Party idealists, but — the average Chinese? Dedicated to the socialist state? Meticulously law-abiding? Selfless and without greed? Disdainful of money? Uninterested in food? After Mao died, the iron vice that held the masses so uncomfortably in its grip slowly melted, China shook itself free of its gyves, and almost at once the more enterprising threw themselves into an orgy of cutthroat competition, bribery and graft, nepotism and corruption, whose laudable object was all too frequently to cheat the government in order to enhance the fortunes of the family.

The principle had venerable origins. The Duke of She said to Confucius,

'With us if a father steals a sheep, an upright son will testify against him.' Confucius retorted, 'With us the son shields his father, and the father shields the son. We see this as upright conduct.' The Chinese chose to take this to justify their basic attitude to society. The family came first and the law and the state nowhere. By extension, therefore, an upright man was one who robbed the state to enrich his relatives, and when he was an official gave them plum jobs in the administration, if necessary creating sinecures for them even when they were halfwits.

Why did Confucius speak as he did? He lived in an era dominated by vicious feuding overlords from rival families who devoted much of their time to murdering each other in vile circumstances. They also treated the ordinary people as disposable tissue, to be overtaxed, stripped any time of their property, and conscripted at the slightest whim as cannon fodder before there were cannons, or forced labour, or ephemeral concubines, according to sex, and then to be discarded once they had outlived their usage or abusage. If the son did denounce his father for stealing a sheep, the poor old man might have his hands and feet lopped off, his nose violently removed along with his testicles, or his legs and arms systematically broken. For more serious crimes he would be banished or executed. Flogging was the mildest of punishments. For aristocrats and farmers alike, therefore, family solidarity was the key to survival at a time when the law was a law unto itself.

A thousand years passed, and then another thousand, but although the laws improved, the tradition was set, and man remained man. Cases were supposed to be decided strictly on their merits, but mandarins were often corrupt and cruel. Litigants were reluctant to seek redress in the courts, notably because both culprit and victim could be punished impartially for disturbing the peace, irrespective of the rights and wrongs of the matter (an equitable practice that in many instances might save the judiciary a great deal of time today). The consequence was that rather than go to the local magistrate, disputing parties left it to the village elders to decide matters between them. The village, like the family, was the honest man's defence against the law — 'the emperor's writ stops at the village gate', it was said.

The attitude towards authority was one of deep distrust. 'Do not fear ghosts, but government,' said Xunzi in his usual cynical vein. The legal system was never fully developed, and was finally dismantled during Mao's Cultural Revolution when most of the judges and lawyers were sent away to do hard labour for their sins. This was understandably a popular move in many quarters in China and might appeal to many in the West today as a move in the right direction, but it left the country almost bereft of a judiciary.

Few cared. China, it has been said (sometimes with pride) is not subject to the rule of Law, but the rule of Man. It is a humanistic society, in which people are more concerned with justice and fairness, and one important aspect of it is *guanxi*, over which Alice and I came to a dead stop — and no wonder since, significantly, there is no precise English translation for the word. Confucius said 'a gentleman wanting to be successful himself, helps others to be successful', and that is the basic principle of *guanxi*, the system of connections and reciprocal favours and mutual backscratching whereby Chinese give each other a hand to get one ahead, sidestepping the law legitimately where it is in the way. With my prudish English conscience, I questioned this last with Ping and was firmly put in my place.

Of course must never actually break the law, do something bad, but who want to bother with it if not necessary, waste so much time, fill in so many form? How many times we get friendly contractor to make changes to our house without applying for licence, build car port, covered terrace, roof over airwell? Guanxi *is good thing as long as private, doesn't hurt the people, not used to get forbidden drugs, or maybe guns to sell to enemy. This is society of human relations. We all help each other.*

Alice naturally believe British High Commissioner can fix visa for old friend because he also your old friend. Is small thing. Where the harm? You try to remember how much my guanxi and guanxi of friends help you as foreign correspondent. In Taiwan you can meet Vice-President Chen Chen because know my brother. You meet Tsao Chu-ren in Hong Kong when he is secretly agent trying to arrange deal between communist leaders and the KMT. You meet secret society chief running gambling den in Kowloon, and old General Zhang

Fagui who always refuse see anybody from newspapers but respect my father, and Red Guards in Hong Kong when the Cultural Revolution, and Malayan Minister of Finance who trusts you because related to my family in China. Even how you get your job with Observer? *Because have friend who is friend of the Editor, David Astor. That is* guanxi. *How can otherwise? The life much easier. You did not bribe him. The Chinese the same. If you suggested bribing someone in China for a recommendation, my father kill you.*

I stood corrected. Sometimes *guanxi* is not a question of personal connections, but of no more than a letter of introduction. For example, we did not know Tsao Chu-ren. We came to him in 1961 with a note from a Chinese friend in Singapore. We had hesitated to telephone him, but Ping admired his writings, so we did — and when we met him were surprised by the warm reception he gave us.

Tsao was a prominent left-wing journalist and happened during the fighting against the Japanese he had been correspondent for New China News Agency and lived in Ganzhou Diqu where Chiang Ching-kuo, the eldest son of Chiang Kai-shek, was introducing a new political system. Ching-kuo asked Tsao to start a new daily paper for him, show he was building a model society. Ching-kuo was KMT, of course, but also inclined to left because just back from study in Moscow. They soon on very good terms. But Tsao also had high-level contacts in Beijing. So later this became foundation for secret contacts between Beijing and Taiwan for arrange the future, with Tsao as intermediary, even neither side trust him completely.

We were astonish Tsao ask us for breakfast at his home in Hong Kong and show lavish hospitality to us, cook all the food himself, including many delicacy dishes D never tasted. Meanwhile he spoke eloquently about secret peace discussions between Beijing and Taiwan, marvellous material for D to write for Observer. *But I felt doubts and suspicious. Wiry he take so much trouble with us? Was he making use of D to spread out his own ideas into international propaganda? Was it all true?*

After checking the story with high-powered sources of Ping in Taiwan, I was reasonably convinced it was, and wrote it. To my astonishment the *Observer* made it the front page lead although the sensational news that weekend was that Yuri Gagarin had circled the earth in a Soviet satellite, becoming the first man to travel in space. My story drew a great deal of flak from the western press and from American Chinawatchers, as a scoop that contradicts everyone else's received opinion usually will. Were they right? Had I been sold a stumer? It was not until 1998 that I knew the answer.

In 1998 Tsao's daughter published his memoirs in the press. There was no doubt they tell the truth. She gave the full details of how her father had accepted the assignment as a secret emissary by Mao Zedong personal order about the years 1960, including exact dates and place where he met Mao and also Zhou Enlai. So his story correct, even if China and Taiwan still enemies. But question still remain: did Tsao make use of D while D made use of Tsao? Only God knew it.

At its best *guanxi* may be an 'old boy' network of neighbours, of schoolmates, army comrades, members of the same club, including friends in official positions (like the British High Commissioner), as Ping said. Or it may bring perfect strangers together but put neither side under an obligation to the other, as in the case of Tsao Chu-ren and myself. But more often than not it is a coldblooded system of mutual exploitation, of exchanges of favours among useful 'contacts', and sentiment does not come into it despite all the backslapping. Favours are strictly reciprocal, and if one Chinese does a service for another, it is on the clear understanding that the other must repay it when the debt is called in. Hand washes hand. It is simply a matter of moral bookkeeping.

Mr Li in Shanghai asks his contact Mr Chang, a senior cadre in Beijing, for an introduction to his minister. Mr Chang complies, and is duly rewarded for this service with an expensive 'gift', which in China does not count as a bribe. Now they are all square. (No cash passes hands — we are all gentlemen here.) Having successfully made the minister's acquaintance, Mr Li then invites him to be guest of honour at a big banquet in a restaurant widely known for its fiendish prices but at which the most luscious delicacies are served. The minister accepts, and is sedulously flattered in the course of the evening. 'You deserve it,' he is told, which when decoded means 'we expect a return'. A week or a month later Mr Li claims his quid pro quo by asking His Excellency to write a 'letter of recommendation' for his son to take up a lucrative post in the Customs Service. Betrayed by his salivary glands, the minister has fallen into the *guanxi* trap. There is no such thing as a free lunch.

In this way the unscrupulous may make use of their contacts — and contacts of their contacts in official circles — to get a lucrative government contract, or a son exempted from military service, or a tax file quietly lost, or a case squashed in the courts, or a massive allocation of a metal in short supply from government stocks. The country is meanwhile full of millions of underpaid cadres ready to make an 'investment' by conniving with an upright son who wants them to allocate a flat in town to his father, or a place in a local school for a younger brother, in return for a 'dividend'. Thus the 'rule of Man' ends up by meaning the rule of influence — and so of cronyism, corruption and nepotism. And no Chinese can escape it. He is not an individual, but part of the system. To stay outside it would be to court oblivion.

This was the China into which foreign investors took their

first hesitant steps in the eighties and nineties to participate in well-named 'joint ventures' with the waiting locals. They were welcomed by their Chinese counterparts who airily waved aside any question of signing tiresome contracts, especially as the legal system was so weak and cumbersome anyway, jovially insisting in the best traditions of *guanxi* that 'we are old friends, we trust each other and need not bother ourselves with small details', a wild assertion difficult to rebut without seeming insulting and risking the whole enterprise. If the foreign investors were mugs enough to work on the basis of this handshake, they would then find that since there was no legal agreement, the Chinese side could legitimately move the goalposts as they pleased.

Before they knew where they were (quite literally), they were being cheated left and right of their investments and their control over the company, and milked for additional 'unexpected' expenses and hidden costs, fees and permits and licences for extra land to be allocated, for water and power to be laid on, anything that could hold up the project if they did not pay. They would also find themselves robbed not only by small-time cadres exacting local toll, but by the men at the top — sometimes 'princelings', rich children of high-ranking Communist Party leaders — who had the wretched aliens in their clutches because when it came to the crunch only through them could they do business at all.

These are the two Chinas as the outsider has seen them in different decades. At one end is the admiring Western academic faced at every turn with disciplined, incorruptible Chinese cadres devoted to the service of the country. At the other is the cursing Western businessman who sees them as a gang of squeeze artists out to cheat the state and himself impartially, and who match the five materialistic Cs of Singapore with their own four Vs — villa, Visa card, vehicle, visits overseas. In his ignorance the foreigner naturally picks out what strikes him at the time or serves his prejudices. Is there an eternal China of the Chinese that embraces all the truths — observed with two eyes, as Ping puts it, and 'not seeing the leopard as a black spot'? Of course. Neither of these others is Ping's China. So then is what Ping picks out as striking in her 'Pingland' anything like my own familiar eternal England?

20

ONCE I am in England I realise it is most curious country in so many ways. For example actually need by law and order, the people obey the regulations, even will queue up when have no queue. Of course when I first go there in 1965 I admire the cathedrals and museums like American middle-aged lady with blue hair. But this is not guidebook. What fascinate me always are those small detail hit the Chinese eye.

For example newspaper seller wanting to go to loo can leave pile of newspapers on street corner and people just take one copy and leave money for it. In Singapore very dangerous. Even man in Mercedes-Benz may stop car and take bunch of them, because something for nothing. So now I begin to understand D fed up with unsocial uncaring behaviour of some local people in our condominium, breaking the bylaws, making noise, letting dog bark day or night, or playing radio too loud, or holding wild late party, or dropping in without warning with two screaming kids.

Because England also quiet. And English house is stronghold. Nobody can walk in without reason. If want to visit friends, must fix in advance. I notice every door in London have different brass knocker, must knock before enter. All this does not mean cold and cheerless, but peaceful. At night London's residential district filled with deathly silence except traffic, even dog dare not bark.

But are we so far apart? Singapore condo may be very open and rowdy sometimes, but the brass door-knockers of London make me remember the quiet alleys in old city of Beijing, where high wall each side shut out all sound, and every house have big vermilion doors with harmonious brass knocker to wake up the doorkeeper. Behind was screen door, protect the peaceful life, then the courtyard with tree where family and friends chat quietly, cool and carefree in the evening. Outside, the alley looked deserted, no traffic, just sometimes cry of pedlar of noodles or hot chestnuts. London and Beijing quite different but got similar noble custom from ancient time for life of tranquillity, make me quite homesick.

I been in America and Canada, in fact have family there. Such a great country. I especially love Niagara Falls, and also especially in Canadian homes wonderful welcoming friendly bathrooms, which mean lot to me because to tell truth I have a shy bottom. Americans have warm hearty manner, easily invite new friends into home for a meal although just meeting for first time. But always in hurry. Halfway through eating the host will start to look at his watch time from time, make guest feel most uncomfortable.

British not like that, and at first seem frigid. Not keen to make friends quickly but once they do, friendship very profound. British, like Chinese, faithful to friends and always be sincere with each other. Once invite you to their home means do everything to make you comfortable, not count the time. When we spend weekend with David Astor, D's Editor, in big, beautiful house on River Thames, he and his wife Bridget do everything for us, and Sunday morning even maid came into the bedroom and serve us perfect breakfast in bed — Oh Heaven, marvellous unforgettable feeling, no one do such thing for me before in my life! But British also polite to strangers, take courtesy seriously, strictly observe etiquette even to someone they hate, therefore of course people admire but say damn hypocrites.

When I go to England 33 years later not much change. I was only there four days, so can only give few impressions of things that strike me. Like for example where are the English? Although I come from multiracial society, huge variety of life with different races of people in London streets make me gasp. Those oriental, including Chinese, Japanese, Korean, Vietnamese, Burmese, could be seen everywhere, and particularly the young people of East and West joy fully together, hand in hand or the man putting his arm around girl's waist and hold her closely giggling even on public street, and Africans male and female in fashionable bright coloured robes walking like a moving flag for their country. Seemed there was no trouble at all, and beautiful city of London make all guests feel at home.

In Piccadilly near the bus stop there was coffeeshop with few small tables on the pavement for pedestrians to take rest or waiting for bus or friend. On cloudy morning, London air heavy, we sat down, D ordered coffee, I a cup of tea, just leisurely and comfortable to watch the people go by. There was a Frenchwoman stood by the door with most charming accent, her facial expression like movie star, with man beside her in excited mood, both shouting with hands, arms, feet and bodies dancing. Two Germans sat next of them, looking angry, as if could not bear the French behave so lively and casual, thinking they had no discipline. And next of the Germans two Vietnamese ordered two cups of coffee; the coffee came quickly and very hot, so when they swallowed it so recklessly their mouths must be badly burned. And next... But there was only one Englishman, who also ordered coffee but let it cool as he quietly read newspaper.

So many different people with different race characters, all talking different languages, each curious, making the society richer! They were like animals make love different ways, orioles sing beautiful songs, crickets chant together, cats give horrible yell. To me all this barbarian life strange and interesting. But the Englishman reading his paper seemed quite at home among the alien voices, and Dennis regarded them serenely and without concern, for this his native town, he was part of its 2,000-year-old traditions which formed him and were not to change for bunch foreigners.

Also imperturbable was a London policeman in standard uniform walking on the pavement and watching the crowd, a big, handsome young chap bravely shouldering his responsibilities among all this medley of races without a gun. People respect these unarmed police, and when in trouble come and complain to them, or ask them solve their problem, and they always ready to help. (Except in one case; they never interfere in quarrelling between man and wife. How clever this custom!)

The English are confident people, because no really poor. I asked Dennis show me poor people once, and he showed me dirty old slum. But those people still affluent compared wretched poor of China. Not even starving. That is because also well looked after by welfare. When a baby born, the government immediately supply free milk. All children enjoy free high school education and even free lunch, and if their academic record excellent also will get scholarship. The English seem to take the young much more seriously than the old. In London, unlike Hong Kong or Singapore, you could not find a teenage boy in street to clean shoes; this job already taken by old men, which according Chinese tradition shows strong lack of respect.

When grow up and starting work, government supplies industrial insurance and all kinds of worker enjoy many holidays. Jobless get help with unemployment pay because do no work, and the public health service looks after everyone even not sick. Any retired person has a pension, and so all provided for. So sons and daughters need not worry about parents' living expenses, but only pay attention to inherit legacy from them. Many of the younger generation after married only once in a while or for festival invite parents to their home for short period. For Chinese all this appear very strange lack of filial piety.

But senior citizens with their pensions always got their dignity and show independent spirit. Therefore you might see them strolling along the street alone, or go to the park or Trafalgar Square to feed pigeons. Pigeons also well looked after. They all overfed by people, getting fat like hen, could hardly fly any more, only sway their body from side to side to closely follow their benefactor. It surprise me to see birds and human beings actually got on very well together. That is because not fattened for the pot. This seems very extraordinary, especially to a Cantonese — it is said even if an alien from outer space came to China, Shanghai people would dissect it for medical research, Beijing people would put it in a museum for education, but Cantonese would cook it with a special dark sauce.

Chinese and English very different in this way. Any Chinese going abroad, doesn't matter where, always homesick for own food, and Singaporeans never forget fish ball, kuey teow, and Hainanese chicken rice, always eat in Chinese restaurants. If have to eat only English food all the time by chance, definitely must lose appetite because the taste too indifferent. Normally every meal starts off with soup, and whether it be onion soup, tomato soup, vegetable soup or whatnot, the soup always the same. Then potatoes usually fried or boiled, or after boil mashed, the vegetables also boiled, absolutely no flavour. Then meat cut into big pieces, the beef reserving some blood after cooked, the mutton still stinking. Always English cooking was monotony.

But breakfast was exception, because rich and practical, including tea, coffee, bread, butter, marmalade, egg, bacon, sausage, beans, porridge — delicious! Only I am against the smell of kipper, but have to accept because I also eat raw onion with sardines for breakfast and D cannot bear. However in general when in London I found best way is to eat Italian food. The dishes with lots herbs smell familiar and nice, and although the noodles changed the name to spaghetti, I still liked it. Did Marco Polo really learn Chinese cooking skills in Beijing, I wondered?

According common saying 'you are what you eat'. Recently Singapore students ate too much McDonald hamburger, deep-fried chicken and ice cream, high percentage of them now evidently overweight, and government seriously ask headmasters to help to reduce it. Likewise English women ate too much butter, potato, cake, pudding, chocolate, means inescapable fate is to get plump waist. Men also addicted to drinking beer and when reach middle-age all became fat. But I enjoy English pubs. Even when cold outside, inside the pub very warm, full of laughing, joking. The men after drink beer, gin, vodka, whisky always forgot the reserved manner, full of witty remarks and humour. It was very popular for male and female went in together, and no need to pay tip.

Wandering through the centre of London we reached Trafalgar Square where we saw one exceptionally energetic pigeon sitting on Nelson's hat. The square is dominated by Nelson's Column and Landseer's lions. At the base of the column were four bronze reliefs cast from captured French cannons, showing scenes of naval battles that made Nelson a national hero. Also four lions facing to different directions. It is very impressive, except that every national culture has own taboos, and Chinese believe stone lions must always face south, because for them to see the sun go down means bad luck. How the Landseer lions felt, I wonder?

When I looked around the square, there was something quite unexpected. The buildings were constructed in a curved line, seeming to enclose the traffic circle. The cars and buses emerged from one street concealed by one imposing block and after roaring around the Nelson's Column disappeared down another street concealed by another block. As I heard the sound of water from the spouting fountains around the column, I had a momentary illusion I was standing on the edge of a river, watching them pouring into the square on a swift current, then circling around in the eddy and suddenly vanishing downstream.

But London is full of circles and circuses and crescents. Ridiculous, I said to Dennis, so many of your streets winding everywhere. How could you build such a vital road system for urban traffic like a snake? 'The rolling English drunkard made the rolling English road,' he quoted to me, sounding very pleased with himself. I know alcohol is most important thing in English life, but a Chinese had also made a remark that a 'rolling mind' meant intelligence and wisdom. Were the English naturally clever or did all the whisky act on the brain, I asked in joke. 'Naturally clever,' he replied with a grin. And after 42 years of guerrilla war with him I believe it.

Hard to imagine the English can build a city in straight lines, like New York. Even the centre of London seems to be constructed around its big parks with their winding paths and wild trees that make the heavy traffic go around them, not straight through. Once you enter them you forget the noise and the bustle of city, and enjoy the birds singing and the greenery — larch, fir, hawthorn, elm, conifer, oak, godknowwhat — the high old trees reaching for the sky, protected through the centuries. You had a good feeling of carefree and peace. There is fourteen times as much green space in London for each person as there is in Tokyo.

In England when the rain permeates the soil, the chalk underneath keeps the water remain there, so will always be moist. Therefore the trees stand upright and graceful, look like immensely big bonsais made by nature. So no matter where you go, the chalk created a marvellous scenery. And that include a huge white horse I saw carved into the hillside near Newbury, magnificent, imposing, and with a serious attitude. It is 374 feet long, and D explained that according tradition it was cut out from the chalk soil to celebrate victory of King Alfred the Great of England in AD 878 over the Danes — pirates in long boats who wore headdress with two ox horns. I did not realise so old. I had thought it must be advertisement for White Horse whisky, which a great favourite among rolling English drunkards.

Chinese gardens and parks must include fish pool fully planted with water lily, a little bridge crossed over it, man-made mountain surrounded by cypress trees and pine forest, a serene pavilion and winding corridors and green bamboo set among colourful flowers adding to the beauty of the artificial landscape. But parks in London not like that; the natural life which is the way the English like it means the scene pure and simple, only trees and a boundless stretch of grassland. It came to me the Chinese garden is for the visitor to go sightseeing, but the English parks are for the English people to rest and relax.

I realised this when I sat on a bench in St James's Park, watching the thousand trees wave in the wind; the weeping willows had lost half of their leaves, and those that still clung to them wiggled like fish caught on the end of a line, dangling over the ducks in the lake. It was a magic moment. Who cared Buckingham Palace at one end and Whitehall at the other?

Sunshine is a rare treasure for the English. When no actual rain, it is 'good weather', and if they see the sun they are delighted and shout 'lovely day' to everyone. I went into one of the parks one bright blue morning when the sky cloudless and the sun shining yellow, and the fine grass looked like a carpet. I was astonished. There was a nip in the air, but there were huge crowds of people. They put blankets on the grass, and sat there chatting and laughing, playing with the children, flying kites, lying on their backs staring at the sun, their hands behind their heads, listening to music, or reading in deck chairs, one young man stripping to the waist to sunbathe, while a married couple passed me pushing a pram with a baby inside, boys and girls happy and temperamentally compatible on the wide expanse of green on that gay and sunny morning.

And some people just walking. English people seem extremely keen on walking. This is said to be due to too much rain, so that they walk quickly and with all strength when they can, and the women all born with a big pair feet, their shoes similar to men's. The famous Chinese author Lin Yu Tang said, 'The most beautiful thing in London is to watch the women wearing low-heel shoes walking through the mist.'

I remembered a friend had told me 'the English grow up in a park'. Now I saw the true situation: the foreigners were all in the streets; the English were all in the parks.

These parks are the true heart of London. In Hyde Park there was the famous 'Speakers' Corner' where people could stand on a soapbox to speak their mind, no matter if communists or conservative, or complain badly about government, all side by side. It remind me of a Chinese market or fair where rival peddlers selling their medicines all made their pitch near to each other, all boasting of their own cures as the most efficacious. But in Hyde Park they were peddling rival political ideas, gathering there to air their beliefs. The English found all this quite natural, but through a foreigner's eye it seemed only after few hundred years of political experience could this happen, and that here in the park was the soul of British freedom and democracy.

But not just like that, of course. All great buildings and streets of London remind me of long, slow history, because never change, remain the same as when I was here 33 years before. Singapore was oriental town when I first arrived and now torn down and replaced with collection glass boxes and towers like any modern city in the world. But not London. And certainly not Oxford, where we spent one of our four days with D's cousin Valerie and her husband Michael, who both studied there.

Oxford is the oldest university in England since before the year 1200, but still kept worldwide reputation for scholarship as a place where most students dream to go. The style and air of Oxford was fragrant with ancient civilisation, and for example the main bookshop was dignified place where staff and buyers both full of the spirit of books, not sordid merchant's attitude. The university had always been a noble institution of higher learning, where students wore quiet dress, put on black gowns to attend lectures, and stayed in the beautiful precincts of colleges where they could absorb real values in an atmosphere of silence and study. (Not like Berkeley

California where I felt I should be dressed like hippy, but that had its own charm.)

I felt at home here. Over a stone archway in the grounds of New College was the inscription of the founder William of Wykeham, 'Manners Makyth Man'. 'Cannot be more Confucian,' I cried, and insisted to take a photo there with both of us. As we walked through the calm and quiet quadrangles and cloisters and visited the Hall and Chapel and gardens of the college, I listened carefully to Valerie's eager answers to my questions. But I was going mad with the beauty of it all.

A young man sitting absolutely still wrapped up in his studies in a sunny courtyard flanked by centuries-old buildings caught my eye. I thought of the many outstanding figures Oxford had bred over so many hundreds of years in this scholarly atmosphere, and whose excellence had contributed in turn to the great prestige of the university. But when I entered the chapels of old colleges dated back to a Catholic England, the soft sunlight through the multicoloured glass windows creating a cool and solemn air, I wondered why so much learning in institutions like this across Europe had led to the folly of a church divided after all those years over whether communion wine was truly the blood of Christ or only a symbol of it. Why the people hate each other so much and fight when Christ said must love each other and even enemies? D said now Catholic and Protestant coexist, even try to get closer, like Communist China and 'democratic' Taiwan. I suddenly remembered Deng Xiaoping had stayed in France long time when young. Had this religious coexistence given him the famous idea of the 'One Country Two Systems' formula for their eventual reunion? D laughed at me. Sometimes my mind flying away too much.

The thought of lunch bring me down to earth. We ate in a small restaurant on the river bank where they also let out boats lying along the shore outside. The river is extremely popular because rowing is the classical outdoor sport of Oxford. But these were flat-bottomed punts propelled with a long pole and remind me at once of ferry boat crossing a river in China which can see in so many Chinese mountain-and-water landscape painting. We hired one of them, and while we relaxed on comfortable cushions, Michael poled us up the shallow waters. The banks of the river thick with bushes and trees whose cold grey branches curved this way and that, sometimes alarm us by leaping outwards at us very low over the water like a kind of reptilian life so that Michael nearly had to prostrate himself to guide the boat underneath.

These boats can be very unsteady, but when Valerie took over the long pole and brought the boat forward, gliding smoothly on the surface in more open water, she stood very straight in the stern, looking exactly like a statue made of bronze, everything absolutely still, only a pair hanging earrings dancing in the breeze beside her face. There were other boats floating up and down leisurely and carefree, and along the bank where the trees leaned to the broken images in the water one of them had stopped in the shadow, two young lovers in it talking in murmurs. The scene very romantic. Brimming with youth generation after generation, this had been a river of love throughout all time, I daydreamed. Everybody knew the Oxford colleges had given the country many great historic figures, including 25 prime ministers, but the river may have give it ten thousand happy unions nobody speaks of.

Would the English think all these idle thoughts of mine frivolous? They could show a solemn face. Standing next to the Houses of Parliament, the clock tower known as 'Big Ben' was built some 150 years ago, the bell inside thirteen-and-a-half tons. That made the chimes so magnificent, so heavy, so beautiful, so serious, and we used to hear them on BBC radio in China, throughout the world, so that one felt as an old friend. 'Ben' in Chinese means stupid, foolish and clumsy. But the Taoist philosopher Laozi said 'a man of great wisdom often appears slow-witted'. When I thought of that, I could see 'Ben' and his solemn chimes might truly represent these enigmatic people.

Because the English not always too easy to understand. For example I naturally imagined the Prime Minister's office and residence at famous Number Ten Downing Street would be another imposing monument to the days of Empire. But if I had not seen a policeman standing outside it when I passed by, I would almost think it was the door of just an ordinary house. How can? These people certainly appeared to know to keep their political leaders in their place, I thought. An English joke? Maybe not. Maybe just by chance. But if I seem suspicious, not surprising. It is to remember I been living more than 42 years not only with the English mind, but with so-called English sense of humour.

21

FORTY-TWO years — forty-four since I walked down rue Catinat in Saigon on that fateful July day. A long time. And the more years that pass with Ping, the more I cringe at the thought that I might have ignored Benny Chau's invitation to stop for a beer and simply walked on to my hotel, losing her forever before I even knew her. Since then so much else has disappeared downstream. Evocative 'Saigon' has long since gone, transmogrified into banal 'Ho Chi Minh City', so has the twice-renamed 'rue Catinat', so has 'Peking', the city of bicycle bells, replaced by 'Beijing', where three million boneshakers are rusting on the scrap heap as the streets fill with honking cars and taxis. Colonial Singapore has become 'Singapore', Europe 'Europe', and the Soviet Union has exploded into fragments. There is no more ominous sound than that of a ticking clock when it has no explosive wired to it.

Have we changed, too — changed each other?

I say 'good morning', Ping still says 'yes', and we sit down at the breakfast table every day, Ping with her fish porridge or sardines and raw onion, myself with Patum Peperium, 'Gentleman's Relish', the anchovy paste that is the mark of the unrepentant Englishman abroad, patented 1828 and a symbol of Empire. The scene is symbolic. For unlike some English-educated Singaporeans, we do not appear to have stirred our two cultures into a uniform mix

— 'English in the head, Chinese in the heart', as someone put it.

I struggle to imitate Ping's calm and her tolerance of human failings as an inevitable part of existence, her Confucian magnanimity against my Christian censoriousness. But then just the other day I fell by the wayside when I caught a middle-aged Chinese woman letting a small white dog run around free in the condominium. 'Why isn't that dog on a lead?' I asked sharply before I could think — the knee-jerk reflex. 'He's only a puppy and he doesn't bite,' the woman replied mildly, 'and if he makes a mess I've got a paper bag to pick it up with.' 'That's not the point,' I said, 'you are not allowed to let dogs loose in Singapore; don't you know it's against the *law*?' 'Oh, law,' she said with a sigh. 'No wonder everyone complains so much ...' Was I never going to learn?

And if I remain myself, Ping remains ineluctably Ping. 'You are interfering barbarian again,' she shoots at me after a short, pregnant silence as the woman wanders off. 'Just a small dog; she calls, he comes; where the harm? Have to accept. Not your business. You are not police.' She is as decisive as ever once she makes a moral judgement, and has never acquired from me the tiresome habit of playing for time by beginning a sentence with 'err', 'urn' or 'well', or using the evasive cop-out 'on this hand, on the other hand'. It comes straight from the shoulder as it always has — *'Do* it.'

She still dresses carefully when visiting a house for the first time, putting to shame the fading seersucker jacket I have reluctantly shrugged on over my T-shirt, and always pre-empts her debt to her hostess by bringing her flowers specially arranged in the market for her. And she remains forever modest in her demands — defeated by the intractable problem of what to give her for a present on her birthday or at Christmas, I now solve it by throwing money at it for her to spend on something 'appropriate'.

She is Confucian to the last.

And Taoist. She remains a health nut, and throws perfectly clean towels into the laundry basket if she finds them lying about — 'never mind, otherwise get some smell,' she says with her own irrefutable logic if I protest. She plays tennis, does a weekly workout at the condominium gym, and as my Chinese herbal doctor becomes ever more imaginative with age — her latest cure for a cough is a repellent concoction based on a creature of dubious provenance that is a worm in winter but seemingly turns into a kind of grass in summer — and looks it. God knows what it was in October when I first tried it. But I must admit that it did no detectable harm. I just went on coughing.

She also grows her own aloes now to rub into my scalp and her own, swearing that they are revitalising, and when through overuse they started to stain my white hair and her black locks a uniform orange, pointed out triumphantly that it made us more alike. The hazards are endless. Yesterday she approached me with a pot of cream and announced that my skin was too dry and she was going to 'fertilise my face' every day. We settled for once a week only. More acceptable is her new prescription for strengthening the legs and relieving arthritis, which consists of a daily ration of ten sultanas soaked in gin. Life does have its compensations occasionally, after all. And I'm still here.

And she remains single-minded, whether concentrating on tennis, gardening, her piano, her English, or my ailments. These days, in consequence, we live the simple life she has always believed in. We do not go out much, we hardly ever see anyone, we are not concerned with the woes of the world, and we do not allow ourselves to be distracted by anything less than a car bomb. The house is clean, but odd things lie about absentmindedly for days, even weeks — a pair of garden shears and a roll of scotch tape on the dining room table, a pile of ageing Chinese newspapers on the sofa. The reason for all that? Ping is wholly absorbed in writing this book and forgets all else.

I get up in the morning to find her already dressed and at her desk, and when I switch off the TV with a sigh of relief at around ten-thirty in the evening she is still there as if glued to the chair. She stops reluctantly for meals, but sits at the table staring wordlessly into the middle distance, her thoughts far away on my early iniquities or other fond memories of times past, the silence punctuated only by a sudden trick question, 'What do you call someone who feeds pigeons — a pigeon-feeder?' Or 'Has England always had kings and queens, like poker?' She is still handicapped by a tendency to say things like 'Now we tea', 'I cannot ready in time', 'We dinner seven', 'You so polite, why?', 'That is I enjoy my room writing'. But it does not faze either of us any more.

The last is in any case the key to her life now. This is the best of times for her, for she has always wanted to write, to express herself, to tell the world. The last time she felt quite like this was when she worked for Radio and Television Singapore and was let loose with a daily programme of her own to say just what she chose to up to a million or more Chinese.

And she remains the happy pessimist who gets the best out of life by expecting the worst. She can enjoy the sun all the more if it comes through after she has gloomily predicted rain, and conversely gives me an I-told-you-so grin when we reach the city in record time by driving down old roads, after she has insisted against all my objections that the new expressway will have seized up with heavy traffic. And she naturally thinks that everyone else is as cynical as she is, except me. 'Don't leave money lying on the dressing table,' she says, 'of course I trust the maid hundred per cent, but she will think you trying to test her.'

Born into the *guanxi* tradition, she has faith only in tried friends, always looks for hidden motives, and — Timeo Danaos

— is particularly suspicious of strangers who come bearing gifts. When a Singapore philanthropist earned widespread praise and publicity by presenting a venerable $100,000 violin to the Singapore Symphony Orchestra after meeting most of the price, I said, 'I didn't know he was interested in music.' 'Mr Wee isn't interested in music,' she said limpidly, 'he's interested in Mr Wee.' All this with a total lack of malice. It is still simply part of her Chinese philosophy of survival in an untrustworthy world.

Her dire predictions are in the same category, but there was one unspoken presentiment she did not even recognise when it came to her. At a crowded cocktail party thrown by our lawyer in his Singapore bungalow she suddenly told me that she felt physically ill with depression, and left the house abruptly to sit by herself in the empty garden. What was wrong? I asked. She did not know. She was shivering, wanted to be left alone. But next day we learned that her old friend P.S. Raman had just collapsed in a Moscow subway station and died of a heart attack.

She had never worked for a non-Chinese until P.S. became her boss on Radio and Television Singapore, but — Confucian and Hindu intellectual — they had been like brother and sister, and it was a savage blow. He was one of those 'outsiders' whose friendship she had learned to treasure. She adored Piroska, who taught her all the tricks of the trade when mixing in polite western society, emerging from the experience, as I have said, with an eagle eye for my shortcomings — 'You are really coolie; why you eat the cake with your fingers when have pastry fork under your nose?' Her first meeting with Gritta Weil, the big-hearted former secretary of the *Observer* who always puts me up and spoils me when I go to England alone, was a case of love at first sight. She even became fond of all her in-laws, my uncles and aunts and cousins, without exception, which is something of a feat in any family. For while remaining essentially Ping, she has slipped comfortably into life with the barbarians and adopted their exotic habits, beginning with polishing brass.

When I first went to England I saw people in West polish copper and brass in the house very seriously, such as doorbell, lamp, even copper nail in the wall, if not will lose face. So when for present we got one big Indian brass jar three feet high, looked like genie inside it, I polished it so often for hours and hours, until I complained to D the work too hard for me. So D painted the jar with colourless lacquer to keep it shining forever, no need to polish. But in fact the jar still tarnish and we find cannot polish the lacquer. So year gone by, the genie jar darker and darker like old gold. But this seemed add some air of classic beauty to it in unique elegant taste, like our marriage getting old, and so no loss of face at all. D so clever even when doesn't know what he is doing.

Ping is now a stickler for custom at Christmas, insisting on all the trimmings from tree to turkey with cranberry sauce and mince pies with brandy butter. She drinks milk and eats most cheeses (double Gloucester, Brie, or Boursin *à l'ail et aux fines herbes* for preference) and raw oysters and smoked salmon, and says that, apart from all else, *prosciutto con melone* alone justifies Italy. She does not even blink at those Celtic delicacies, Welsh rarebit and Scotch eggs. And meanwhile she has allowed herself to be seduced by some of the more bizarre western superstitions.

When we are walking in the evening suddenly I saw a new moon rise up and can't help to shout 'Quick! Turn over coin.' D lifted his head to look, and in the same time release my hand and put his into his trouser's pocket. According English superstition, turn over coin when new moon appear can make a wish come true. So D's trouser pocket with the coin turning inside just like throwing it into Rome's fountain. I don't know why. (Nor does D.)

And I? Apart from incidents like my lapse over the little white dog, I seem to have succeeded in going some way towards meeting her, so that although I remain myself, she says I am more Chinese than many Chinese. I am told that when a farmer finds he has an obstreperous horse on his hands, he puts a quiet mare into the field alongside it, and she teaches it civilised behaviour. Perhaps it has been a little like that with us. I am now less explosive, more concerned with common sense than that ass, the law, and generally take things as they are.

I can read the horror stories of human silliness that pass for news in the *Straits Times* every day without muttering or shouting or screwing up the paper any more. If Shutup Charlie barks during the night, I presume he has his reasons. If the maid breaks a favourite glass, I say accidents will happen. I am entirely at home in a house full of Chinese pictures and ornaments, including arcane and apparently meaningless objects that are supposed to bring health and good luck. I no longer strive unnecessarily to improve the world, understanding that even if man invented a better mousetrap, it would only produce a smarter mouse. The turtle is at last wagging his tail in the mud.

One might think it is age — I am 80 as I write — but even the Chinese do not always relax when old. Deng Xiaoping jealously preserved his job as master of China and his love of power into his nineties, and so have other geriatric communist leaders. No, it is Ping, not age or China, that has influenced me, just as it is I, not England, that have influenced her. We have kept our separate identities, but acquired a part of each other, making it our own, as in the Taoist circle that symbolises Oneness — the white segment that represents *yang* has a black spot in the middle, and the black segment that represents *yin* has a white one.

Our differences are not in conflict, but complementary, just as they are in more mundane matters: her nose for property has balanced my nose for news in keeping both above water, and we find as we write this book that her feminine memory for detail matches my memory for the names she can never recollect — 'The man who bought our old car was called Eccles, but I can't recall anything else about him,' I may say. 'Oh, yes, of course, Eccles, thank you now remind me. Don't you remember? He had a racehorse with a white patch and he wore a wig. His wife ran away with a Brazilian diplomat, and he went to Africa to grow coffee. But it was no good.' We have even synchronised our walking.

D has long legs, and in old days when he walks as if on wings I have to run two gasping for breath with my small feet if want to keep up. But now we can stroll comfortably together in step. It is symbolic. I said 'you miss your joyful quick walk when I am not with you', but he answered 'walk slowly with you and Charlie is another kind of joy'. I recall when we were young, love was like fanatical burning sun. Now the mood like rosy clouds in evening sky. We have come out of intense emotion of past to go into the quiet life, live in peace with each other. Walking slowly hand in hand in silence after supper to enjoy the breeze and admire the night, I feel I drank glass wine and forget my small feet altogether.

We read each other's minds with unnerving frequency, we have similar tastes, and conspire when it comes to deciding how to rid ourselves of the hideous objects that people present us with from time to time. ('The downstairs loo for this one, I think.' 'Right.') The fact that we are from the same generation is more important now than the fact that we are from different ends of the earth, so that we hold the same views about modern manners and mayhem in a world in which spectacle sports include oral sex in high places (if that is not a contradiction in terms).

We like to discuss all sorts of affairs, because our ideas similar, but for same reason most of the time we are happy to be silent, due to we understand each other deeply, even without say one word.

So which is the barbarian now? There is none. Nor need there be anywhere between East and West. Contrary to the boasts of scholarly Chinese chauvinists, the same so-called 'Asian values' are to be found in England and the US as in China — thrift, loyalty, hard work, honesty and the rest of the cliches — and the ultimate teaching of all major religions is the same — 'be good'. Meanwhile the same vices are also to be found in the 'Confucian' East and the 'Christian' West. The Americans have no monopoly on 'greed is good'; it was this doctrine that inspired the profligate bank lending, the official corruption and quick-buck cronyism that contributed so heavily to the downfall of the South Korean and Japanese economies, among others, in 1997. The difference depends only on whether you heed the voice of the angel sitting on your right shoulder or the voice of the devil sitting on your left, not whether you come from this or that hemisphere.

But — to keep things in perspective — ours is a domestic drama about two individuals, not even about any Chinese woman married to any Anglo-Saxon man, but specifically Ping and myself. So as I wrote in the Preface, we hope it has something to say in the East-West context, but there is no suggestion that it can be projected onto a wider screen. It does not mean that with globalisation China and America will eventually come to resemble some heraldic beast with the head of an eagle and the tail of a dragon (or vice versa). God forbid. The monster would have to be put to sleep.

Nor will they be like the two one-winged birds of Chinese legend that can fly only when joined together, for the imbalance between them would cause them to go in ever-decreasing circles with the usual regrettable results. But the day could come when they went beyond the trading of ubiquitous Big Macs for ubiquitous Chinese takeaways to an understanding and acceptance of each other's ways, until each was like a contrasting dot in the segment of the other, interacting in the circle symbolising world unity.

Anything is possible, given time. Ping and I might still come up against a blank wall of incomprehension sometimes, even when arguing over this book. But as we stood gazing across London towards St Paul's Cathedral in August 1998, and decided to be remarried in the OBE Chapel on our Golden Wedding anniversary, we held hands tightly. We knew the secret of our long marriage It was an open mind, a shedding of all preconceived ideas, a refusal to listen to what others said, a rejection of all the misinformed dogma propagated by the pundits about each other's people. And we held the proof.

Since more than 40 years passed, we still have a marriage based nine days acquaintance. Even though not rich or noble, still happy, so what more I want? When D suggest maize a party for our ruby wedding, I told him I really faneyjust candlelight dinner together, celebrate our two person world, why trouble friends. Even 40 years on, I feel like a bride, my heart beating fast.

The Chinese astrologers in their infinite wisdom had laid down consolingly that if someone born in the Year of the Rabbit (Ping) married someone born in the Year of the Ram (myself), they could at least rub along as friends thanks to their similar artistic bents, even given that there could be no love between them. Laugh?